THE
EVERYDAY
WRITER

THE EVERYDAY WRITER

A Brief Reference

Andrea Lunsford
THE OHIO STATE UNIVERSITY

Robert Connors
UNIVERSITY OF NEW HAMPSHIRE

with a section for
multilingual writers by

Franklin E. Horowitz
TEACHERS COLLEGE
COLUMBIA UNIVERSITY

ST. MARTIN'S PRESS
New York

Publisher: Marilyn Moller
Development editor: Kristin Bowen
Managing editor: Patricia Mansfield Phelan
Project editor: Diane Schadoff
Editorial assistant: Griff Hansbury
Production supervisor: Joe Ford
Art director: Lucy Krikorian
Text design: Anna George
Cover design: Lucy Krikorian

Library of Congress Catalog Card Number: 95-73167

Manufactured in the United States of America.

1   0   9   8   7
f   e   d   c   b   a

For information, write:
St. Martin's Press, Inc.
175 Fifth Avenue
New York, NY 10010

ISBN: 0-312-09569-4

Acknowledgments

Robert Frost. Excerpt from "The Road Not Taken" from *The Poetry of Robert Frost.* Copyright © 1923, 1969 by Henry Holt & Company, Inc. Reprinted by permission of Henry Holt & Company, Inc.

D. Letticia Galindo. "Bilingualism and Language Variation" from *Language Variation in North American English,* edited by A. Wayne Glowka and Donald M. Lance. New York: MLA, 1993: 202. Reprinted by permission of the Modern Language Association of America.

Acknowledgments and copyrights are continued at the back of the book on page 415, which constitutes an extension of the copyright page.

CONTENTS

HOW TO USE THIS BOOK

Our goal in *The Everyday Writer* is to provide a "short and sweet" writing reference you can use easily on your own—at work, in class, even on the run. Small enough to tuck into a backpack or briefcase, this text has been designed to help you find information quickly, efficiently, and with minimal effort.

Ways into the book

- The *quick access menu* inside the front cover gives a quick list of the book's contents. Once you find the general topic you are looking for on the Quick Access Menu, it will point you to the section of the book where you'll find your information. Turn then to that tabbed section, and check the menu on the tabbed divider for the exact page.

- The *index* lists everything covered in the book. You can find information here by looking up a topic ("articles," for example) or, if you're not sure what your topic is called, by looking up the word you need help with (*a* or *the*, for example).

- Two *tables of contents* list chapters and main headings in detail—the complete contents on pp. vii–xviii and the Brief Contents on the inside back cover.

- *Boxed editing tips* at the beginning of most chapters will help you check your drafts with a critical eye and edit as need be.

- *Frequently Asked Questions (FAQs)* about writing are covered in the first tabbed section, with brief explanations, hand-edited examples, and cross references to other places in the book where you'll find more detail.

- *Documentation models* are easy to find in two tabbed sections—one for MLA style and the other for APA and CBE styles.

- *Tips for multilingual writers* appear in a separate tabbed section and in boxes throughout the book. You can also find a list of the topics covered, including language-specific tips, on the tabbed divider for that section.

- *Revision symbols* are listed in the back of the book. If your instructor uses these symbols to mark your drafts, consult this list.
- A *glossary of usage* (Chapter 28) gives quick advice on commonly confused and misused words.

We hope that this book will prove to be an everyday reference — and that these reference features will lead you quickly and easily to whatever information you need.

PREFACE

The Everyday Writer rests on two simple insights. First, writing surrounds us: it's not something we do just in school or on the job but something that is as familiar and everyday as a pair of worn sneakers, or the air we breathe. We want to acknowledge this "everydayness" of writing and to encourage users of this book to act on Gloria Anzaldúa's advice—to "write in the kitchen, lock yourself up in the bathroom. Write on the bus or the welfare line, on the job or during meals. . . ." Second, all learning, including learning to write, grows out of what we already know and understand, linking our "everyday" knowledge to something new—whether that something new is a form of punctuation, a sentence pattern, a stylistic choice, or a method of research. Thus *The Everyday Writer* speaks to students in everyday language about how to use what they already know to expand their writing repertoires.

Specifically, *The Everyday Writer* aims to enact the two principles described above by providing a quick and simple reference writers can easily use on their own, on the run even, as they work on writing tasks on the bus, in the computer lab, in the library, in between classes, on the job. Small enough to fit in a backpack, and with a binding that allows the book to open flat, *The Everyday Writer* can go anywhere, anytime.

Highlights

Attention to everyday language *in* everyday language. Each chapter opens with a brief example showing the everyday use of that chapter's subject. Everyday language pervades the book, giving students clear, straightforward answers they can understand, with examples from school, from the workplace, and from home.

Best online coverage. Chapter 39 offers unique coverage of the language of the digital world from *Wired Style: Principles of English Usage in the Digital Age,* the new style guide by the editors of *Wired.* Guidelines for using and evaluating electronic sources are in Chapter 42, Conducting Research, and Chapter 43, Evaluating and Using Sources. In addition, we provide guidelines for citing and documenting Internet sources in MLA, APA, and CBE styles. The guidelines for MLA and APA are from the most comprehensive and up-to-date system we could find, developed by Andrew Harnack and Eugene Kleppinger.

Quick guidelines on the most common errors. A "crisis-control center" provides practical answers to the most frequently asked questions (FAQs) about writing, with questions gleaned from nationwide research into student writing patterns and teacher responses to the writing of first-year college students. This study identified mistakes in the grammar, syntax, and use of standard written English writers are most likely to make as well as the larger rhetorical concerns readers are most likely to comment on. This tabbed section opens the book in brief, everyday language and provides hand-edited examples to help students recognize and edit for these problem areas.

Boxed editing tips. Detailed editing tips, usually at the beginning of each chapter, help students work with their own writing. All handbooks provide rules, but only *The Everyday Writer* gives tips to help students apply the rules to their own drafts.

Unique coverage of language variety. Chapter 26 helps students "shift language gears," as they often need to do, among ethnic, regional, occupational, and standard varieties of English.

Other significant features

A complete section for multilingual writers. Written by Franklin Horowitz of Teachers College, Columbia University, this section covers grammatical and rhetorical issues of concern to multilingual writers, including ESL writers. Boxed tips throughout the book offer advice on topics where ESL writers need extra help. Whenever possible we give language-specific advice, with special tips for 15 languages.

Special attention to matters of style. Brief style boxes help writers with the kinds of stylistic choices they must make as they move among various communities, fields, jobs, and disciplines.

A complete chapter on writing about literature. Chapter 53 presents a text-based approach to interpreting a literary work, with a sample student essay and a glossary of literary terms.

Help with many common everyday writing tasks. Today's writing tasks are many and varied, and *The Everyday Writer* offers help with some of the most important ones: email (Chapter 54), professional and business writing (Chapter 54), oral presentations (Chapter 52), collaboratively produced projects (Chapter 5).

And because writing situations and needs are changing constantly, we have *The Everyday Writer* Web site, which will feature FAQs about writing, links to other writer-friendly sites, even a chat space. Join us at *www.smpcollege.com/smp_english.everyday_writer*.

Acknowledgments

During the years we have worked on *The Everyday Writer*, we have had the benefit of much wisdom, advice, and help. Of special significance to us in this extensive collaboration have been Francine Weinberg, whose legendary abilities to condense and clarify enabled us to realize the goal of writing a brief handbook; Kristin Bowen, whose meticulous attention to even the smallest detail is reflected on every single page; Marilyn Moller, who is simply our *sine qua non* of editors (and friends); Diane Schadoff, who is calm patience personified; Griff Hansbury, whose quiet support has been deeply appreciated; George Scribner, whose imaginative marketing sense has helped us, we hope, reach a very wide audience; Steve Debow, whose creative and daring thinking has challenged and inspired us; and Lucy Krikorian and Anna George, to whom we owe the wonderful cover and interior designs.

We are also especially grateful to the students in Andrea's autumn 1995 English 167 class, who commented extensively on what they wanted and needed in a brief handbook; to students and colleagues at Bread Loaf School of English, whose incisive questions about *The St. Martin's Handbook* prompted so much thought and revision; to Melissa Goldthwaite and Matthew Taylor, who helped search for quotations and other necessary source material — and helped in innumerable other ways as well; to Carolyn Wilkins, secretary for the Rhetoric and Composition program at Ohio State, who helped expedite more express mail packages than anyone else we know; to Frank Horowitz for his continuing meticulous work on the chapters for multilingual writers; to Andrew Harnack and Eugene Kleppinger for making (excellent) sense of electronic citation and documentation systems; and to *Wired* magazine for graciously allowing us to reprint part of *Wired Style*.

We have benefited mightily from a group of particularly astute and helpful reviewers, including Kelly Merrill Austin, Brigham Young University; Kathleen Bell, University of Central Florida; Grant Boswell, Brigham Young University; Sandra Councilman, University of North Texas; David E. Fear, Valencia Community College; Charles Fisher, Aims Community College; Blythe Forcey, North Carolina State University; Judith E. Funston, State University of New York at Potsdam; Ann Mace Futrell, Louisiana Tech University; Sara Garnes, The Ohio State University; Russell Greer, University of Georgia; Trenton Hickman, Brigham Young University; Michael Keller, South Dakota State University; Joan S. Latchaw, North Dakota State University; Joan Livingston-Webber, Western Illinois University; Victor Luftig, Brandeis University; Scott McClintock, Loyola Marymount University; Elaine Marshall, Barton College; Gretchen Flesher Moon, Gustavus Adolphus College; Mark S. Newman, Scott Community College; Rai Peterson, Ball State University; Donna Qualley, Western Washington University; Kathryn Rosser Raign, University of North Texas; Thomas Recchio, University of Connecticut; Priscilla Reiser, University of North Texas; Wendy Rider, Brigham Young University; Shirley Rose, Purdue University; Ann M. Salak, Pierce College; Mary Sauer, Indiana University Purdue University, Indianapolis; Karen Scriven, Barton College; Dickie Spurgeon, Southern Illinois University, Edwardsville; Ethel F. Taylor, North Carolina Agricultural and Technical State University; Meredith Walker, Clemson University; and Kristin R. Woolever, Northeastern University.

And we wish especially to thank the following students who responded thoughtfully, thoroughly, and helpfully to early drafts of *The Everyday Writer*: Penny S. DiCamilto, Aims Community College; Amanda Farish, Clemson University; Kristen Ham, Louisiana Tech University; Jeanine Jewell, Western Washington University; Adrienne C. Jones, Ball State University; Amy Bryan Killingsworth, Louisiana Tech University; Libbi Levine, Brandeis University; Rebekah K. Little, University of Nebraska, Omaha; Christopher Daniel MacDonald, Valencia Community College; Elizabeth Mace, Pierce College; Kyle Parker, Ball State University; Beverly K. Poll, University of Nebraska, Omaha; Jeffrey L. Reaser, North Carolina State University; Alisa Anne Sachs, Western Washington University; Alexandra Stokman, Brandeis University; J'nyne Tucker, Valencia Community College; and Stephanie Van Parys, University of Georgia.

Andrea Lunsford
Robert Connors

THE
EVERYDAY
WRITER

FREQUENTLY
ASKED
QUESTIONS

Q: What is most difficult for you in
writing?
A: Starting a piece seems to be
extremely difficult for me. . . .
Perhaps the reason is that good
writing is based on clear thinking,
which is the hardest thing we have
to do. It's as plain as that. It's hard
to start to write because what you
have to do is start to think.

— ROGER ANGELL

FREQUENTLY ASKED QUESTIONS

The Everyday Writer builds on research identifying the precise error patterns that characterize student writing today and that seem most important to instructors. We began by gathering a nationwide sample of more than twenty thousand student essays to which instructors had responded and carefully analyzing a scientifically stratified sample of the essays to identify the twenty most common error patterns. All turned out to be sentence-level issues. Then, we examined the essays a second time for larger rhetorical issues, identifying the ten issues of content and organization that instructors comment on most. Not surprisingly, the errors we discovered corresponded closely to the problems our students have — and to the questions about writing they frequently ask. To help with what may be your own frequently asked questions (FAQs) about writing, Chapters 1–3 provide guidelines for recognizing, understanding, and revising these most common errors.

Broad Content Issues

As a writer, you are in some ways like a bandleader. You must orchestrate all the elements of your writing into a persuasive performance, assembling your ideas, words, and evidence into one coherent structure. Readers expect you to be their guide — to help them understand your meaning. To meet these expectations, you must pay careful attention to several broad content issues: whether your purpose is clear, who your audience is, which points need to be fully established, and so on. Instructors reading college essays most often comment on these five content issues: (1) use of supporting evidence, (2) use of sources, (3) achievement of purpose, (4) attention to audience, and (5) overall impression. Look at the examples of such questions and comments in this chapter to help you understand responses to content issues that readers have to your own writing.

1a Check your use of supporting evidence.

Effective writing needs to accomplish two basic goals: to make a claim and to prove it. Readers expect that a piece of writing will make one or more points clearly and will support those points with ample evidence—good reasons, examples, or other details. When you use evidence effectively, you help readers understand your point, making abstract concepts concrete and offering "proof" that what you are saying is sensible and worthy of attention. (In fact, this issue of supporting evidence is the one readers in our research asked students about *most often*, accounting for 56 percent of all the comments we analyzed.) When readers make statements such as the following ones, they are referring to or questioning your use of supporting evidence:

> This point is underdeveloped.
>
> The details here don't really help me see your point.
>
> I'm not convinced—what's your authority?
>
> The three reasons you offer are very persuasive.
>
> Good examples. Can you offer more?

For more discussion of the use of good reasons, examples and precedents, and citing authority, see 6b. Providing supporting details in paragraphs is covered in 7b.

1b Check your use of sources.

One important kind of supporting evidence comes from source materials. To back up the points you are making, you need to choose possible sources, evaluate them, and decide when to quote, when to summarize, and when to paraphrase them. Using sources competently not only helps support your claim but also builds your credibility as a writer: you demonstrate that you understand what others have to say about a topic and that you are fully informed about these varying perspectives. When readers make comments such as the following ones, they are referring to or questioning your use of sources:

> Only two sources? You need at least several more.
>
> Who said this?
>
> One of the clearest paraphrases I've seen of this crucial passage.
>
> Your summary leaves out three of the writer's main points.
>
> Your summary is just repetition — it doesn't add anything new.
>
> This quotation beautifully sums up your argument.
>
> Why do you quote at such length here? Why not paraphrase?
>
> You cite only sources that support your claim — citing one or two with differing views would help show me you've considered other opinions.

For further discussion of choosing, reading, and evaluating sources, see 43a–d; for more on quoting, paraphrasing, and summarizing, see 43e. Incorporating source materials in your text is covered in 44c.

1c Check to see that you achieve your purpose.

The purposes for writing vary widely. You might, for example, write to ask for an appointment or a job interview, to send greetings or condolences, to summarize information for a test, or to trace the causes of World War II for an essay. In college writing, you need to pay careful attention to what an assignment asks you to do, noting particularly any key terms in the assignment, such as *analyze, argue, define,* and *summarize.* Such words are important if you are to meet the requirements of the assignment, stay on the subject, and achieve your purpose. Readers' questions often reveal how well you have achieved your primary purpose. Here are some reader comments that refer to purpose.

> Why are you telling us all this?
>
> What is the issue here, and what is your stand on it?
>
> Very efficient and thorough discussion! You explain the content very clearly and thus reveal your understanding of the article.
>
> Why simply give a lot of plot summary here—it does little to analyze character development.

For guidelines on considering purposes, see 4b.

1d Check your attention to audience.

All writing is intended to be read, even if only by the writer. The most effective writers are sensitive to readers' backgrounds, values, and needs. They pay attention to their audience by taking the time to define terms readers may not know, providing necessary background information, and considering readers' perspectives on and feelings about a topic. Following are some typical reader comments on audience:

> Careful you don't talk down to your readers.
>
> You've left me behind here. I can't follow.
>
> Your level of diction is perfect for relating to the board of trustees.
>
> I'm really enjoying reading this!
>
> Don't assume everyone shares your opinion about this issue.

For guidelines on considering your audience, see 4c and Chapter 25.

1e   Check for overall impression.

When friends, colleagues, or instructors read your writing, they often give you information about the overall impression it makes, perhaps noting how it is improving or how it needs to be improved. You will do well to note such responses carefully and to analyze them to determine your strengths and weaknesses as a writer. Setting up a conference with a writing tutor or your instructor is one way to explore these general responses. Readers tend to give their overall impressions at the very beginning or the very end of an essay, saying things like this:

> I was looking for more critical analysis from you, and I've found it!
>
> Much improved over your last essay.
>
> Your grasp of the material here is truly impressive.
>
> What happened here? I can't understand your point in this essay.
>
> Good job—you've convinced me!

For more specific ways of assessing the overall impression your writing creates, see 8a and 8b.

2

Organization and Presentation

The most important or brilliant ideas in the world will have little effect on an audience if they are difficult to recognize, read, or follow. Indeed, our research confirms that readers depend on writers to organize and present their material in ways that aid understanding. In regard to organization and presentation, the instructors in our study most often asked questions about or commented on these features, in order of frequency: (1) overall organization, (2) sentence structure and style, (3) paragraph structure, (4) format, and (5) documentation.

2a   Check the overall organization.

Readers expect a writer to provide organizational patterns and signals that will help them follow what the writer is trying to say. Sometimes such organizational cues are simple. If you are giving directions, for example, you might give chronological cues (first you do A, then B, and so on), and if you are describing a place, you might give spatial cues (at the north end is A, in the center is B, and so on). But complex issues often call for complex organizational patterns. For example, you may need to signal readers that you are moving from one problem to several possible solutions or that you are moving through a series of comparisons and contrasts. Here are some common teacher comments concerning organizational features.

> I'm confused here—what does this point have to do with the one before it?
>
> Your most important point is buried here in the middle. Why not move it up front?
>
> Organization here is chronological rather than topical; as a result, you summarize but do not analyze.
>
> How did we get here? You need a transition.
>
> Very clear, logical essay. A joy to read.

For more discussion on writing out a plan, see 6c. For more on effective patterns of development, see 7c; and on using transitions to aid organization, see p. 47.

2b Check sentence structure and style.

Effective sentences form the links in a chain of writing, guiding readers' understanding each step along the way. If you have never taken a close look at how well your sentences serve to guide your readers, spend a little time examining them now. How long do your sentences tend to be? Do you use strings of short sentences? Do your sentences flow logically from one thought to another, or do you make the reader work to figure out the connections between them? Do your long sentences confuse the reader or wander off the topic? How do your sentences usually begin? How do you link them to one another? Following are some typical questions about and comments on sentences:

> The pacing of your sentences here really keeps me reading—excellent variation of length and type.
>
> Can you combine sentences to make the logical connection explicit here?
>
> Your use of questions helps clarify this complex issue.
>
> This is not effective word order for a closing sentence—I've forgotten your main point. Can you find a better sentence?
>
> These sentences all begin with nouns—the result is a kind of dull clip-clop, clip-clop.

> Too many short, simple sentences here. This reads like a grocery list rather than an explanation of a complex issue.
>
> This sentence goes on forever—how about dividing it up?

For a more detailed discussion of sentence types, see Chapter 16. Sentence conciseness is covered in Chapter 14, and sentence variety in Chapter 15.

2c   Check paragraph structure.

Paragraph structure can help readers follow the thread of thought in a piece of writing. You may tend to paragraph by feel, so to speak, without thinking very much about paragraph structure as you write. In fact, the best time to examine your paragraphs is generally *after* you have completed a draft. Here are some typical readers' questions and comments about paragraphs.

> Why the one- and two-sentence paragraphs? Elaborate!
>
> Your introductory paragraph immediately gets my attention and gives an overview of the essay—good!
>
> I can't follow the information in this paragraph. Can you reorder it?
>
> What is the main idea of this paragraph?
>
> Very effective ordering of details in this paragraph.
>
> This paragraph skips around two or three points. It has enough ideas for three paragraphs.

For guidelines on editing paragraphs, see p. 39. For more detailed information on paragraph development in general, see Chapter 7.

2d   Check format.

An attractive, easy-to-read format makes a reader's job pleasant and efficient. Therefore, you should pay close attention to the physical presentation of your materials and to the visual effect they create. Part of your job as a writer is to know what format is most appropriate for a particular task. In the research conducted for this book, readers made the following kinds of comments about format:

> You need a title, one that gets across your meaning.
>
> Why use this tiny single-spaced type? It is almost impossible to read.
>
> Number pages—these were not in the right order.

Your headings helped me follow this report. Why not use subheadings as well?

Never turn in a computer-printed essay without separating the pages and tearing off the tractor holes.

For more discussion of format, see Chapter 40 on document design.

2e Check documentation.

Any writing that uses source materials requires careful documentation — in-text citations, endnotes, footnotes, lists of works cited, bibliographies — to guide readers to your sources and let them know you have carried out accurate research. While very few writers carry documentation guidelines around in their heads, smart writers know which guidelines to use and where to find them. Here are some readers' questions and comments that focus on documentation.

I checked my copy of *Emma* and this quotation's not on the page you list.

What are you paraphrasing here? Your introduction merely drops readers into the middle of things. *Introduce the material paraphrased.*

What are you summarizing here? Where do these ideas come from?

I can't tell where this quotation ends.

Keep in-text citations as simple as possible — see information in handbook.

Why aren't works listed in alphabetical order?

This is *not correct* MLA citation style. Check your book!

What is the date of this publication?

For more information on documenting sources according to MLA style, see Chapters 45–48. APA and CBE styles are covered in Chapters 49–51.

3

The Twenty Most Common Errors

Grammar, punctuation, and other sentence-level matters will seldom draw much attention unless they interfere with the meaning you're trying to get across. Because they do get in the way, however, they are important to your success as a writer.

What kinds of surface errors are you likely to find in your writing, and how will readers respond to them? Our study of college writing patterns revealed that spelling errors are by far the most common type of error, even with spell checkers, by a factor of more than three to one. (A list of the words most often misspelled can be found in Chapter 27.) Our study also showed that not all surface errors disturb readers, nor do instructors always mark all of them. Finally, not all surface errors are consistently viewed as errors. In fact, some of the patterns identified in our research are considered errors by some readers but stylistic options by others.

While many people think of correctness as absolute, based on hard and fast unchanging "rules," instructors and students know better. We know that there are rules, but that the rules change all the time. "Is it okay to use *I* in essays for this class?" asks one student. "My high school teacher wouldn't let us." "Will more than one comma error lower my grade?" asks another. Such questions show that rules clearly exist but that they are always shifting and thus need our ongoing attention.

Our research shows some of the shifts that have occurred in the last century alone. Some mechanical and grammatical questions that are of little or no concern today used to be perceived as extremely important. In the late-nineteenth century, for instance, instructors at Harvard said that their students' most serious writing problem was the inability to distinguish between the proper uses of *shall* and *will*. Similarly, split infinitives represented a serious problem for many instructors of the 1950s. Nowadays, at least since the starship *Enterprise* set out "to boldly go" where no one has gone before, split infinitives seem to wrinkle fewer brows.

These examples of shifting standards do not mean that there is no such thing as "correctness" in writing — only that *correctness always depends on some context*. Correctness is not so much a question of absolute right or wrong as it is a question of the way the choices a writer makes are perceived by readers. As writers, we are all judged by the words we put on the page. We all want to be considered competent and careful, and writing errors work against that impression. The world judges us by our control of the conventions we have agreed to use, and we all know it. As Robert Frost once said of poetry, trying to write without honoring the conventions and agreed-upon rules is like playing tennis without a net.

A major goal of this book is to help you understand and control the surface conventions of academic and professional writing. Since you already know most of these rules, the most efficient way to proceed is to focus on those that are still unfamiliar or puzzling.

To aid you in this process, we have identified the twenty error patterns (other than misspelling) that were most common among U.S. college students in the late 1980s and list them here in order of frequency. These twenty errors are likely to cause you the most trouble, so it is well worth your effort to check for them in your writing. Here are brief explanations and examples of each error pattern, along with cross-references to other places in this book where you can find more detail and additional examples.

1 Missing comma after an introductory element

When a sentence opens with an introductory word, phrase, or clause, readers usually need a small pause between the introductory element and the main part of the sentence. Such a pause is most often signaled by a comma. Try to get into the habit of using a comma after every introductory element, be it a word, a phrase, or a clause. When the introductory element is very short, you don't always need a comma after it. But you're never wrong if you do use a comma after an introductory element, and sometimes the comma is necessary to prevent a misreading.

▶ Frankly, we were baffled by the committee's decision.

▶ In fact, the Philippines consists of more than eight thousand islands.

▶ To tell the truth, I have never liked the Mets.

▶ Determined to get the job done, we worked all weekend.

▶ Because of its isolation in a rural area surrounded by mountains, Crawford Notch doesn't get many visitors.

▶ Though I gave advice for revising, his draft became only worse.

The comma is needed here to prevent a misreading; without the comma, we might read the clause as *Though I gave advice for revising his draft.*

▶ **In German, nouns are always capitalized.**
^

This sentence would at first be misunderstood if it did not have a comma. Readers would think the introductory phrase was *In German nouns* rather than *In German*.

For guidelines on editing for commas after introductory elements, see p. 194. For more on commas and introductory elements in general, see 15b, 16l, and 29a.

2   Vague pronoun reference

Pronouns are words such as *he, she, it, they, this, that, which,* and *who* that replace another word so that it does not have to be repeated. Pronouns should refer clearly to a specific word or words (called the *antecedent*) elsewhere in the sentence or in a previous sentence, so that readers can be sure whom or what the pronoun refers to. There are two common kinds of vague pronoun reference. The first occurs when there is more than one word that the pronoun might refer to; the second, when the reference is to a word that is implied but not explicitly stated.

POSSIBLE REFERENCE TO MORE THAN ONE WORD

▶ **Transmitting radio signals by satellite is a way of overcoming the**
                                                    the airwaves
problem of scarce airwaves and limiting how ~~they~~ **are used.**
                                                    ^

What is being limited — the signals or the airwaves?

▶ **Before Mary Grace physically and verbally assaulted Mrs. Turpin,**
the latter
~~she~~ **was a judgmental woman who created her own ranking system of**
^
people and used it to justify her self-proclaimed superiority.

Whom does *she* refer to — Mary Grace or Mrs. Turpin? As edited, there is no doubt.

REFERENCE IMPLIED BUT NOT STATED

▶ **The troopers burned a refugee camp as a result of the earlier attack.**
     destruction of the camp
This was the cause of the war.
^

What does *this* refer to? The editing makes clear what caused the war.

a policy
▶ Company policy prohibited smoking, ~~which~~ many employees resented.
‸

What does *which* refer to — the policy or smoking? The editing clarifies the sentence.

For guidelines on editing for clear pronoun reference, see p. 134. For more on pronoun reference, see 21g.

3 Missing comma in a compound sentence

A compound sentence is made up of two or more parts that could each stand alone as a sentence. When the parts are joined by *and, but, so, yet, nor,* or *for,* insert a comma to indicate a pause between the two thoughts.

▶ We wish dreamily upon a star‚ and then we look down to find
‸
ourselves standing in mud.

▶ The words "I do" may sound simple‚ but they mean a life commitment.
‸

In very short sentences, the comma is optional if the sentence can be easily understood without it. But you'll never be wrong to use a comma, and sometimes a comma is necessary to prevent a misreading.

▶ Meredith wore jeans‚ and her feet were bare.
‸

Without the comma, readers might at first think that Meredith was wearing her feet.

For guidelines on editing for commas in compound sentences, see p. 194. For further discussion and examples, see 16h and 29b.

4 Wrong word

"Wrong word" errors can involve mixing up words that sound somewhat alike or using a word with the wrong shade of meaning or using a word with a completely wrong meaning. Many "wrong word" errors are due to the improper use of homonyms — words that are pronounced alike but spelled differently, such as *their* and *there*.

▶ The Pacers played ~~there~~ *their* best, but that was not good enough.

▶ *Paradise Lost* contains many ~~illusions~~ *allusions* to classical mythology.

▶ He noticed the ~~stench~~ *fragrance* of roses as he entered the room.

> Wrong shade of meaning: a *stench* is a disagreeable smell; a *fragrance* is a pleasing odor.

▶ Working at a computer all day often means being ~~sedate~~ *sedentary* for long periods of time.

> Wrong meaning: *sedate* means "composed, dignified," and *sedentary* means "requiring much sitting."

For guidelines on editing for words, see p. 155. For information about choosing the right word for your meaning, see Chapter 24. For discussion of choosing respectful words, see Chapter 25.

5 Missing comma(s) with a nonrestrictive element

Use commas to set off any part of a sentence that tells more about a word in the sentence but that your reader does *not* need in order to understand the word or sentence. A nonrestrictive element is one that is not essential to the basic meaning of the sentence.

▶ Marina, who was the president of the club, was first to speak.

> The reader does *not* need the clause *who was the president of the club* to know the basic meaning of the sentence: who was first to speak. As a nonrestrictive (or nonessential) element, the clause is set off by commas.

▶ Louis was forced to call a session of the Estates General, which had not met for 175 years.

> The reader does *not* need the clause *which had not met for 175 years* to understand which assembly the sentence is talking about because the *Estates General* has already been named. This clause is *not* essential to the basic meaning of the sentence and should be set off by a comma.

▶ Kristin's first doll, Malibu Barbie, is still her favorite.
   ^   ^

The reader knows which doll is Kristin's favorite — her *first* one; *Malibu Barbie* is thus not essential to the meaning of the sentence and needs to be set off by commas.

For guidelines on editing for commas with nonrestrictive elements, see p. 194. For additional explanation, see 29c.

6 Wrong or missing verb ending

It is easy to forget the verb endings *-s* (or *-es*) and *-ed* (or *-d*) because they are not always pronounced clearly when spoken. In addition, some varieties of English care for using these endings in ways that are different from uses in standard academic English. Be on the lookout for these omitted endings, and check carefully for them when you edit.

                uses
▶ Eliot ~~use~~ feline imagery throughout the poem.
        ^

                        dropped
▶ The United States ~~drop~~ two atomic bombs on Japan in 1945.
                    ^

For more on verb endings, see 17a and 17c. For subject-verb agreement, see Chapter 18.

7 Wrong or missing preposition

Many words in English are regularly used with a particular preposition to express a particular meaning. For example, throwing a ball *to* someone is different from throwing a ball *at* someone: the first ball is thrown to be caught; the second, to hurt someone. Using the wrong preposition in such expressions is a common error. Because many prepositions are short and are not stressed or pronounced clearly in speech, they are often left out accidentally in writing. Proofread carefully, and check a dictionary when you're not sure about the preposition to use.

        on   *in*
▶ We met ~~in~~ Union Street ~~at~~ San Francisco.
        ^   ^

In and *at* both show place, but use *on* with a street and *in* with a city.

▶ Nixon compared the United States ~~with~~ a "pitiful, helpless giant."

to (inserted above "with")

Compare to is used to note similarities; *compare with* is used to note similarities and differences.

▶ Who called the game yesterday?

off (inserted above, before "the")

Adding *off* makes clear that the game was canceled. To "call" a game can mean either to postpone it or announce it.

For guidelines on checking for prepositions, see p. 405. For additional information about choosing the correct preposition, see 16g.

8   Comma splice

A comma splice occurs when only a comma separates clauses that could each stand alone as a sentence. To correct a comma splice, you can insert a semicolon or period, add a word like *and* or *although* after the comma, or restructure the sentence.

▶ Westward migration had passed Wyoming by; even the discovery of gold in nearby Montana failed to attract settlers.

▶ I was strongly attracted to her, *for* she had special qualities.

▶ I was strongly attracted to her, *although* she had no patience with children.

▶ *Having* ~~They always had~~ roast beef for Thanksgiving, ~~this~~ was a family tradition.

For guidelines on revising comma splices, see p. 143. For additional information about ways to avoid or revise comma splices, see Chapter 22.

9   Missing or misplaced possessive apostrophe

To make a noun possessive, you must add either an apostrophe and an -s (*Ed's book*) or an apostrophe alone (*the boys' gym*). Possessive personal pronouns, however, do *not* take apostrophes: *hers, his, its, ours, yours.*

▶ Overambitious parents can be very harmful to a ~~childs~~ well-being.
   child's

▶ Ron Guidry was once one of the ~~Yankee's~~ most electrifying pitchers.
   Yankees'

▶ Garnet Hill is pleased to announce ~~it's~~ spring white sale.
   its

For guidelines on editing for possessive apostrophes, see p. 210. For additional explanation, see 32a.

10 Unnecessary shift in tense

Verb tenses tell readers when actions take place: saying "Willie *went* to school" indicates a past action whereas saying "he *will go*" indicates a future action. When you shift from one tense to another with no clear reason, you can confuse readers; sometimes they have to guess which tense is the right one.

▶ Joy laughs until she ~~cried~~ at that episode of *Seinfeld*.
   cries

▶ Lucy was watching the great blue heron take off. Then she ~~slips~~ and ~~falls~~ into the swamp.
   slipped *fell*

▶ Kathy is in charge of finance; she ~~will~~ always ~~keep~~ her office locked.
   keeps

For guidelines on editing unnecessary shifts in tense, see p. 73. For more on using verb tenses in sequences, see 17g.

11 Unnecessary shift in pronoun

An unnecessary pronoun shift occurs when a writer who has been using one kind of pronoun to refer to someone or something shifts to another pronoun for no apparent reason. The most common shift in pronoun is from *one* to *you* or *I*.

▶ When one first sees a painting by Georgia O'Keeffe, ~~you are~~ impressed
   one is

   by a sense of power and stillness.

▶ If we had known about the ozone layer, ~~you~~ ^{we} could have banned aerosol sprays long ago.

For guidelines on editing for confusing pronoun shifts, see p. 73. For more on shifts in pronouns, see 12d.

12 Sentence fragment

A sentence fragment is a part of a sentence that is written as if it were a whole sentence, with a capital letter at the beginning and a period, question mark, or exclamation point at the end. A fragment may lack a subject, a complete verb, or both. Or a fragment may begin with a subordinating word such as *because*, which indicates that it depends for its meaning on another sentence.

NO SUBJECT

▶ Marie Antoinette spent huge sums of money on herself and her favorites. *Her extravagance helped* ~~Helped~~ bring on the French Revolution.

NO COMPLETE VERB

▶ The old aluminum boat *was* sitting on its trailer.

Sitting cannot function alone as the verb of the sentence. Adding the auxiliary verb *was* turns it into a complete verb, *was sitting*, indicating continuing action. Now this is a sentence.

BEGINNING WITH SUBORDINATING WORD

▶ We returned to the drugstore, *where* ~~Where~~ we waited for our parents.

For guidelines on editing for sentence fragments, see p. 149. For more detailed information on sentence fragments, see Chapter 23.

13 Wrong tense or verb form

Errors of wrong tense or wrong verb form include using a verb that does not indicate clearly when an action or condition is, was, or will be completed—for example, using *walked* instead of *had walked*, or *will go* instead of *will have gone*. Some varieties of English use the verbs *be* and *have* in ways that differ significantly from their use in standard academic or professional English; these uses may also be labeled as wrong verb forms. Finally, many errors of this kind involve verbs with irregular forms (like *begin, began, begun* or *break, broke, broken*). Errors may occur when a writer confuses these forms or treats these verbs as if they followed the regular pattern—for example, using *beginned* instead of *began*, or *have broke* instead of *have broken*.

▶ By the time Ian arrived, Jill ~~died~~. *had*

> The verb *died* does not clearly indicate that the death occurred *before* Ian arrived.

▶ The poet ~~be~~ looking at a tree when she has a sudden inspiration. *is*

▶ Florence Griffith Joyner has ~~broke~~ many track records. *broken*

▶ The Greeks ~~builded~~ a wooden horse that the Trojans ~~taked~~ into the city. *built* *took*

> The verbs *build* and *take* have irregular past-tense forms.

For guidelines on editing verb tenses, see p. 115. For more detailed information about verb tenses and forms, see 16b and Chapters 17 and 18.

14 Lack of subject-verb agreement

A verb must agree with its subject in number and person. In many cases, the verb must take a form depending on whether the subject is singular or plural: *The old man is angry and stamps into the house,* but *The old men are angry and stamp into the house.* Lack of subject-verb agreement is often just a matter of leaving the *-s* ending off the verb out of carelessness, or of using a form of English that does not have this ending. Sometimes, however, this error results from particular sentence constructions.

When other words come between a subject and a verb, be careful: the noun nearest to the verb is not always the verb's subject.

▶ A central part of my life goals ~~have~~ been to go to law school.
  ^*has*^

The subject is the singular noun *part*, not *goals*.

▶ The two main goals of my life ~~is~~ to be generous and to have no
  ^*are*^

regrets.

Here, the subject is the plural noun *goals*, not *life*.

If a subject has two or more parts connected by *and*, the subject is almost always plural. Sometimes the parts of the subject refer to the same person or thing; in such cases, as in the second example below, the subject should be treated as singular.

▶ The senator and her husband commutes every day from suburban

Maryland.

▶ Our senator and friend ~~commute~~ every day from Maryland.
  ^*commutes*^

If a subject has two or more parts joined by *or* or *nor*, the verb should agree with the part nearest to the verb.

▶ My brothers or my sister ~~come~~ every day to see Dad.
  ^*comes*^

Here, the noun closest to the verb is a singular noun. The verb must agree with that singular noun. If this construction sounds awkward, consider the next edit.

▶ My ~~brothers~~ or my ~~sister~~ commute every day from Louisville.
  ^*sister*^   ^*brothers*^

Now the noun closest to the verb is a plural noun, and the verb agrees with it.

Collective nouns such as *committee* and *jury* can be treated as singular or plural, depending on whether they refer to a single unit or multiple individuals.

▶ The committee ~~was~~ taking all the responsibility themselves.
  ^*were*^

▶ The committee ~~were~~ honored for its fund-raising.
  ^*was*^

Some writers stumble over words like *measles* and *mathematics*, which look plural but are singular in meaning.

▶ Measles ~~have~~ become much less common in the United States.
    has

Pronoun subjects cause problems for many writers. Most indefinite pronouns such as *each, either, neither,* or *one* are always singular and take a singular verb. The indefinite pronouns *both, few, many, others,* and *several* are always plural and take plural verb forms. Several indefinite pronouns (*all, any, enough, more, most, none, some*) can be singular or plural depending on the context in which they are used.

▶ Each of these designs ~~coordinate~~ with the others.
    coordinates

▶ Many of these designs coordinate/ with the others.

The relative pronouns *who, which,* or *that* take verbs that agree with the word the pronoun refers to.

▶ Johnson was one of the athletes who ~~was~~ disqualified.
    were

For guidelines on editing for subject-verb agreement, see p. 119. For additional information about subject-verb agreement, see Chapter 18.

15   Missing comma in a series

When three or more items appear in a series, they should be separated from one another with commas. Many newspapers do not use a comma between the last two items, but the best advice is that you'll never be wrong to use a series comma, because a sentence can be ambiguous without one.

▶ Sharks eat mostly squid, shrimp, crabs, and other fish.

For guidelines on editing for series commas, see p. 194. For more on parallel structures in a series, see 11a, or on using commas in a series, see 29d.

16 Lack of agreement between pronoun and antecedent

Pronouns are words such as *I, it, you, her, this, themselves, someone,* and *who* that replace another word (the antecedent) so that it does not have to be repeated. Pronouns must agree with their antecedents in gender (for example, using *he* or *him* to replace *Abraham Lincoln,* and *she* or *her* to replace *Queen Elizabeth*) and in number (for example, using *it* to replace *a book,* and *they* or *them* to replace *fifteen books*).

Some problems occur with words like *each, either, neither,* and *one,* which are singular and take singular pronouns.

▶ Each of the puppies thrived in ~~their~~ *its* new home.

Problems can also occur with antecedents that are joined by *or* or *nor.*

▶ Neither Jane nor Susan felt that ~~they~~ *she* had been treated fairly.

Some problems involve words like *audience* and *team,* which can be either singular or plural depending on whether they are considered a single unit or multiple individuals.

▶ The team frequently changed ~~its~~ *their* positions to get varied experience.

Because *team* refers to the multiple members of the team rather than to the team as a single unit, *its* needs to change to *their.*

The other kind of antecedent that causes problems is an antecedent such as *each* or *employee,* which can refer to either men or women. Use *he or she, him or her,* and so on, or rewrite the sentence to make the antecedent and pronoun plural or to eliminate the pronoun altogether.

▶ Every student must provide his *or her* own uniform.

▶ ~~Every student~~ *All students* must provide ~~his~~ *their* own ~~uniform.~~ *uniforms*

▶ Every student must provide ~~his own~~ *a* uniform.

For guidelines on editing for pronoun-antecedent agreement, see p. 134. For additional information about pronoun-antecedent agreement, see 21f.

17 Unnecessary comma(s) with a restrictive element

A restrictive element is one that is essential to the basic meaning of the sentence. It is *not* set off from the rest of the sentence with a comma or commas.

▶ **People/who wanted to preserve wilderness areas/opposed the plan to privatize national parks.**

The reader needs the clause *who wanted to preserve wilderness areas* because it announces which people opposed the plan. As an essential element, the clause should not be set off by commas.

▶ **Shakespeare's tragedy/*Othello*/deals with the dangers of jealousy.**

The reader needs to know which of Shakespeare's many tragedies this sentence is talking about. The title *Othello* is therefore essential and should not be set off by commas.

For guidelines on editing out unnecessary commas with restrictive elements, see p. 194. For additional information about restrictive phrases and clauses, see 29c and 29j.

18 Fused sentence

A fused sentence (also called a run-on sentence) is created when clauses that could each stand alone as a sentence are joined with no punctuation or words to link them. Fused sentences must either be divided into separate sentences or joined by adding words or punctuation.

▶ The current was swift. ~~he~~ *He* could not swim to shore.

▶ Klee's paintings seem simple, *but* they are very sophisticated.

▶ She doubted the value of meditation; *nevertheless,* she decided to try it once.

▶ I liked the movie very much, *for* it made me laugh throughout.

For guidelines on revising fused sentences, see p. 143. For more information about ways to revise fused sentences, see Chapter 22.

19   Misplaced or dangling modifier

Check every modifier (whether a word, phrase, or clause) to make sure that it is as close as possible to the word it describes or relates to. Be on the lookout for misplaced modifiers that may confuse your readers by seeming to modify some other word, phrase, or clause.

▶ ~~T~~hey could see the eagles swooping and diving. ~~with~~ *With* binoculars~~.~~ ,

Who was wearing the binoculars—the eagles?

▶ ~~H~~e had decided he wanted to be a doctor. ~~when~~ *When* he was ten years old~~.~~ ,

What kind of doctor would he be at age ten?

▶ The architect (only) considered using pine paneling.

Did the architect only consider but then reject pine paneling?

A dangling modifier hangs precariously from the beginning or end of a sentence, attached to no other word in the sentence. The word that it modifies may exist in your mind but not on paper. Proofread carefully to ensure that each modifier refers to some other word in the sentence.

▶ A doctor should check your eyes for glaucoma every year if *you are* over fifty.

▶ Looking down the sandy beach, *we see that* people are tanning themselves.

For guidelines on editing misplaced and dangling modifiers, see p. 131.

20   *Its/It's* confusion

Use *its* to mean *belonging to it*; use *it's* only when you mean *it is* or *it has*.

▶ The car is lying on ~~it's~~ *its* side in the ditch.

▶ ~~Its~~ *It's* a white 1986 Buick.

For more on distinguishing *its* and *it's*, see 32b.

COMPOSING AND REVISING

... write in the kitchen, lock
yourself up in the bathroom. Write
on the bus or the welfare line, on
the job or during meals. . . .
— GLORIA ANZALDÚA

COMPOSING AND REVISING

4

Considering Purpose and Audience

What do a magazine article, a letter to MasterCard complaining about an error on your bill, and an engineering report have in common? All are written to achieve a specific purpose with a particular audience. As a careful and effective writer, you will want to understand as much as possible about your purposes for writing and about the readers you are addressing. Whether you are writing for a class assignment, as part of your job, or to communicate with a friend, you need to consider your purpose and audience.

Consider your task or assignment.

- If you have a specific writing assignment, what does it ask you to do? Look for words such as *analyze, classify, compare, contrast, describe, discuss, define, explain*, and *survey*. Keep in mind that these words may differ in meaning from discipline to discipline or from job to job: *analyze* might mean one thing in literature and something rather different in biology — and something else still in a corporate report.
- What information do you need to complete the assignment? Do you need to do any research?
- Should you limit — or broaden — the subject you're writing about to make it more compelling to you and your audience? What problem(s) does the topic suggest to you? If you wish to redefine the assignment in any way, check with the person who made the assignment.
- What are the assignment's specific requirements? Consider length, format, organization, design, and deadline.

Consider your purpose.

- What is the primary purpose the assignment calls for? to explain, to summarize, to persuade, to recommend, to entertain — or some other purpose? If you are unclear about the primary purpose, think about what you want to accomplish or talk with the person who made the assignment. Are there any secondary purposes to keep in mind?
- What is the purpose of the person who gave you this assignment — to make sure you have read or understood certain materials? to evaluate your thinking and writing abilities? to determine whether you can evaluate certain materials critically? How can you fulfill these expectations?

- What are your own purposes in this piece of writing — to respond to a question adequately and accurately? to learn as much as possible about a topic? to communicate your ideas clearly and forcefully? to make recommendations? to express certain feelings? How can you achieve these goals?

4c   Consider your audience.

- Whom do you most want to reach? people already sympathetic to your views? people unsympathetic to your views? members of a group you belong to — or don't belong to?

- In what ways are the members of your audience different from you? from one another? Think in terms of education, region, age, gender, occupation, social class, ethnic and cultural heritage, politics, religion, marital status, sexual orientation, and other factors.

- What assumptions can you legitimately make about your audience? What might they value? Think of qualities such as brevity, originality, conformity, honesty, adventure, wit, seriousness, thrift, and so on.

- What languages and varieties of English does your audience use? What special language, if any, will they expect you to use? What knowledge do they have about your topic? Do you need to provide any special background information or define any terms?

- What response(s) do you want to evoke?

5

Exploring Ideas

The point is so simple that we often forget it: we write best about topics we know well. One of the most important parts of the entire writing process, therefore, is choosing a topic that will engage your strengths and your interest and then exploring that topic — surveying what you know and determining what you need to find out.

5a   Try brainstorming.

One of the best ways to begin exploring a topic is also the most familiar: *talk it over* with others. One way to begin is in a brainstorming session. Used widely in business and industry, brainstorming means tossing out ideas—often with several others, either in person or online. You can also brainstorm by yourself. All you need is a pen and blank paper, or a computer.

1. Within a time limit of five or ten minutes in a group with several others, list *every* word or phrase that comes to mind about the topic. Just jot down key words and phrases, not sentences. No one has to understand the list but you and your group. Don't worry about whether or not something will be useful. Just list as much as you can in this brief span of time.
2. If very little occurs to you and your group, try calling out thoughts about the opposite side of your topic. If you are trying, for instance, to think of reasons to reduce tuition and are coming up blank, try concentrating on reasons to *increase* tuition. Once you start generating ideas in one direction, you can usually move back to the other side of the topic fairly easily.
3. When the time is up, stop and read over the lists you have made. If anything else comes to mind, add it to your list. Then reread the list, looking for patterns of interesting ideas or one central idea.

Here is what one student came up with after brainstorming with her classmates for an essay on prejudice.

Some prejudice in everyone

Where does it come from?

Learned—we aren't born with it

Examples: against some races or other groups

against some ways of thinking

against some ways of dressing

5b Try freewriting.

Freewriting, a kind of brainstorming in writing, is a method of exploring a topic by writing about it for a period of time *without stopping*.

1. Write for ten minutes or so. Think about your topic, and let your mind wander; write down whatever occurs to you. Don't stop, and don't worry about grammar or spelling. If you get stuck, write anything—just don't stop.
2. When the time is up, look at what you have written. You may discover some important insights and ideas.

5c   Try clustering.

Clustering is a way of generating ideas using a visual scheme or chart. It is especially helpful for understanding the relationships among the parts of a broad topic and for developing subtopics.

1. Write down your topic in the middle of a blank piece of paper and circle it.
2. In a ring around the topic circle, write down what you see as the main parts of the topic. Circle each one, and draw a line from it to the topic.
3. Think of more ideas, examples, facts, or other details relating to each main part. Write each of these near the appropriate part, circle each one, and draw a line from it to the part.
4. Repeat this process with each new circle until you can't think of any more details. Some trails may dead-end, but you will still have various trains of thought to follow and many useful connections among ideas.

Here is an example of the clustering one student did for an essay about prejudice.

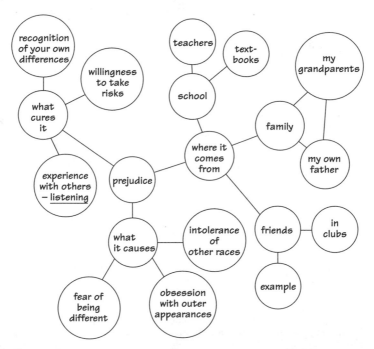

5d Try looping.

Looping is a kind of directed freewriting that narrows a topic through a process of five-minute stages, or loops.

1. Spend five minutes freewriting about your topic *without stopping*. This is your first loop.
2. Look at what you have written. Find the central or most intriguing thought, and summarize it in a single sentence. The student who came up with the brainstorming list in 5a used it as her first loop and chose the final example, prejudice against ways of dressing, to guide a second loop about prejudice.
3. Starting with the summary sentence from your first loop, spend another five minutes freewriting. This second loop circles around the first loop, just as the first loop circled around your topic. Look for the central idea within your second piece of freewriting, which will form the basis of a third loop.
4. Keep this process going until you discover a clear angle on your topic, or something about the topic that you can pursue in a full-length piece of writing.

5e Ask questions.

Another basic strategy for exploring a topic and generating ideas is simply to ask and answer questions. Here are two widely used sets of questions to get you started.

Questions to describe a topic

Originally developed by Aristotle, the following questions can help you explore a topic by carefully and systematically describing it:

1. *What is it?* What are its characteristics, dimensions, features, and parts?
2. *What caused it?* What changes occurred to create your topic? How is it changing? How will it change?
3. *What is it like or unlike?* What features differentiate your topic from others? What analogies does your topic support?
4. *What larger system is your topic a part of?* How is your topic related to this system?
5. *What do people say about it?* What reactions does your topic arouse? What about the topic causes those reactions?

Questions to explain a topic

These are the well-known questions that ask *who, what, when, where, why,* and *how.* Widely used by news reporters, these questions are especially helpful for explaining a topic.

1. *Who* is doing it?
2. *What* is at issue?
3. *When* does it begin and end?

4. *Where* is it taking place?
5. *Why* does it occur?
6. *How* is it done?

5f Work collaboratively.

Most work today is done collaboratively, whether that work is on a basketball court, at a corporate meeting, or in a classroom. Writers often work together to come up with ideas, to respond to one another's drafts, or even to coauthor something. Following are some strategies for working with others:

1. Fix a regular meeting time and a system for contacting one another.
2. If you are working over a computer network, exchange email addresses, and consider exchanging ideas and drafts electronically.
3. Establish ground rules for the group. The first might be that every member have an equal opportunity—and responsibility—to contribute.
4. Assign duties at each meeting: one person to take notes, another to keep discussion on track, and so on.
5. With final deadlines in mind, set an agenda for each group meeting.
6. Listen carefully to what each person says. If disagreements arise, try paraphrasing to see if everyone is hearing the same thing.
7. Use group meetings to work together on particularly difficult problems. If an assignment is complex, have each member explain one section to all the others. If the group has trouble understanding part of the task, check with whoever made the assignment.
8. Expect disagreement, and remember that the goal is not for everyone just to "go along." The challenge is to get a really spirited debate going and to argue through all possibilities.
9. If you are preparing a group-written document, divide up the drafting duties. As a group, set reasonable deadlines for each stage of the work. Schedule at least two meetings to iron out the final draft, reading it aloud and working for consistency of tone. When the final draft is ready, have everyone proofread it, assigning one person to make the corrections.
10. If the group will be making a presentation, be sure you know exactly how much time you will have. Decide how each member will con-

tribute to the presentation, making sure everyone has a role. Leave time for at least two practice sessions.

11. Make a point of assessing the group's effectiveness. What has the group accomplished? What has it done best? What has it been least successful at? What has each member contributed? How could the group function more effectively?

6

Drafting

One of our students defines drafting as that time in a writing project "when the rubber meets the road." In this sense, drafting begins the moment you start shaping your ideas for presentation to your readers. As you decide on your main idea, organize materials to support that idea, and sketch out a plan for your writing, you have already begun the drafting process.

6a Establish a working thesis.

A thesis states the main idea of a piece of writing. Most academic or professional writing contains a thesis statement, often near the beginning. The thesis functions as a promise to the readers, letting them know what the writer will discuss. Though you may not have a final thesis when you begin to write, you should establish a tentative working thesis early on in your writing process.

The word *working* is important here because the working thesis may well change as you write. Even so, a working thesis focuses your thinking and research, and helps keep you on track.

A working thesis should have two parts: a topic part, which states the topic, and a comment part, which makes an important point about the topic.

▶ ┌──────TOPIC──────┐ ┌──────COMMENT──────┐
Recent studies of depression suggest that it is much more closely

related to physiology than scientists had previously thought.

▶ ┌──────TOPIC──────┐ ┌──────COMMENT──────┐
The current health care crisis arises from three major causes.

A successful working thesis has three characteristics:

1. It is potentially *interesting* to the intended audience.
2. It is as *specific* as possible.
3. It limits the topic enough to make it *manageable*.

You can evaluate a working thesis by checking it against each of these characteristics, as in the following example:

PRELIMINARY WORKING THESIS

▶ **Theories about global warming are being debated around the world.**

INTERESTING? The topic itself holds interest, but it seems to have no real comment attached to it. The thesis merely states a bare fact, and the only place to go from here is to more bare facts.

SPECIFIC? The thesis is not specific. Who is debating these theories? What is at issue in this debate?

MANAGEABLE? The thesis is not manageable; it would require research on global warming in many countries.

ASSESSMENT: This thesis can be narrowed by the addition of a stronger comment and a sharper focus.

REVISED WORKING THESIS

▶ **Scientists from several countries have challenged global-warming theories, claiming that they are more propaganda than science.**

6b   Develop support for your thesis.

Gathering information

Writing will often call for research. An assignment may specify that you conduct research on your topic and cite your sources. Or you may find that you do not know enough about your topic to write about it effectively without doing some research. Sometimes you need to do research at various stages of the writing process — early on, to help you understand or define your topic, or later on, to find additional examples to support your thesis. Once you have a working thesis, consider what additional information you might need. (For more on conducting research and working with sources, see Chapters 41 and 42.)

Giving good reasons

In effecting real changes in minds and hearts, we need to rely on good reasons that establish credibility. Once you state your working thesis — that is, once you make a claim about a topic — you have to support that claim. Doing so requires that you explore your ideas fully, and that you identify good reasons for making the claim.

Citing examples and precedents

Just as a picture can sometimes be worth a thousand words, a well-conceived example can be extremely valuable in supporting a point and in helping readers understand abstractions. "Famine," for instance, may be difficult to think about in the abstract, but a graphic description of a drought-stricken community, its riverbed cracked and dry, its people listless, emaciated, and with stomachs bloated by hunger, speaks directly to our understanding.

Precedents are particular kinds of examples taken from the past. Although the most common use of precedent occurs in law, where an attorney may argue a case by citing the precedent of past decisions, precedent appears in everyday life as well. If you urge your best friend to work your shift because you worked her shift the last time she needed some time off, you are supporting your position on the basis of precedent.

In college writing, you usually must list your sources for any examples or precedents not based on your own knowledge (43f).

Citing authority

Another way to support a position is to cite an authority. As young children, we were easily swayed by authority; it was right to do something simply because our parents (the authorities) said so. In recent years, the use of authority has figured prominently in the dramatic impact of the U.S. surgeon general's 1963 announcement that smoking is hazardous to health. At the time, many people quit smoking, largely convinced by the authority of the person offering the evidence.

But as with other strategies for building support for a position, citing authorities demands careful consideration. You might consider the following questions to be sure you are using authorities effectively:

- Is the authority timely? (The argument that the United States should pursue a policy just because it was supported by Thomas Jefferson will probably fail because Jefferson's time was so radically different from ours.)
- Is the authority qualified to judge the topic at hand? (To cite a biologist in an essay on linguistics is not likely to strengthen your argument.)
- Is the authority likely to be known and respected by readers? (To cite an unfamiliar authority without some identification will lessen the impact of the evidence.)

6c Write out a plan.

At this point, you may find it helpful to write out a plan or informal outline. To do so, simply write down your thesis, review your exploratory notes and research materials, and then list all the good reasons you have to support the claim. Here, for example, is one writer's plan.

WORKING THESIS

▶ **Increased motorcycle use demands reorganization of parking lots.**

INTRODUCTION

give background and overview (motorcycle use up dramatically)
state purpose — to fulfill promise of thesis by offering solutions

BODY

describe the current situation (tell of my research at area parking lots)
describe the problem in detail (report on statistics; cars vs. cycles)
present two possible solutions (enlarge lots or reallocate space)

CONCLUSION

recommend against first solution because of cost and space
recommend second solution, and summarize benefits of it

Outlines

Even if you have made an informal written plan before drafting, you may also wish to prepare a formal outline, which can help you to see exactly how the parts of your writing will fit together — how your ideas relate, where you need examples, what the overall structure of your work will be.

Most formal outlines follow a conventional format of numbered and lettered headings and subheadings, using roman numerals, capital letters, arabic numerals, and lowercase letters to show the levels of importance of the various ideas and their relationships. Each new level is indented to show its subordination to the preceding level.

Thesis statement
  I. First main topic
    A. First subordinate idea
      1. First supporting detail
      2. Second supporting detail
      3. Third supporting detail
    B. Second subordinate detail
      1. First supporting detail
      2. Second supporting detail
  II. Second main topic
    A. First subordinate idea
      1. First supporting detail
      2. Second supporting detail
    B. Second subordinate idea
      1. First supporting detail
      2. Second supporting detail
        a. First supporting detail
        b. Second supporting detail

Each level contains at least two parts, so there is no *A* without a *B*, no *1* without a *2*. Comparable items are placed on the same level — all capital letters, for instance, or all arabic numerals. Each level develops the idea before it. Points *1* and *2* under *A*, for example, are the points that develop, explain, or demonstrate *A*. Headings are stated in parallel form — either all sentences or all grammatically parallel structures.

Whatever form your plan takes, you may want or need to change it along the way. Writing has a way of stimulating thought, and the process of drafting may generate new ideas. Or you may find that you need to reexamine some data or information or gather more material.

Outlining on a computer

Outlining on a computer will allow you to rearrange or experiment with various options easily and efficiently. In addition, your software may have an outline template and the capability to produce a complete table of contents based on the headings and subheadings you use in your draft.

6d Write out a draft.

No matter how good your planning, investigating, and organizing have been, chances are you will need to do more work as you draft. This fact of life leads to the first principle of successful drafting: be flexible. If you see that your plan is not working, do not hesitate to alter it. If some information now seems irrelevant, leave it out, even if you went to great lengths to obtain it. Throughout the drafting process, you may need to refer to points you have already written about. You may learn that you need to do more research, that your whole thesis must be reshaped, or that your topic is too broad and should be narrowed. Very often you will continue planning, investigating, and organizing throughout the process.

Some Guidelines for Drafting

- Have all your information close at hand and arranged according to your plan.
- Try to write in stretches of at least thirty minutes. Writing can provide momentum, and once you get going, the task becomes easier.
- Don't let small questions bog you down. As you write, questions will come up that need to be answered. But unless they are major ones, just make a note of them or a tentative decision, and move on.
- Remember that a first draft need not be perfect. In order to keep moving and get a draft done, you often must sacrifice some fine points of writing at this stage. Concentrate on getting all your ideas down on paper.
- Stop writing at a logical place—where you know exactly what will come next. If you do, it will be easier for you to start writing when you return to the draft.

7

Constructing Paragraphs

Paragraphs serve as signposts, pointers that help guide readers through a piece of writing. A look at your favorite magazine will show paragraphs working this way: the first paragraph almost always aims to get our attention and convince us to read on, and subsequent ones often indicate a new point or a shift in focus or tone.

Put simply, a paragraph is a group of sentences or a single sentence set off as a unit. Usually the sentences in a paragraph all revolve around one main idea. This chapter explores some of the ways in which writers can create a variety of effective paragraphs.

Editing Paragraphs

- Is there a sentence that makes the main idea of each paragraph clear? If not, should there be? (7a)

- Within each paragraph, how does each sentence relate to the main idea? Revise or eliminate any that do not. (7a)

- How completely does each paragraph develop its main idea? What details are used? Are they effective? Do any paragraphs need more detail? (7b) What other methods of development might be used? narration? description? comparison and contrast? analogy? (7c)

- Does the first sentence of each paragraph let readers know what that paragraph is about? Does the last sentence in some way conclude that paragraph's discussion? If not, does it need to?

- How does the introductory paragraph catch readers' interest? (7f)

- How does the last paragraph draw the piece to a conclusion? (7f)

- Is each paragraph organized in a way that is easy for readers to follow? Are sentences within each paragraph clearly linked? Do any of the transitions try to create links between ideas that do not really exist? (7e)

- Are the paragraphs clearly linked to one another? Do any more links need to be added? From one paragraph to another, are any of the transitions artificial? (7e)

7a   Focus on a main idea.

An effective paragraph generally focuses on one main idea. A good way to achieve such paragraph unity is to state the main idea clearly in one sentence and then relate all the other sentences in the paragraph to that idea. The sentence that presents the main idea is called the topic sentence.

Announcing the main idea in a topic sentence

The following paragraph opens with a clear topic sentence, and the rest of the paragraph builds on the idea stated in that sentence:

> *Our friendship was the source of much happiness and many memories.* We danced and snapped our fingers simultaneously to the soul tunes of the Jacksons and Stevie Wonder. We sweated together in the sweltering summer sun, trying to win the championship for our softball team. I recall the taste of pepperoni and sausage pizza as we discussed the highlights of our team's victory. Once we even became attracted to the same person, but luckily we were able to share his friendship.

A topic sentence does not always come at the beginning of a paragraph; it may come at the end. Occasionally a paragraph's central idea is so obvious that it need not be stated explicitly in a topic sentence.

Relating each sentence to the main idea

Whether the main idea of a paragraph is stated in a topic sentence or is only implied, make sure that all other sentences in the paragraph contribute to the main idea. The first sentence in the following paragraph announces the topic. All of the other sentences clearly relate to that topic, resulting in a unified paragraph.

> When I was a teenager, there were two distinct streams of popular music: one was black, and the other was white. The former could only be heard way at the end of the radio dial, while white music dominated everywhere else. This separation was a fact of life, the equivalent of blacks sitting in the back of the bus and "whites only" signs below the Mason-Dixon line. Satchmo might grin for days on "The Ed Sullivan Show" and certain historians hold forth *ad nauseam* on the black contribution to American music, but the truth was that our worlds rarely twined.
> – MARCIA GILLESPIE, "They're Playing My Music, but Burying My Dreams"

7b Provide details.

An effective paragraph develops its main idea by providing enough details to hold the readers' interest. Without such development, a paragraph may seem lifeless and abstract.

A POORLY DEVELOPED PARAGRAPH

No such thing as "human nature" compels people to behave, think, or react in certain ways. Rather, from the time of our infancy to our death, we are constantly being taught, by the society that surrounds us, the customs, norms, and mores of our distinct culture. Everything in culture is learned, not genetically transmitted.

This paragraph is boring. Although its main idea is clear and its sentences hold together, it fails to gain our interest or hold our attention because it lacks any specific examples or details. Now look at the paragraph revised to include needed specifics.

THE SAME PARAGRAPH, REVISED

Imagine a child in Ecuador dancing to salsa music at a warm family gathering, while a child in the United States is decorating a Christmas tree with bright, shiny red ornaments. Both of these children are taking part in their country's cultures. It is not by instinct that one child knows how to dance to salsa music, nor is it by instinct that the other child knows how to decorate the tree. No such thing as "human nature" compels people to behave, think, or react in certain ways. Rather, from the time of our infancy to our death, we are constantly being taught, by the society that surrounds us, the customs, norms, and mores of our distinct culture. A majority of people feel that the evil in human beings is "human nature." However, the Tasaday, a "Stone Age" tribe discovered not long ago in the Philippines, do not even have equivalents in their language for the words *hatred, competition, acquisitiveness, aggression,* and *greed*. Such examples suggest that everything in culture is learned, not genetically transmitted.

Though both paragraphs argue the same point, only the second one comes to life. It does so by bringing in specific details *from* life. We want to read this paragraph, for it appeals to our senses (a child dancing; bright, shiny red ornaments) and our curiosity (who are the Tasaday?).

 7c Use effective patterns of development.

Here are several common patterns you can use to develop paragraphs.

Narration

A narrative paragraph uses a story to develop a main idea. Here is one student's narrative paragraph that tells a personal story to support a point about the dangers of racing bicycles with flimsy alloy frames.

People who have been exposed to the risk of dangerously designed bicycle frames have paid too high a price. I saw this danger myself in the 1984 Putney Race. A Stowe-Shimano graphite frame failed, and the rider was catapulted onto Vermont pavement at fifty miles per hour. The pack of riders behind him was so dense that other racers crashed into a tangled, sliding heap. The aftermath: four hospitalizations. I got off with some stitches, a bad road rash, and severely pulled tendons. My Italian racing bike was pretzled, and my racing was over for that summer. Others were not so lucky. An Olympic hopeful, Brian Stone of the Northstar team, woke up in a hospital bed to find that his cycling was over—and not just for that summer. His kneecap had been surgically removed. He couldn't even walk.

Description

A descriptive paragraph uses specific details to create a clear impression. Thus, descriptive paragraphs often *show* rather than tell, using sensory details to help the reader see what something looks like, and perhaps how it sounds, smells, tastes, or feels. Notice how the following paragraph includes details about an old schoolroom; they convey a strong impression of a room where "time had taken its toll."

> The professor's voice began to fade into the background as my eyes wandered around the classroom in the old administration building. The water-stained ceiling was cracked and peeling, and the splitting wooden beams played host to a variety of lead pipes and coils. My eyes followed these pipes down the walls and around corners until eventually I saw the electric outlets. I thought it was strange that they were exposed, and not built in, until I realized that there probably had been no electricity when the building was built. Below the outlets the sunshine was falling in bright rays across the hardwood floor, and I noticed how smoothly the floor was worn. Time had taken its toll on this building.

Definition

You may often need to write an entire paragraph in order to define a word or concept, as in the following paragraph:

> Economics is the study of how people choose among the alternatives available to them. It's the study of little choices ("Should I take the chocolate or the strawberry?") and big choices ("Should we require a reduction in energy consumption in order to protect the environment?"). It's the study of individual choices, choices by firms, and choices by governments. Life presents each of us with a wide range of alternative uses of our time and other resources; economists examine how we choose among those alternatives.
>
> – TIMOTHY TREGARTHEN, *Economics*

Example

One of the most common ways of developing a paragraph is by illustrating a point with one or more examples.

The Indians made names for us children in their teasing way. Because our very busy mother kept my hair cut short, like my brothers', they called me Short Furred One, pointing to their hair and making the sign for short, the right hand with fingers pressed close together, held upward, back out, at the height intended. With me this was about two feet tall, the Indians laughing gently at my abashed face. I am told that I was given a pair of small moccasins that first time, to clear up my unhappiness at being picked out from the dusk behind the fire and my two unhappy shortcomings made conspicuous.

– Mari Sandoz, "The Go-Along Ones"

Division and classification

Division breaks a single item into parts. Classification groups many separate items according to their similarities. A paragraph evaluating a history course might divide the course into several segments — textbooks, lectures, assignments — and examine each one in turn. A paragraph giving an overview of history courses might classify the courses in a number of ways — by time periods, by geographic areas, by the kinds of assignments demanded, by the number of students enrolled, or by some other principle.

DIVISION

We all listen to music according to our separate capacities. But, for the sake of analysis, the whole listening process may become clearer if we break it up into its component parts, so to speak. In a certain sense, we all listen to music on three separate planes. For lack of a better terminology, one might name these: (1) the sensuous plane, (2) the expressive plane, (3) the sheerly musical plane. The only advantage to be gained from mechanically splitting up the listening process into these hypothetical planes is the clearer view to be had of the way in which we listen.

– Aaron Copland, *What to Listen for in Music*

CLASSIFICATION

Many people are seduced by fad diets. Those who have always been overweight turn to them out of despair; they have tried everything, and yet nothing seems to work. A second group to succumb appear perfectly healthy but are baited by slogans such as "look good, feel good." These slogans prompt self-questioning and insecurity — do I really look good and feel good? — and as a direct result, many healthy people fall prey to fad diets. With both types of people, however, the problems surrounding such diets are numerous and dangerous. In fact, these diets provide neither intelligent nor effective answers to weight control.

Comparison and contrast

When you compare two things, you look at their similarities; when you contrast two things, you focus on their differences. You can structure paragraphs that compare or contrast in two basic ways. One way is to present all the information about one item and then all the information about the other item, as in the following paragraph:

> You could tell the veterans from the rookies by the way they were dressed. The knowledgeable ones had their heads covered by kerchiefs, so that if they were hired, tobacco dust wouldn't get in their hair; they had on clean dresses that by now were faded and shapeless, so that if they were hired they wouldn't get tobacco dust and grime on their best clothes. Those who were trying for the first time had their hair freshly done and wore attractive dresses; they wanted to make a good impression. But the dresses couldn't be seen at the distance that many were standing from the employment office, and they were crumpled in the crush.
>
> – MARY MEBANE, "Summer Job"

Or you can switch back and forth between the two items, focusing on particular characteristics of each in turn.

> Malcolm X emphasized the use of violence in his movement and employed the biblical principle of "an eye for an eye and a tooth for a tooth." King, on the other hand, felt that blacks should use nonviolent civil disobedience and employed the theme "turning the other cheek," which Malcolm X rejected as "beggarly" and "feeble." The philosophy of Malcolm X was one of revenge, and often it broke the unity of black Americans. More radical blacks supported him, while more conservative ones supported King. King thought that blacks should transcend their humanity. In contrast, Malcolm X thought they should embrace it and reserve their love for one another, regarding whites as "devils" and the "enemy." King's politics were those of a rainbow, but Malcolm X's rainbow was insistently one color—black. The distance between Martin Luther King Jr.'s thinking and Malcolm X's was the distance between growing up in the seminary and growing up on the streets, between the American dream and the American reality.

Analogy

Analogies (comparisons that explain an unfamiliar thing in terms of another) can also help develop paragraphs. In the opening sentences of the following paragraph, the writer draws an unlikely analogy— between dogs and laboratories—to introduce readers to an examination of what keeps laboratories young.

Like dogs, laboratories age considerably faster than people. But while dogs age at a factor of seven, I would say labs age at a factor of 10, which makes the MIT Media Lab 100 years old last month. When we officially opened our doors for business in October 1985, we were the new kids on the block, considered crazy by most. Even *The New York Times* called us "charlatans." While I was slightly hurt at being referred to as "all icing and no cake," it secretly pleased me because I had no doubt that computing and content would merge together into everyday life. Now, 10 years later, "multi-media" is old hat. The term appears in the names and advertising jingles of some of the most staid corporations. But becoming part of the establishment is a lot less fun than experiencing the risk and abuse of pioneering.

– NICHOLAS NEGROPONTE, "Being Digital"

Cause and effect

You can often develop paragraphs by explaining the causes of something or the effects that something brings about. The following paragraph discusses the effects of television on the American family:

Television's contribution to family life has been an equivocal one. For while it has, indeed, kept the members of the family from dispersing, it has not served to bring them together. By its domination of the time families spend together, it destroys the special quality that distinguishes one family from another, a quality that depends to a great extent on what a family does, what special rituals, games, recurrent jokes, familiar songs, and shared activities it accumulates.

– MARIE WINN, *The Plug-in Drug: Television, Children, and the Family*

Process

Paragraphs often serve to depict or explain a process, sometimes using chronology to order the stages in that process.

By the late 20s, most people notice the first signs of aging in their physical appearance. Slight losses of elasticity in facial skin produce the first wrinkles, usually in those areas most involved in their characteristic facial expressions. As the skin continues to lose elasticity and fat deposits build up, the face sags a bit with age. Indeed, some people have drooping eyelids, sagging cheeks, and the hint of a double chin by age 40 (Whitbourne, 1985). Other parts of the body sag a bit as well, so as the years pass, adults need to exercise regularly if they want to maintain their muscle tone and body shape. Another harbinger of aging, the first gray hairs, is usually noticed in the 20s and can be explained by a reduction in the number of pigment-producing cells. Hair may become a bit less plentiful, too, because of hormonal changes and reduced blood supply to the skin.

– KATHLEEN STASSEN BERGER, *The Developing Person Through the Life Span*

7d   Consider paragraph length.

Paragraph length is determined by content and purpose. Paragraphs should develop an idea, create any desired effects (such as suspense or humor), and advance the larger piece of writing. Fulfilling these aims will sometimes require short paragraphs, sometimes long ones. For example, if you are writing a persuasive piece, you may put all your evidence into one long paragraph to create the impression of a solid, overwhelmingly convincing argument. In a story about an exciting event, on the other hand, you may use a series of short paragraphs to create suspense, to keep the reader rushing to each new paragraph to find out what happens next.

Reasons to start a new paragraph

- to turn to a new idea
- to emphasize something (such as an idea or an example)
- to change speakers (in dialogue)
- to lead readers to pause
- to take up a subtopic
- to start the conclusion

7e   Make paragraphs flow.

A paragraph has coherence (or flows) if its details fit together clearly in a way that readers can easily follow. Here are five ways to achieve paragraph coherence.

Using spatial order

Paragraphs organized in spatial order look at something from top to bottom, left to right, or near to far. Spatial order is a common way of organizing descriptive paragraphs, as in the descriptive paragraph in 7c.

Using chronological order

Paragraphs organized chronologically arrange events as they occurred, from the earliest event to later ones. Chronological order is used frequently in narrative paragraphs, as in the process paragraph in 7c.

Using a general-to-specific pattern

Paragraphs organized in a general-to-specific pattern usually open with a general or abstract idea, which is followed by a number of more specific points that substantiate or elaborate on the generalization. See the narrative paragraph in 7c for an example.

Using parallelism

Parallel structures can help connect the sentences within a paragraph. As readers, we feel pulled along by the force of the parallel structures in the following example:

> William Faulkner's "Barn Burning" tells the story of a young boy trapped in a no-win situation. If he betrays his father, he loses his family. If he betrays justice, he becomes a fugitive. In trying to free himself from his trap, he does both.

Using transitions

Transitions are words such as *so, however,* and *thus* that signal relationships between sentences. Transitions help guide the reader from one idea to another. To understand how important transitions are in directing readers, try reading the following paragraph, from which all transitions have been removed.

A PARAGRAPH WITH NO TRANSITIONS

> In "The Fly," Katherine Mansfield tries to show us the "real" personality of "the boss" beneath his exterior. The fly helps her to portray this real self. The boss goes through a range of emotions and feelings. He expresses these feelings to a small but determined fly, whom the reader realizes he unconsciously relates to his son. The author basically splits up the story into three parts, with the boss's emotions and actions changing quite measurably. With old Woodifield, with himself, and with the fly, we see the boss's manipulativeness. Our understanding of him as a hard and cruel man grows.

We can, if we work at it, figure out the relationship of these sentences to one another, for this paragraph is essentially unified by one major idea. But the lack of transitions results in an abrupt, choppy rhythm; the paragraph lurches from one detail to the next, dragging the confused reader behind. See how much easier the passage is to read and understand with transitions added.

THE SAME PARAGRAPH WITH TRANSITIONS

In "The Fly," Katherine Mansfield tries to show us the "real" personality of "the boss" beneath his exterior. The fly in the story's title helps her to portray this real self. In the course of the story, the boss goes through a range of emotions. At the end, he finally expresses these feelings to a small but determined fly, whom the reader realizes he unconsciously relates to his son. To accomplish her goal, the author basically splits up the story into three parts, with the boss's emotions and actions changing measurably throughout. First with old Woodifield, then with himself, and last with the fly, we see the boss's manipulativeness. With each part, our understanding of him as a hard and cruel man grows.

Commonly used transitions

TO SIGNAL SEQUENCE

again, also, and, and then, besides, finally, first . . . second . . . third, furthermore, last, moreover, next, still, too

TO SIGNAL TIME

after a few days, after a while, afterward, as long as, as soon as, at last, at that time, before, earlier, immediately, in the meantime, in the past, lately, later, meanwhile, now, presently, simultaneously, since, so far, soon, then, thereafter, until, when

TO SIGNAL COMPARISON

again, also, in the same way, likewise, once more, similarly

TO SIGNAL CONTRAST

although, but, despite, even though, however, in contrast, in spite of, instead, nevertheless, nonetheless, on the contrary, on the one hand . . . on the other hand, regardless, still, though, yet

TO SIGNAL EXAMPLES

after all, for example, for instance, indeed, in fact, of course, specifically, such as, the following example, to illustrate

TO SIGNAL CAUSE AND EFFECT

accordingly, as a result, because, consequently, for this purpose, hence, so, then, therefore, thereupon, thus, to this end

TO SIGNAL PLACE

above, adjacent to, below, beyond, closer to, elsewhere, far, farther on, here, near, nearby, opposite to, there, to the left, to the right

TO SIGNAL CONCESSION

although it is true that, granted that, I admit that, it may appear that, naturally, of course

TO SIGNAL SUMMARY, REPETITION, OR CONCLUSION

as a result, as has been noted, as I have said, as we have seen, as mentioned earlier, in any event, in conclusion, in other words, in short, on the whole, therefore, to summarize

---

❋ **For Multilingual Writers: Distinguishing among Transitions**

Distinguishing among some very similar common transition words can be difficult. The difference between *however* and *nevertheless*, for example, is a subtle one: while each introduces statements that contrast with what comes before it, *nevertheless* emphasizes the contrast whereas *however* tones it down. Check the usage of transitions in *The American Heritage Dictionary of the English Language*, which provides usage notes for easily confused words.

7f Work on opening and closing paragraphs.

Opening paragraphs

Even a good piece of writing may remain unread if it has a weak opening paragraph. In addition to announcing your topic, an introductory paragraph must engage readers' interest and focus their attention on what is to follow. At their best, introductory paragraphs serve as hors d'oeuvres, whetting the appetite for the following courses.

One common kind of opening paragraph follows a general-to-specific sequence, ending with a thesis. In such an introduction, the writer opens with a general statement and then gets more and more specific, concluding with the most specific sentence in the paragraph — the thesis. The following paragraph illustrates such an opening:

> Throughout Western civilization, places such as the ancient Greek agora, the New England town hall, the local church, the coffeehouse, the village square, and even the street corner have been arenas for debate on public affairs and society. Out of thousands of such encounters, "public opinion" slowly formed and became the context in which politics was framed. Although the public sphere never included everyone, and by itself

did not determine the outcome of all parliamentary actions, it contributed to the spirit of dissent found in a healthy representative democracy. Many of these public spaces remain, but they are no longer centers for political discussion and action. They have largely been replaced by television and other forms of media — forms that arguably isolate citizens from one another rather than bringing them together.

> – MARK POSTER, "The Net as a Public Sphere"

In this paragraph, the opening sentence introduces a general subject, sites of public debate throughout history; subsequent sentences focus more specifically on the roles public spaces have played in democratic societies; and the last sentence presents the thesis, which the rest of the essay will develop.

OTHER EFFECTIVE WAYS OF OPENING

- with a quotation
- with an anecdote
- with a question
- with an opinion

Concluding paragraphs

A good conclusion wraps up a piece of writing in a meaningful and memorable way. If a strong opening paragraph arouses readers' curiosity, a strong concluding paragraph satisfies readers.

A common strategy for concluding is to restate the main idea (but not word for word) and then move to several more general statements. The following paragraph uses this strategy, opening with a final point of contrast, specifying it in several sentences, and then ending with a much more general statement:

> Lastly, and perhaps greatest of all, there was the ability, at the end, to turn quickly from war to peace once the fighting was over. Out of the way these two men behaved at Appomattox came the possibility of a peace of reconciliation. It was a possibility not wholly realized, in the years to come, but which did, in the end, help the two sections to become one nation again . . . after a war whose bitterness might have seemed to make such a reunion wholly impossible. No part of either man's life became him more than the part he played in this brief meeting in the McLean house at Appomattox. Their behavior there put all succeeding generations of Americans in their debt. Two great Americans, Grant and Lee — very different, yet under everything very much alike. Their encounter at Appomattox was one of the great moments of American history.
>
> – BRUCE CATTON, "Grant and Lee: A Study in Contrasts"

OTHER EFFECTIVE WAYS OF CONCLUDING

- with a quotation
- with a question
- with a vivid image
- with a call for action
- with a warning

A Matter of Style: Reiterating

One pattern you may recognize from political discourse and some forms of preaching is known as reiterating. In this pattern, the writer states the main point of a paragraph and then reiterates it in a number of different ways, hammering home the point and often building in intensity as well. This strategy finds particular power in the writing and preaching of Martin Luther King Jr., as in the following example:

> We are on the move now. The burning of our churches will not deter us. We are on the move now. The bombing of our homes will not dissuade us. We are on the move now. The beating and killing of our clergymen and young people will not divert us. We are on the move now. The arrest and release of known murderers will not discourage us. We are on the move now. Like an idea whose time has come, not even the marching of mighty armies can halt us. We are moving to the land of freedom.
>
> – MARTIN LUTHER KING JR., "Our God Is Marching On"

8

Revising and Editing

Whether you are writing a wedding invitation, an email to a client, or a history essay, you will want to make time to revise and edit what you write. Revising involves taking a fresh look at a draft, making sure that it includes all the necessary information and that the presentation is clear and effective. Editing involves fine-tuning your prose, attending to details of grammar, usage, punctuation, and spelling. Finally, careful proofreading aims at a perfect copy.

✳ **For Multilingual Writers:**
Asking a Native Speaker to Review Your Draft

One good way to make sure that your writing is well developed and easy to follow is to have someone else read it. You might find it especially helpful to ask a native speaker to read over your draft and to point out any words or patterns that are unclear or not idiomatic. (See Chapter 57 for more on words used idiomatically.)

8a Revising

If at all possible, put the draft away for a day or two to clear your mind and get some distance from your writing.

Rereading for meaning

At this point, don't worry about small details. Instead, concentrate on your message and how clearly you have expressed it. Note any places where the meaning seems unclear.

Remembering your purpose

Does your draft achieve its purpose? If you wrote for an assignment, go back to it to see that you did what was asked. If you set out to prove something, make sure you have done so. If you intended to propose a solution to a problem, make sure you have indeed set forth a well-supported solution rather than, for instance, an analysis of the problem.

Considering your audience

How appropriately do you address your audience? Think carefully about your audience's experiences and expectations. Will you catch their interest, and will they be able to follow your discussion? Is the language formal or informal enough for these readers? Have you defined any terms they may not know? What objections might they raise?

Getting response

In addition to your own critical appraisal and that of an instructor or supervisor, you may want to get response to either your printed or online draft from friends, classmates, or colleagues.

The following questions can be used to respond to someone else's draft or to analyze your own. If you ask other people to evaluate your draft, be sure that they know your assignment, intended audience, and purpose.

Some Guidelines for Peer Response

- *Purpose.* Does the draft carry out the assignment? Does it accomplish its purpose?
- *Title and introduction.* Does the title tell readers what the draft is about? How does it catch readers' interest? What does the opening accomplish? Does it make readers want to continue? How else might the draft begin?
- *Thesis.* What is the main idea? Is it stated explicitly? Should it be?
- *Audience.* How does the draft interest and appeal to its audience? Is it written at the right level for the intended readers?
- *Supporting points.* List the main points and review them one by one. How does each one support the thesis? Do any need to be explained more or less fully? Do any seem confusing or boring? Do any make you want to know more? Should any points be eliminated or added? How well is each point supported by evidence, examples, or details?
- *Organization and flow.* Is the writing easy to follow? Are the ideas presented in an order that will make sense to readers?
- *Transitions.* Are there effective transitions within sentences, between paragraphs, and from one idea to the next?
- *Conclusion.* Does the draft conclude in a memorable way, or does it seem to end abruptly or trail off into vagueness? How else might it end?
- *Final thoughts.* What are the main strengths and weaknesses of the draft? What might still be confusing to readers? What is the single most important thing you say in the draft? What will readers want to know more about?

8b Editing

Once you have revised a draft for content and organization, it is time to look closely at your sentences and words. Turning a "blah" sentence into a memorable one — or finding exactly the right word to express a thought — can result in writing that is really worth reading.

Examining your sentences

Good sentences keep readers engaged and ready for more. As with life, variety is the spice of sentences. You can add variety to your sentences by looking closely at their length, structure, and opening patterns.

Varying sentence length

Too many short sentences, especially one after another, can sound like a series of blasts on a car horn, whereas a steady stream of long sentences may tire or confuse readers. Most writers aim for some variety in length, breaking up a series of fairly long sentences with a very brief one.

In examining the following paragraph, the writer found that all five of its sentences were almost exactly the same length. See how varying the lengths of two sentences makes the paragraph easier to read:

The incident, which occurred when I was six and my sister was seven, has changed me in many ways. ~~Primarily as a~~ *One* result of ~~the~~ *that* harsh appraisal ~~my father's acquaintance~~ *has been an extreme concern for* ~~gave me, I have always been very concerned about~~ my appearance. Conceivably, a concern about my appearance can be beneficial; however, at times it is a bit of an obsession. I have become overly critical of my own appearance, but even more critical of the appearance of those around me. I instantly judge a person by the way he or she looks, a ~~prejudice that includes everyone, not~~ *practice that is the basis for prejudice and one that* ~~just minorities.~~ *limits my appreciation of myself as well as of others.*

Varying sentence openings

Opening sentence after sentence in the same way results in a jerky, abrupt, or choppy rhythm. You can vary sentence openings by beginning with a dependent clause, a phrase, an adverb, a conjunctive adverb, or a coordinating conjunction (15b).

The following paragraph provides vivid description and imaginative dialogue, but see how revising some of the openings improves the flow and makes the entire paragraph easier to read and more memorable.

> "Your daughter is absolutely beautiful!" the woman
> *A*
> gushed as she talked to my father. ~~She was a~~ friend of
> *she*
> his from work, ~~and~~ had heard much about my sister Tracy
> and me, but had never met us before. I could tell that
> she was one of those blunt, elderly women, the type that
> pinches cheeks, because as soon as she finished appraising
> my sister, she turned to me with a <u>deductive</u> look in her
> *Beady*   *traveling*
> eye. Her face said it all. ~~Her beady~~ brown eyes ~~traveled~~
> slowly from my head to my toe*,* ~~as~~ she sized me up and
> said rather condescendingly, "Oh, and she must be the
> smart one." I looked down at my toes as I rocked
> nervously back and forth. Then, looking at my sister I
> realized for the first time that she was very pretty, and
> I was, well, the smart one.

Checking for sentences opening with it *and* there

As you go over the opening sentences of your draft, look especially at those beginning with *it* or *there*. Sometimes these words can create a special emphasis, as in "It was a dark and stormy night." But they can also easily be overused or misused. Another, more subtle problem with these openings is that they may be used to avoid taking responsibility for a statement. The following sentence can be improved by editing:

> *The university must*
> ▶ ~~It is necessary to~~ raise student fees.
> ^

Examining words

The words you choose allow you to put a personal stamp on your writing. Study your word choice carefully, making sure you get the most mileage out of each word. Because word choice is highly individual, general guidelines are hard to provide. Nevertheless, the following questions should help you think about the kinds of words you use:

- Are the nouns primarily abstract and general or concrete and specific? Too many abstract and general nouns can result in boring prose. To say that you bought a new car is much less memorable and interesting than to say you bought a new red convertible or a new Nissan.

- Are there too many nouns in relation to the number of verbs? The *effect* of the *overuse* of *nouns* in *writing* is the *placing* of too much *strain* on the inadequate *number* of *verbs* and the resultant *prevention* of *movement* of the *thought*. In the preceding sentence, one tiny verb (*is*) has to drag along the entire weight of eleven nouns. The result is a heavy, boring sentence. Why not say instead, *Overusing nouns places a big strain on the verbs and consequently slows down the prose?*

- How many verbs are forms of *be—be, am, is, are, was, were, being, been?* If *be* verbs account for more than about a third of your total verbs, you are probably overusing them (17a, b).

- Are verbs *active* wherever possible? Passive verbs are harder to read and remember than active ones. Although the passive voice has many uses, often your writing will be stronger, more lively, and more energetic if you use active verbs (17g).

- Are your words *appropriate?* Check to be sure they are not too fancy — or too casual.

Using spell checkers and style checkers

While these software tools won't catch every spelling error or identify all problems of style, they can be very useful. Most professional writers use their spell checkers religiously. Remember, however, that spell checkers are limited; they don't recognize most proper names, foreign words, or specialized language and they do not recognize homonym errors (misspelling *there* as *their*, for example). Most commercial style checkers will highlight cliches, repetitions, or expressions like *it is* and *there are*.

Examining tone

Tone refers to the attitude that a writer's language conveys toward the topic and the audience. In examining the tone of your draft, think about the nature of the topic, your own attitude toward it, and that of your intended audience. Check for connotations, or specific associations, of words as well as slang, jargon, emotional language, and the level of formality. Is your language creating the tone you want to achieve (humorous, serious, impassioned, and so on), and is that tone an appropriate one, given your audience and topic? You may discover from examining the tone of your draft that your own attitude toward the topic is different from what you originally thought.

Proofreading the final draft

Take time for one last, careful proofreading, which means reading to correct any typographical errors or other slips, such as inconsistencies in spelling and punctuation. To proofread most effectively, read through the copy aloud, making sure that punctuation marks are used correctly and consistently, that all sentences are complete, and that no words are left out. Then go through it again, this time reading backward so that you can focus on each individual word and its spelling. This final proofreading aims to make your written product letter-perfect, something you can be proud of.

SENTENCE STYLE

When you start writing—and I think
it's true for a lot of beginning
writers—you're scared to death that
if you don't get that sentence right
that minute it's never going to show
up again. And it isn't. But it doesn't
matter—another one will, and it'll
probably be better.

— TONI MORRISON,
The Sight of Memory

SENTENCE STYLE

9

Consistency and Completeness

If you listen carefully to the conversations around you, you will hear inconsistent and incomplete structures all the time, particularly during a lively or heated discussion. For instance:

> "The Bulls are . . . They must be . . . Man, they are absolutely the very best team . . . not in the League even . . . in the world."
>
> "Wait till the Sonics take them. Because you know that Shawn Kemp will be more lethal than . . . he will be up to Jordan . . . for sure . . . just wait!"

In the flow of informal conversation, such structures pose few problems for speakers or listeners. But in writing, these "sentences" can seem mixed up, incoherent, or nonsensical. This chapter provides guidelines for recognizing and editing mixed and incomplete structures.

Editing for Consistency and Completeness

- If you find an especially confusing sentence, check to see whether it has a subject (*The athletes swam and ran*) and a predicate (*The athletes swam and ran*). If not, revise as necessary. (9a) If you find both a subject and a predicate, and you are still confused, see whether the subject and verb make sense together. If not, revise so that they do. (9b)

- Revise any *is when*, *is where*, and *reason is because* constructions. (9b)
  > the city
  > ▶ Rio is where I learned Portuguese.
  >   ^

- Check all comparisons for completeness. (9e)
  >   we like
  > ▶ We like Marian better than Margaret.
  >   ^

9a Make grammatical patterns consistent.

One inconsistency that poses problems for writers and readers is a mixed structure, which results from beginning a sentence with one grammatical pattern and then switching to another one. For example:

MIXED   The fact that I get up at 5:00 A.M., a wake-up time that explains why I'm always tired in the evening.

The sentence starts out with a subject (*The fact*) followed by a dependent clause (*that I get up at 5:00 A.M.*). The sentence needs a predicate to complete the independent clause but instead it moves to another phrase followed by a dependent clause (*a wake-up time that explains why I'm always tired in the evening*). Thus the independent clause is never completed, and what results is a fragment, or incomplete sentence.

REVISED   The fact that I get up at 5:00 A.M. explains why I'm always tired in the evening.

Deleting *a wake-up time that* changes the rest of the sentence into a predicate.

REVISED   I get up at 5:00 A.M., a wake-up time that explains why I'm always tired in the evening.

Deleting *The fact that* turns the beginning of the sentence into an independent clause.

9b   Make subjects and predicates consistent.

Another kind of mixed structure, called faulty predication, occurs when a subject and predicate do not fit together grammatically or simply do not make sense together. Many cases of faulty predication result from using forms of *be* when another verb would be stronger.

▶ A characteristic that I admire is ~~a person who is generous.~~ *generosity.*

A person is not a characteristic.

▶ The rules of the corporation ~~expect~~ *require that* employees ~~to~~ be on time.

Rules cannot expect anything.

Is when, is where, *and* reason is because

These illogical constructions are inappropriate in academic or professional writing.

▶ A stereotype is ~~when someone characterizes~~ *an unfair characterization of* a group ~~unfairly.~~.

▶ A confluence is ~~where~~ *a place* two rivers join to form one.

▶ ~~The reason~~ I like to play soccer ~~is~~ because it provides aerobic exercise.

9c Use elliptical structures carefully.

Sometimes writers omit certain words in compound structures. When the omission is common to all parts of the compound, this type of structure, known as an elliptical structure, is appropriate. In the following sentence, the omitted word is in brackets:

▶ That bell belonged to the figure of Miss Duling as though it grew directly out of her right arm, as wings grew out of an angel or a tail [grew] out of the devil. – EUDORA WELTY, *One Writer's Beginnings*

If the omitted word does not match all parts of the compound, readers might be confused, and so the omission is inappropriate.

▶ His skills are weak, and his performance only average.
is

The omitted verb *is* does not match both parts of the compound (*skills are . . . performance is*), and so the writer must include it.

9d Check for missing words.

The best way to catch inadvertent omissions is to proofread carefully, reading each sentence slowly — and aloud.

▶ The professor's heavy German accent made difficult for the class understand her lectures.
it   *to*

9e Make comparisons complete, consistent, and clear.

Check comparisons. When you compare two or more things, the comparison must be complete, logically consistent, and clear.

▶ I was embarrassed because my parents were so different/
from my friends' parents.

Different from what? Adding *from my friends' parents* tells readers what the comparison is being made to.

                                          the one by

▶ **Woodberry's biography is better than Fields.**
                                         ^

This sentence illogically compares a book with a person. The editing makes the comparison logical.

UNCLEAR   Ted always felt more affection for his brother than his sister.

Did Ted feel more affection for his brother than his sister did — or more affection for his brother than he felt for his sister?

CLEAR   Ted always felt more affection for his brother than *he did for* his sister.

CLEAR   Ted always felt more affection for his brother than his sister *did.*

10

Coordination and Subordination

If you think about how you build sentences, you may notice a difference between your spoken and your written language. In speech, people tend to use *and* and *so* as all-purpose connectors.

I'm going home now, and I'll see you later.

The meaning of this sentence may be perfectly clear in speech, which provides clues with voice, facial expressions, and gestures. But in writing, the actual meaning might not be clear. It could, for instance, have two rather different meanings.

Because I'm going home now, I'll see you later.

I'm going home now because I'll see you later.

The first sentence links two ideas with *and*, a coordinating conjunction; the other two sentences link ideas with *because*, a subordinating conjunction. These examples show two different ways of combining ideas in a sentence: coordinating conjunctions give the ideas equal emphasis; and subordinating conjunctions emphasize one idea more than another.

Editing for Coordination and Subordination

How do your ideas flow from one sentence to another? Do they connect smoothly and clearly? Are the more important ideas given more emphasis than less important ones? These guidelines will help you edit with such questions in mind.

- How often do you link ideas with *and*? If you use *and* excessively, decide whether all the ideas are equally important. If they are not equal, edit to subordinate the less important ones. (10b)

- Look for strings of short sentences that might be combined to join related ideas. (10a)

  ▶ The report was short. It was persuasive. It changed my mind.

  but it   *;*

- Are the most important ideas in independent clauses? If not, edit so that they are. (10b)

  Even though the
  ▶ ~~The~~ report was short, ~~even though~~ it changed my mind.

10a Use coordination to relate equal ideas.

When you want to give equal emphasis to different ideas in a sentence, link them with a coordinating conjunction (*and, but, for, nor, or, so, yet*) or a semicolon. The following sentences all use coordination: the precise relationship between the different ideas in each sentence is expressed by a coordinating conjunction or a semicolon.

▶ They acquired horses, *and* their ancient nomadic spirit was suddenly free of the ground.

▶ There is perfect freedom in the mountains, *but* it belongs to the eagle and the elk, the badger and the bear.

▶ No longer were they slaves to the simple necessity of survival; they were a lordly and dangerous society of fighters and thieves, hunters and priests of the sun.

– N. Scott Momaday, The Way to Rainy Mountain

Coordination can help make explicit the relationship between two separate ideas.

▶ My son watches *The Simpsons* religiously/;̷ F̷orced to choose, he
would probably choose Homer Simpson over his sister.

Connecting these two sentences with a semicolon strengthens the connection between two closely related ideas.

When you connect ideas in a sentence, make sure that the relationship
between the ideas is clear.

▶ Moderate breezes can roll and slide these grains along a sandy bed,
but it takes a fresh wind to lift sand grains into the air flow.
 – FRANK PRESS AND RAYMOND SIEVER, *Understanding Earth*

▶ Watching television is a common way to spend leisure time, a̷n̷d̷ *but* it
makes viewers apathetic.

The relationship between the two ideas in the original sentence is unclear:
what does being a common form of leisure have to do with being
apathetic? Changing *and* to *but* better relates the two ideas.

10b Use subordination to emphasize main ideas.

Subordination allows you to distinguish major points from minor
points or to bring in supporting details. If, for instance, you put your
main idea in an independent clause, you might then put any less significant ideas in dependent clauses, phrases, or even single words. The
following sentence shows the subordinated point in italics:

▶ Mrs. Viola Cullinan was a plump woman *who lived in a three-*
bedroom house somewhere behind the post office.
 – MAYA ANGELOU, "My Name Is Margaret"

The dependent clause adds important information about Mrs. Cullinan, but it is subordinate to the independent clause, which carries the
main idea: *Mrs. Viola Cullinan was a plump woman.*
　　Notice that the choice of what to subordinate rests with the writer
and depends on the intended meaning. Angelou might have given the
same basic information differently.

▶ Mrs. Viola Cullinan, *a plump woman,* lived in a three-bedroom house
somewhere behind the post office.

Subordinating the information about Mrs. Cullinan's size to that about her house would suggest a slightly different meaning, of course. As a writer, you must think carefully about what you want to emphasize and subordinate information accordingly.

Subordination also establishes logical relationships among ideas. These relationships are often specified by subordinating conjunctions.

SOME COMMON SUBORDINATING CONJUNCTIONS

after	if	though
although	in order that	unless
as	once	until
as if	since	when
because	so that	where
before	than	while
even though	that	

Look now at one more sentence by Maya Angelou, which is shown with the subordinate clause italicized and the subordinating conjunction underlined.

▶ She usually rested her smile until late afternoon *when her women friends dropped in and Miss Glory, the cook, served them cold drinks on the closed-in porch.* – MAYA ANGELOU, "My Name Is Margaret"

Using too many coordinate structures can be monotonous and can make it hard for readers to recognize the most important ideas. Subordinating lesser ideas can help highlight the main ideas.

▶ Many people come home tired in the evening, and so they turn on the
  Though they
TV to relax. ~~They~~ may intend to watch just the news, ~~but then~~ a game
  ^   which
show comes on next, ~~and~~ they decide to watch ~~it~~ for just a short
  Eventually,   ^
while~~,~~ ~~and~~ they get too comfortable to get up, and they end up
  ^
spending the whole evening in front of the TV.

The editing subordinates some of the less important ideas in the passage and makes clear to the reader that some of the ideas are more important than others.

A Matter of Style: Subordination

Carefully used subordination can create powerful effects. Some particularly fine examples come from Martin Luther King Jr.

> Perhaps it is easy for those who have never felt the stinging darts of segregation to say, "Wait." But *when* you have seen vicious mobs lynch your mothers and fathers at will and drown your sisters and brothers at whim; *when* you have seen hate-filled policemen curse, kick, and even kill your black brothers and sisters; . . . *when* you have to concoct an answer for a five-year-old son who is asking: "Daddy, why do white people treat colored people so mean?"; *when* you take a cross-country drive and find it necessary to sleep night after night in the uncomfortable corners of your automobile because no motel will accept you; . . . *when* your first name becomes "nigger," your middle name becomes "boy" (however old you are) and your last name becomes "John," and your wife and mother are never given the respected title "Mrs."; . . . *when* you are forever fighting a degenerating sense of "nobodiness" — then you will understand why we find it difficult to wait.
>
> – MARTIN LUTHER KING JR., "Letter from Birmingham Jail"

Subordinating less important ideas

▶ ~~Our~~ **new boss can be difficult, ~~although~~ she has revived and maybe**
  ^
  even saved the division.

Although our
(appears above as insertion)

The editing puts the more important information — that she has saved part of the company — in an independent clause and subordinates the other information.

Excessive subordination

When too many subordinate clauses are strung together, readers may have trouble keeping track of the main idea expressed in the independent clause.

TOO MUCH SUBORDINATION

▶ **Philip II sent the Spanish Armada to conquer England, which was ruled by Elizabeth, who had executed Mary because she was plotting to overthrow Elizabeth, who was a Protestant, whereas Mary and Philip were Roman Catholics.**

The long string of subordinate clauses makes the relationship of the ideas hard to follow — and also makes the main idea (in the independent clause at the beginning) hard for readers to remember.

REVISED

▶ **Philip II sent the Spanish Armada to conquer England, which was ruled by Elizabeth, a Protestant. She had executed Mary, a Roman Catholic like Philip, because Mary was plotting to overthrow her.**

Putting the facts about Elizabeth executing Mary into an independent clause makes key information easier to recognize.

11
Parallelism

Parallel grammatical structures are used in many of our most familiar phrases: *sink or swim, rise and shine, shape up or ship out.* If you look and listen for these structures, you will see parallelism in everyday use. Bumper stickers often use parallel grammatical structures to make their messages memorable (*Children on board; parents on Valium*), as do song lyrics and jump-rope rhymes. This chapter will help you use parallel structures to create pleasing rhythmic effects in your own writing.

Editing for Parallelism

- Look for any series of three or more items, and make all of the items parallel in structure. If you want to emphasize one particular item, try putting it at the end of the series. (11a)
- Check for places where two ideas are compared, contrasted, or otherwise paired in the same sentence. Often these ideas will appear on either side of *and, but, or, nor, for, so,* or *yet,* or after each part of *both . . . and, either . . . or, neither . . . nor, not only . . . but also, whether . . . or,* or *just as . . . so.* Edit to make the two ideas parallel in structure. (11b)
- Check all parallel structures to be sure you have included all necessary words — articles, prepositions, the *to* of the infinitive, and so on. (11c)
- Be sure items in lists are parallel in form. (11a)
- Be sure all headings are parallel in form. (40b)

11a Make items in a series or list parallel.

All items in a series should be in parallel form — all nouns, all verbs, all prepositional phrases, and so on. Such parallelism makes a series both graceful and easy to follow.

> ▶ The enchantment grew not out of anything that happened or was performed but out of something that seemed to go round and around and around with the girl, attending her, a steady gleam in the shape of a circle — a ring *of ambition, of happiness, of youth.*
> – E. B. WHITE, "The Ring of Time"

> Just as the young woman goes "round and around and around," balanced easily on her horse, so the sentence circles rhythmically too, balanced by a series of parallel phrases.

In the sentences below, note how the revisions make all items in the series parallel.

> ▶ The quarter horse skipped, pranced, and ~~was sashaying~~ *sashayed* onto the track.

> ▶ The children ran down the hill, skipped over the lawn, and *jumped* into the swimming pool.

> ▶ The duties of the job include baby-sitting, house-cleaning, and ~~preparation of~~ *preparing* meals.

Items in a list and on a formal outline should be parallel (6c).

> ▶ Kitchen rules: (1) Coffee to be made only by library staff. (2) Coffee service to be closed at 4:00 P.M. (3) Doughnuts to be kept in cabinet. (4) ~~No faculty members should handle coffee materials.~~ *Coffee materials not to be handled by faculty.*

11b Use parallel structures to pair ideas.

Parallel structures can help you pair two ideas effectively. The more nearly parallel the two structures are, the stronger the connection between the ideas will be.

▶ **History became popular, and historians became alarmed.**
— WILL DURANT

▶ **We die. That may be the meaning of life. But we *do* language. That may be the measure of our lives.** — TONI MORRISON

the flesh
▶ **Writers are often more interesting on the page than in ~~person.~~**
^

In these examples, the parallel structures all help to point up an important contrast between two ideas or acts.

With coordinating conjunctions

When you link ideas with *and, but, or, nor, for, so,* or *yet,* try to make the ideas parallel in structure.

who is
▶ **Consult a friend in your class or who is good at math.**
^

accepts
▶ **The wise politician promises the possible and ~~should accept~~ the**
^
inevitable.

In both sentences, the editing links the two ideas by making them parallel.

With correlative conjunctions

Use the same structure after both parts of the following correlative conjunctions: *either . . . or, both . . . and, neither . . . nor, not . . . but, not only . . . but also, just as . . . so,* and *whether . . . or.*

live in
▶ **I wanted not only to go away to school but also to New England.**
^

Balancing *to go* with *to live* links the two ideas and makes the sentence easier to read.

11c Include all necessary words.

In addition to making parallel elements grammatically similar, be sure to include any words—prepositions, articles, verb forms, and so on— that are necessary for clarity, grammar, or idiom.

▶ We'll move to a town in the Southwest or *in* Mexico.

To a town in Mexico or to Mexico in general? The editing clarifies the meaning.

A Matter of Style: Parallelism

Parallel structures can help a writer emphasize important ideas, as Joan Didion does in the following sentence:

> I would like to promise her that she will grow up with a sense of her cousins and of rivers and of her great-grandmother's teacups, would like to pledge her a picnic on a river with fried chicken and her hair uncombed, would like to give her *home* for her birthday, but we live differently now and I can promise her nothing like that.
>
> – JOAN DIDION, "On Going Home"

The first two parallel phrases—*would like to promise her, would like to pledge her*—introduce a series of specific concrete details and images that lead up to the general statement in the last phrase, that she *would like to give her* daughter a sense of "home." Although Didion could have stated this general point first and then gone on to illustrate it with concrete details, she achieves greater emphasis by making it the last in a series of parallel structures.

12

Shifts

A shift in writing is an abrupt change of some sort that results in inconsistency. Sometimes writers shift deliberately, as Dave Barry does in saying he "would have to say that the greatest single achievement of the American medical establishment is nasal spray." Barry's shift in tone from the serious (the American medical establishment) to the banal (nasal spray) makes us laugh, as Barry wishes us to. Although writers sometimes deliberately make such shifts for good reasons, unintentional shifts can be jolting and confusing to readers. This chapter helps you edit out unintentional shifts in verbs, pronouns, and tone.

Editing for Confusing Shifts

- If you shift from one verb tense to another, check to be sure there is a reason for doing so. (12a)
- Do you see any shifts in mood—perhaps from an indicative statement to an imperative—and if so, are they necessary? (12b)
- Check for shifts from active (*She asks questions*) to passive voice (*Questions are asked*). Are they intentional—and if so, for what reason? (12c)
- Do you see any shifts in point of view—from *we* to *you*, for example—and if so, what are the reasons for the shifts? (12d)
- Check your writing for consistency in tone. If your tone is serious, is it consistently so? (12f)

12a Check for unnecessary shifts in tense.

If the verbs in a passage refer to actions occurring at different times, they may require different tenses. Be careful, however, not to change tenses for no reason.

> ▶ A few countries produce almost all of the world's illegal drugs, but
>   *affects*
>   addiction ~~affected~~ many countries.
>   ^

12b Check for shifts in mood.

Be careful not to shift from one mood to another without good reason. The mood of a verb can be indicative (he *closes* the door), imperative (*close* the door), or subjunctive (if the door *were closed*). (17h) Notice how the original version of the following sentence shifts unnecessarily from the imperative to the indicative:

> ▶ Keep your eye on the ball, and ~~you should~~ bend your knees.

The writer's purpose is to give orders, and the editing makes both verbs imperative.

12c   Check for shifts in voice.

Do not shift without reason between the active voice (she *sold* it) and the passive voice (it *was sold*). Sometimes a shift in voice is justified, but often it may only confuse readers (17g).

▶ Two youths approached ~~me, and I was~~ asked ^me^ for my wallet.

> The original sentence shifts from the active (*youths approached*) to the passive (*I was asked*), so it is unclear who asked for the wallet. Making both verbs active clears up the confusion.

12d   Check for shifts in point of view.

Unnecessary shifts between first-person point of view (*I, we*), second-person (*you*), and third-person (*he, she, it, one,* or *they*), or between singular and plural subjects can be very confusing to readers.

▶ ^You^ ~~One~~ can do well on this job if you budget your time.

> It was not clear whether the writer was making a general statement or giving advice to someone. Eliminating the shift eliminates this confusion.

▶ Nurses receive much less pay than doctors, even though ^nurses have^ ~~a nurse has~~ the primary responsibility for daily patient care.

> The writer had no reason to shift from third-person plural (*nurses*) to third-person singular (*a nurse*).

12e   Check for shifts between direct and indirect discourse.

When you quote someone's exact words, you are using direct discourse: *She said, "I'm an editor."* When you report what someone says without repeating the exact words, you are using indirect discourse: *She said she is an editor.* Shifting between direct and indirect discourse in the same sentence can cause problems, especially with questions.

▶ Bob asked what ^he^ could ~~he~~ do to help~~?~~.

> The editing eliminates an awkward shift by reporting Bob's words. It could be edited to quote him: *Bob asked, "What can I do to help?"*

12f Check for shifts in tone and diction.

Tone (a writer's attitude toward a topic or audience) is related to diction, or word choice, and to overall formality or informality. Watch out for shifts in your tone or diction that could confuse readers and leave them wondering what your real attitude is (8b).

INCONSISTENT TONE

The question of child care forces a society to make profound decisions about its economic values. Can most families with children actually live adequately on only one salary? If some conservatives had their way, June Cleaver would still be stuck in the kitchen baking cookies for Wally and the Beaver and waiting for Ward to bring home the bacon, except that with only one income, the Cleavers would be lucky to afford hot dogs.

In the first version, the first two sentences set a serious, formal tone, discussing child care in fairly general, abstract terms. But in the third sentence, the writer shifts suddenly to sarcasm and to references to television characters of an earlier era. Readers cannot tell whether the writer is presenting a serious analysis or preparing for a humorous satire. See how the passage was revised to make the tone consistent.

REVISED

The question of child care forces a society to make profound decisions about its economic values. Can most families with young children actually live adequately on only one salary? Some conservatives believe that women with young children should not work outside the home, but many are forced to do so for financial reasons.

INCONSISTENT DICTION

Since taking office, Prime Minister Chretien has been bombarded with really gross news, including tons of strikes, record unemployment, several scandals, and even bitching from colleagues in his own party.

REVISED

Since taking office, Prime Minister Chretien has been bombarded with unrelenting bad news, including a wave of strikes, record unemployment, several scandals, and even sniping from colleagues in his own party.

The shift in diction from formal to highly informal gives an odd, disjointed feeling to the passage. As revised, the passage is easier to read because the words are consistently formal.

13

Emphasis

In everyday speaking, emphasis is easy to achieve by raising our voices, putting extra stress on an important word, or drawing out a phrase. And much of the writing we see around us — in advertisements, on Web sites, in magazines — gains emphasis in similar fashion, with color or graphics or bold type, for instance.

Much academic or professional writing, however, can't rely on such graphic devices for emphasis. Luckily, writers have other tools at their disposal. This chapter will help you write emphatic sentences that put the spotlight on main ideas, letting readers know which elements are most important.

Editing for Sentence Emphasis

As you revise a draft, follow these steps to make sure that each sentence emphasizes the ideas you *want* emphasized.

- Identify the word or words you want to receive special emphasis. If those words are buried in the middle of a sentence, edit the sentence to change their position. Remember that the end and the beginning are generally the most emphatic. (13a)
- Note any sentences that include a series of three or more words, phrases, or clauses. Could the items in the series be arranged in climactic order, with the most important item last? (13b)

13a Use closing and opening positions for emphasis.

When you read a sentence, what are you likely to remember? Other things being equal, you remember the ending. This is the part of the sentence that should move the writing forward by providing new information, as it does in the following example:

▶ To protect her skin, she took along *plenty of sunblock lotion.*

A less emphatic but still important position in a sentence is the opening, which hooks up the new sentence with what has come before.

▶ **When Rosita went to the beach, she was anxious not to get a sunburn. *To protect her skin,* she took along plenty of sunblock lotion.**

The second sentence would lose emphasis if the key words, *plenty of sunblock lotion,* were buried in the middle, as in the following version:

▶ **To protect her skin, she took along *plenty of sunblock lotion,* and she also planned to stay under an umbrella most of the time.**

If you place relatively unimportant information in the memorable closing position of a sentence, you may undercut what you want to emphasize or give more emphasis to the closing words than you intend.

▶ *Last month, she* ~~She~~ gave $500,000 ~~to~~ the school capital campaign ~~last month.~~

Moving *$500,000* to the end of the sentence emphasizes the *amount.*

13b Use climactic order to emphasize important ideas.

Presenting ideas in climactic order means arranging them in order of increasing importance, power, or drama so that your writing builds to a climax.

▶ **After they've finished with the pantry, the medicine cabinet, and the attic, [neat people] will throw out the red geranium (too many leaves), sell the dog (too many fleas), and send the children off to boarding school (too many scuffmarks on the hardwood floors).**
> – SUSANNE BRITT,
> "Neat People vs. Sloppy People"

This statement saves its most dramatic item for last, making its point forcefully. The original version of the next sentence fails to achieve strong emphasis because its verbs are not sequenced in order of increasing power; the editing provides climactic order.

▶ **Soap operas** assault our eyes, damage our brains ~~,~~ *and* ~~and~~ **offend our ears** ~~,~~

14

Conciseness

You can see the importance of conciseness in directions, particularly those on medicines. Consider the following directions found on one common prescription drug:

> Take one tablet daily. Some drugs may aggravate your condition, so read all labels carefully. If any include a warning, check with your doctor.

These directions aim to state the message as clearly and concisely as possible to relay important information on a small label. Squeezing words onto a three-inch label is probably not your ordinary writing situation, but more often than not, you will want to write as concisely as you can.

Editing for Conciseness

- Look for redundant words. If you are unsure about a word, read the sentence without it; if meaning is not affected, leave the word out. (14b)
- Look for empty or meaningless words—words like *aspect* or *factor*, *definitely* or *very*. If your meaning would not change without them, take them out. (14c)
- Do you use any wordy phrases? If so, see if you can replace them with a single word. Instead of *because of the fact that*, try *because*. (14d)
- Reconsider any sentences that begin with *it is* or *there is/are*. Unless they create special emphasis, try recasting the sentences without these words. (14e)

14a Eliminate unnecessary words.

Usually you'll want to make your point in the fewest possible words. Compare the following sentence with its revision:

> ▶ Her constant and continual use of vulgar expressions with obscene meanings indicated to her pre-elementary supervisory group that she was rather deficient in terms of her ability to interact in an efficient manner with peers in her potential interaction group.

Why write that sentence when you could instead write the following?

▶ Her constant use of four-letter words told the day-care workers she might have trouble getting along with other four-year-olds.

14b Eliminate redundant words.

Sometimes writers add words for emphasis, saying that something is large *in size* or red *in color* or that two ingredients should be combined *together*. The italicized words are redundant, or unnecessary for meaning, as are the deleted words below.

▶ ~~Compulsory~~ ^A^ttendance at assemblies is required.

▶ The auction featured ~~contemporary~~ "antiques" made recently.

▶ Many different forms of hazing occur, such as physical ~~abuse~~ and mental abuse.

14c Eliminate empty words.

Empty words are those that contribute no real meaning. In general, delete them.

EMPTY WORDS

angle, area, aspect, case, character, element, factor, field, kind, nature, scope, situation, thing, type

Many modifiers are so common that they have become empty words, adding no meaning to a statement.

MEANINGLESS MODIFIERS

absolutely, awesome, awfully, central, definitely, fine, great, literally, major, quite, really, very

Because empty words tend to make writing dull as well as wordy, use them sparingly. When you cannot simply delete them, try to think of a more specific way to say what you mean.

▶ The ~~h~~^H^ousing ~~situation~~ can ~~have a really significant impact on the~~ ^strongly influence^ ~~social aspect of~~ ^social^ a student's life.

14d Replace wordy phrases.

Wordy phrases are those that can be reduced to a word or two with no loss in meaning.

WORDY	CONCISE
at all times	always
at the present time	now/today
at that point in time	then
due to the fact that	because
in order to	to
in spite of the fact that	although
in the event that	if
for the purpose of	for

14e Simplify sentence structure.

Using the simplest grammatical structures possible will tighten and strengthen your sentences considerably.

▶ Kennedy, ~~who was~~ only the second Roman Catholic ~~to be~~ nominated

for the presidency by a major party, had to handle the religion issue
delicately.
~~in a delicate manner.~~
　^
Reducing a clause to an appositive, deleting unnecessary words, and replacing four words with one tighten the sentence and make it easier to read.

Using strong verbs

Be verbs (*is, are, was, were, been*) often result in wordiness.

　　　　　　　　　　　　　　　　harms
▶ A high-fat, high-cholesterol diet ~~is bad for~~ your heart.
　　　　　　　　　　　　　　　　　^

Avoiding expletives

Words such as *there is*, *there are*, and *it is* often add excess words to a sentence. Sometimes these expletive constructions are an effective way to introduce a topic; often, however, your writing will be better without them.

▶ ~~There are~~ M̃any people ~~who~~ fear success because they believe they do
not deserve it.

▶ ~~It is necessary for~~ P̃residential candidates ^need^ to perform well on
television.

Using active voice

Try to use the active voice whenever possible. Some writing situations
call for the passive voice, but it is always wordier than the active — and
often makes for dull or even difficult reading.

▶ ~~In Gower's research, it was~~ ^Gower^ found that pythons often dwell in trees.

15

Sentence Variety

Row upon row of trees identical in size and shape may appeal at some
level to our sense of orderliness, but in spite of that appeal, the rows
soon become boring. Constant uniformity in anything, in fact, soon gets
tiresome, while its opposite, variation, is usually pleasing to readers.
Variety is important in sentence structures, while too much uniformity
results in dull, listless prose. This chapter examines ways to use some
traditional foes of boring sentences — variety in length and in openings.

> **Editing for Sentence Variety**
>
> • Count the words in each sentence, and underline the longest and short-
>   est sentences in each paragraph. If the difference between the longest
>   and shortest sentences is fairly small — say, five words or fewer — try
>   revising the paragraph to create greater variety in sentence length.
>   (15a)
>
> • If many sentences have fewer than ten words, consider whether any of
>   them need more detail or should be combined with other sentences.
>
> • How do your sentences open? If all or most of them open with a sub-
>   ject, try recasting some sentences to begin with a transition, a phrase,
>   or a dependent clause. (15b)

15a Vary sentence length.

When you vary the length of your sentences, your prose becomes more readable and interesting, and you create a pleasing rhythmic effect. Deciding how and when to vary sentence length, however, is not always easy. How short is too short? How long is too long? Is there a "just right" length for a particular sentence or idea? The answers depend on, among other things, your purpose, intended audience, and topic. Frequent alternation in sentence length characterizes much memorable writing. After one or more long sentences with complex ideas or images, the punch of a short sentence can be refreshing.

▶ **The fire of, I think, five machine-guns was pouring upon us, and there was a series of heavy crashes caused by the Fascists flinging bombs over their own parapet in the most idiotic manner. It was intensely dark.**   **– George Orwell, *Homage to Catalonia***

15b Vary sentence openings.

Varying the way sentences open can make your writing readable and interesting. In fact, if sentence after sentence begins with the subject, a passage may become monotonous or even hard to read.

▶ **The way football and basketball are played is as interesting as the**
Because football
players. F̶o̶o̶t̶b̶a̶l̶l̶ is a game of precision/, ᴇ̆ach play is diagrammed to
  ^
accomplish a certain goal. Basketball, is a game of endurance.
however,
   ^
In fact, a
A̶ basketball game looks like a track meet; the team that drops of
 ^
exhaustion first loses. Basketball players are often compared to artists/,
their
T̶h̶e̶ p̶l̶a̶y̶e̶r̶s̶' moves and slam dunks a̶r̶e̶ their masterpieces.
 ^

The editing adds variety by using subordinating words (*Because* in the second line) and a prepositional phrase (*In fact* in the fourth line), and by linking sentences. Varying sentence openings prevents the passage from seeming to jerk or lurch along.

You can add variety to your sentence openings by using transitions, various kinds of phrases, and introductory dependent clauses.

TRANSITIONAL EXPRESSIONS

▶ *In contrast,* **our approach will save time and money.**

▶ *Nevertheless,* **the show must go on.**

PHRASES

▶ *At each desk,* **a computer printout provides necessary data.**

▶ *Frustrated by the delays,* **the drivers started honking their horns.**

▶ *To qualify for flight training,* **one must be in good physical condition.**

▶ *Our hopes for snow shattered,* **we started home.**

▶ *Baton raised in a salute,* **the maestro readied the orchestra.**

DEPENDENT CLAUSES

▶ *What they want* **is a place to call home.**

▶ *Because the hills were dry,* **the fire spread rapidly.**

A Matter of Style: Technical Style

For some types of writing, varying sentence structure and length is not always appropriate. Many technical writers, particularly those who write manuals that will be translated into other languages, must follow stringent rules for sentence structure and length. Technical writers working for Hewlett-Packard, for example, must adhere to a strict subject-verb-object order and limit all sentences to a maximum length of fifteen words. You will want to understand the style conventions of your field as fully as possible, then, and bring them to bear on your own sentence revisions.

SENTENCE
GRAMMAR

As we mature, we learn a great deal
about grammar from reading — and
not grammar books but newspapers,
novels, poetry, magazines, even the
labels on cereal boxes.

— LYNN Z. BLOOM,
Strategic Writing

SENTENCE GRAMMAR

16

Basic Grammar

The grammar of our first language comes to us almost automatically, without our thinking much about it or even being aware of it. Listen in, for instance, on a conversation between two six-year-olds.

> CHARLOTTE: My new bike that Grandma got me has a red basket and a loud horn, and I love it.
>
> ANNA: Can I ride it?
>
> CHARLOTTE: Sure, as soon as I take a turn.

This simple conversation features sophisticated grammar—the subordination of one clause to another, a compound object, a series of adjectives—used effortlessly. Though native speakers know the basic grammatical "rules," these rules can produce a broad range of sentences, some more effective and artful than others. Understanding the grammatical structures presented in this chapter can help you produce sentences that are grammatical—and appropriate and effective as well.

16a The basic grammar of sentences

A sentence is a grammatically complete group of words that expresses a thought. To be grammatically complete, a group of words must contain a subject, which identifies what the sentence is about, and a predicate, which says or asks something about the subject or tells the subject to do something.

SUBJECT	PREDICATE
I	have a dream.
The rain in Spain	stays mainly in the plain.
Puff, the magic dragon,	lived by the sea.

Some brief sentences have a one-word predicate with an implied, or "understood," subject (for example, *Stop!*). Most sentences, however, contain additional words that expand the basic subject and predicate. In the preceding example about the dragon, for instance, the subject might have been simply *Puff*; the words *the magic dragon* tell us more about the subject. Similarly, the predicate of that sentence could grammatically be *lived*; the words *by the sea* expand the predicate by telling us where Puff lived.

PARTS OF SPEECH

All English words belong to one or more of eight grammatical categories called parts of speech: verbs, nouns, pronouns, adjectives, adverbs, prepositions, conjunctions, and interjections. Many English words regularly function as more than one part of speech. Take the word *book*, for example: when you *book a plane flight*, it is a verb; when you *take a good book to the beach*, it is a noun; and when you *have book knowledge*, it is an adjective.

16b Verbs

Verbs are among the most important words because they move the meaning of sentences along. Verbs show action of body or mind (*glance, speculate*), occurrence (*become, happen*), or a state of being (*be, seem*). They can also change form to show *time, person, number, voice,* and *mood.*

TIME	we *work*, we *worked*
PERSON	I *work*, she *works*
NUMBER	one person *works*, two people *work*
VOICE	she *asks*, she *is asked*
MOOD	we *see*, if we *saw*

Auxiliary verbs (also called helping verbs) combine with other verbs (often called main verbs) to create verb phrases. Auxiliaries include the various forms of *be, do,* and *have* (which can also be used as main verbs) and the words *can, could, may, might, must, shall, should, will,* and *would.*

▶ You *do need* some sleep tonight!

▶ I *could have danced* all night.

▶ She *would prefer* to learn Italian rather than Spanish.

See Chapter 17 for a complete discussion of verbs.

16c Nouns

Nouns name persons (*aviator, child*), places (*lake, library*), things (*truck, suitcase*), and concepts (*happiness, balance*). Proper nouns name specific persons, places, things, and concepts: *Bill, Iowa, Supreme Court, Buddhism.* Collective nouns name groups: *team, flock, jury* (18d).

You can change most nouns from singular (one) to plural (more than one) by adding *-s* or *-es: horse, horses; kiss, kisses.* Some nouns, however, have irregular plural forms: *woman, women; alumnus, alumni; mouse, mice; deer, deer.* Noncount nouns, such as *dust, peace,* and *prosperity,* do not have a plural form because they name something that cannot easily be counted (27c).

To show ownership, nouns take the possessive form by adding an apostrophe plus -*s* to a singular noun or just an apostrophe to a plural noun: *the horse's owner, the boys' dilemma* (32a).

Nouns are often preceded by the articles *a, an,* or *the* (also known as determiners): *a rocket, an astronaut, the launch* (55c, d).

✳ **For Multilingual Writers: Count and Noncount Nouns**

Is the hill covered with grass or grasses? See 55a for a discussion of count and noncount nouns.

16d Pronouns

Pronouns often take the place of nouns, serving as short forms so that you do not have to repeat a noun that you have already mentioned. A noun that a pronoun replaces or refers to is the antecedent of the pronoun. (See Chapter 21.)

ANTECEDENT   PRONOUN
▶ *Caitlin* **refused the invitation even though** *she* **wanted to go.**

Here are the categories of pronouns.

PERSONAL PRONOUNS

Personal pronouns refer to specific persons or things.

I, me, you, he, she, him, it, we, they

▶ **After the scouts made camp,** *they* **ran along the beach.**

POSSESSIVE PRONOUNS

Possessive pronouns indicate ownership.

my, mine, your, yours, her, hers,
his, its, our, ours, their, theirs

▶ *My* **roommate lost** *her* **keys.**

REFLEXIVE PRONOUNS

Reflexive pronouns refer to the subject of the sentence or clause in which they appear. They end in *-self* or *-selves*.

> myself, yourself, himself, herself, itself, oneself, ourselves, yourselves, themselves

▶ **The seals sunned** *themselves* **on the warm rocks.**

INTENSIVE PRONOUNS

Intensive pronouns have the same form as reflexive pronouns. They emphasize a noun or another pronoun.

▶ **He decided to paint the apartment** *himself*.

INDEFINITE PRONOUNS

Indefinite pronouns do not refer to specific nouns, although they may refer to identifiable persons or things. The following is a partial list:

> all, another, anybody, both, each, either, everything, few, many, most, neither, none, no one, nothing, one, some, something

▶ *Somebody* **screamed when the lights went out.**

DEMONSTRATIVE PRONOUNS

Demonstrative pronouns identify or point to specific nouns.

> this, that, these, those

▶ *These* **are Peter's books.**

INTERROGATIVE PRONOUNS

Interrogative pronouns are used to ask questions.

> who, which, what

▶ *Who* **can help set up the chairs for the meeting?**

RELATIVE PRONOUNS

Relative pronouns introduce dependent clauses and "relate" the dependent clause to the rest of the sentence (16m).

> who, which, that, what, whoever, whichever, whatever

▶ **Margaret owns the car** *that* **is parked by the corner.**

The interrogative pronoun *who* and the relative pronouns *who* and *whoever* have different forms depending on how they are used in a sentence. (See Chapter 21.)

RECIPROCAL PRONOUNS

Reciprocal pronouns refer to individual parts of a plural antecedent.

each other, one another

▶ **The business failed because the partners distrusted** *each other.*

16e Adjectives

Adjectives modify (limit the meaning of) nouns and pronouns, usually by describing, identifying, or quantifying those words.

▶ **The** *red* **Corvette ran off the road.** [describes]
▶ *That* **Corvette needs to be repaired.** [identifies]
▶ **We saw** *several* **Corvettes race by.** [quantifies]

In addition to their basic forms, most descriptive adjectives have other forms that allow you to make comparisons; *small, smaller, smallest; foolish, more foolish, most foolish, less foolish, least foolish* (19c). Many of the words functioning as pronouns (16d) can function as adjectives when they are followed by a noun.

▶ *That* **is a dangerous intersection.** [pronoun]
▶ *That* **intersection is dangerous.** [adjective]

Adjectives usually precede the words they modify, though they may follow linking verbs.

▶ **The car was** *defective.*

Other kinds of adjectives that identify or quantify are articles (*a, an, the*) and numbers (*three, sixty-fifth*).

Proper adjectives are adjectives formed from or related to proper nouns (*Egyptian, Emersonian*). Proper adjectives are capitalized (35b).

16f Adverbs

Adverbs modify verbs, adjectives, other adverbs, or entire clauses. Many adverbs have an *-ly* ending, though some do not (*always, never, very, well*), and some words that end in *-ly* are not adverbs but adjectives (*friendly, lovely*). One of the most common adverbs is *not*.

▶ **David and Rebecca *recently* visited Maine.** [modifies the verb *visited*]

▶ **They had an *unexpectedly* exciting trip.** [modifies the adjective *exciting*]

▶ **They *very* soon discovered lobster.** [modifies the adverb *soon*]

▶ ***Frankly*, they would have liked to stay another month.** [modifies the independent clause that makes up the rest of the sentence]

Many adverbs, like many adjectives, have other forms that can be used to make comparisons: *forcefully, more forcefully, most forcefully, less forcefully, least forcefully* (19c).

Conjunctive adverbs modify an entire clause and help connect the meaning between that clause and the preceding clause (or sentence). Examples of conjunctive adverbs include *however, furthermore, therefore,* and *likewise* (16h).

16g Prepositions

Prepositions are important structural words that express relationships between nouns or pronouns and other words in a sentence. Prepositions may show relationships of space (*beyond*) or time (*after*) or some other kind of relationship (*as, regarding*).

▶ **We did not want to leave *during* the game.**

▶ **The contestants waited nervously *for* the announcement.**

▶ **Drive *across* the bridge, go *down* the avenue *past* three stoplights, and then turn left *before* the Gulf station.**

SOME COMMON PREPOSITIONS

about	at	down	near	since
above	before	during	of	through
across	behind	except	off	toward
after	below	for	on	under
against	beneath	from	onto	until
along	beside	in	out	up
among	between	inside	over	upon
around	beyond	into	past	with
as	by	like	regarding	without

SOME COMPOUND PREPOSITIONS

according to	except for	instead of
as well as	in addition to	next to
because of	in front of	out of
by way of	in place of	with regard to
due to	in spite of	

16h Conjunctions

Conjunctions connect words or groups of words to each other and tell something about the relationship between these words.

Coordinating conjunctions

Coordinating conjunctions join equivalent structures—two or more nouns, pronouns, verbs, adjectives, adverbs, prepositions, conjunctions, phrases, or clauses (10a).

▶ A strong *but* warm breeze blew across the desert.

▶ Please print *or* type the information on the application form.

▶ Kristin worked two shifts today, *so* she is tired tonight.

COORDINATING CONJUNCTIONS

and	for	or	yet
but	nor	so	

Correlative conjunctions

Correlative conjunctions join equal elements; these conjunctions come in pairs.

▶ *Both* Bechtel *and* Kaiser submitted bids on the project.

▶ Jeff *not only* sent a card *but also* visited me in the hospital.

CORRELATIVE CONJUNCTIONS

both . . . and	neither . . . nor
either . . . or	not only . . . but also
just as . . . so	whether . . . or

Subordinating conjunctions

Subordinating conjunctions introduce adverb clauses and signal the relationship between an adverb clause and another clause, usually an independent clause (10a, 16m). For instance, in the following sentence, the subordinating conjunction *while* signals a time relationship between the two events in the sentence, letting us know that they both happened simultaneously:

▶ Sweat ran down my face *while* I frantically searched for my child.

SOME SUBORDINATING CONJUNCTIONS

after	if	though
although	in order that	unless
as	once	until
as if	since	when
because	so that	where
before	than	whether
even though	that	while

Conjunctive adverbs

Conjunctive adverbs signal a logical relationship between parts of a sentence and, when used with a semicolon, can link independent clauses (16m).

▶ The cider tasted bitter; *however,* each of us drank a tall glass of it.
▶ The cider tasted bitter; each of us, *however,* drank a tall glass of it.

SOME CONJUNCTIVE ADVERBS

also	indeed	now
anyway	instead	otherwise
besides	likewise	similarly
certainly	meanwhile	still
finally	moreover	then
furthermore	namely	therefore
however	nevertheless	thus
incidentally	next	undoubtedly

16i   Interjections

Interjections express surprise or emotion: *oh, ouch, ah, hey*. Interjections often stand alone, as fragments. Even when interjections are part of a sentence, they do not relate grammatically to the rest of the sentence.

▶ **The problem suggested, *alas*, no easy solution.**

PARTS OF SENTENCES

Knowing a word's part of speech helps us understand how to use that word. But we also need to look at the way the word functions in a particular sentence. Consider, for instance, the word *description*.

         SUBJECT
▶ **This *description* evokes the ecology of the Everglades.**

         DIRECT OBJECT
▶ **I need a *description* of the ecology of the Everglades.**

Description is a noun in both sentences, yet in the first it serves as the subject of the verb *evokes*, while in the second it serves as the direct object of the verb *need*.

Basic sentence patterns

1. SUBJECT/VERB

    S   V
▶ **Babies cry.**

2. SUBJECT/VERB/SUBJECT COMPLEMENT

    S   V   SC
▶ **Babies seem fragile.**

3. SUBJECT/VERB/DIRECT OBJECT

    S   V   DO
▶ **Babies drink milk.**

4. SUBJECT/VERB/INDIRECT OBJECT/DIRECT OBJECT

    S   V   IO   DO
▶ **Babies give grandparents pleasure.**

5. SUBJECT/VERB/DIRECT OBJECT/OBJECT COMPLEMENT

    S   V   DO   OC
▶ **Babies make parents proud.**

16j Subjects

The subject of a sentence identifies what the sentence is about. The simple subject consists of one or more nouns or pronouns; the complete subject consists of the simple subject (SS) with all its modifiers.

┌─── COMPLETE SUBJECT ───┐
              SS
▶ *Sailing over the fence, the ball* **crashed through Mr. Wilson's window.**

┌── COMPLETE SUBJECT ──┐
   SS
▶ *Stadiums with real grass* **are hard to find these days.**

┌──COMPLETE SUBJECT──┐
   SS
▶ *Those who sit in the bleachers* **have the most fun.**

A compound subject contains two or more simple subjects joined with a coordinating conjunction (*and, but, or*) or a correlative conjunction (*both . . . and, either . . . or, neither . . . nor*).

▶ *Baseball and softball* **developed from cricket.**
▶ *Both baseball and softball* **developed from cricket.**

The subject usually comes before the predicate, or verb, but not always. Sometimes writers reverse this order to achieve a particular effect.

▶ **Up to the plate stepped** *Casey.*

In imperative sentences, which express requests or commands, the subject *you* is almost always implied but not stated.

▶ **(***You***) Keep your eye on the ball.**

In questions and certain other constructions, the subject usually appears between the auxiliary verb (16b) and the main verb.

▶ **Did** *Casey* **save the game?**

In sentences beginning with *there* or *here* followed by a form of *be*, the subject always follows the verb. *There* and *here* in such sentences are never the subject.

▶ **There was no *joy* in Mudville.**

16k Predicates

In addition to a subject, every sentence has a predicate, which asserts or asks something about the subject or tells the subject to do something. The "hinge," or key word, of a predicate is the verb. The simple predicate (SP) of a sentence consists of the main verb and any auxiliaries (16b); the complete predicate includes the simple predicate plus any modifiers of the verb and any objects or complements and their modifiers.

```
         ┌──── COMPLETE PREDICATE ────┐
         ┌──── SP────┐
```
▶ **Both of us *are planning to work at home.***

On the basis of how they function in predicates, verbs can be divided into three categories: linking, transitive, and intransitive.

Linking verbs

A linking verb links, or joins, a subject with a subject complement. A subject complement is a word or group of words that identifies or describes the subject.

```
         ┌─── S ───┐ ┌V┐ ┌────SC────┐
```
▶ **Christine is a single mother.**

```
         ┌S┐ ┌V┐ ┌ SC ┐
```
▶ **She is patient.**

If it identifies the subject, the complement is a noun or pronoun (*a single mother*). If it describes the subject, the complement is an adjective (*patient*).

The forms of *be*, when used as main verbs rather than as auxiliary verbs, are linking verbs (like *are* in this sentence). Other verbs, such as *appear, become, feel, grow, look, make, seem, smell,* and *sound,* can also function as linking verbs, depending on the sense of the sentence.

Transitive verbs

A transitive verb expresses action that is directed toward a noun or pronoun. This noun or pronoun that receives the action is called the direct object of the verb.

```
  S ┌──── V ──┬──── DO ────┐
```
▶ **I will analyze three poems.**

In the preceding example, the subject and verb do not express a complete thought. The direct object completes the thought, saying *what* I will analyze. In other sentences, the direct object may complete a thought by identifying the receiver of an action.

A direct object may be followed by an object complement, a word or word group that describes or identifies the direct object. Object complements may be adjectives, as in the next example, or nouns, as in the second example.

```
  S ┌──V──┬┌────────── DO ──────────┐┌── OC──┐
```
▶ **I consider Marianne Moore's poetry exquisite.**

```
  ┌──────────── S ────────────┐┌─V─┐┌─DO─┐┌── OC ──┐
```
▶ **Her poems and personality made Moore a celebrity.**

A transitive verb may also be followed by an indirect object, which tells to whom or what, or for whom or what, the verb's action is done. You might say the indirect object is the recipient of the direct object.

```
  ┌──────────────── S ────────────┐┌─V─┬─IO─┐┌────── DO ──────┐
```
▶ **Moore's poems about the Dodgers give me considerable pleasure.**

```
  ┌──S ──┐┌─V ─┬┌────── IO ──────┐┌─DO─┐
```
▶ **Brooklyn owes Marianne Moore a lot.**

Intransitive verbs

An intransitive verb expresses action that is not directed toward an object. Therefore, an intransitive verb does not have a direct object, though it is often followed by an adverb.

```
  ┌────S ────┬┌───V──┐
```
▶ **The Red Sox persevered.**

```
  ┌───S ──┬─V──┐
```
▶ **Their fans watched helplessly.**

The action of the verb *persevered* has no object (it makes no sense to ask, *persevered what?* or *persevered whom?*), and the action of the verb *watched* is directed toward an object that is implied but not expressed.

161 Phrases

A phrase is a group of words that lacks either a subject or a predicate or both. Phrases function as adjectives, adverbs, or nouns to add information to a sentence.

Noun phrases

A noun phrase consists of a noun and all its modifiers. In a sentence, a noun phrase can function as a subject, object, or complement.

> ┌─────── SUBJECT ───────┐
> ▶ *Delicious, gooey peanut butter* is surprisingly healthful.

> ┌─ OBJECT ─┐
> ▶ Dieter prefers *green salad.*

> ┌─COMPLEMENT─┐
> ▶ A tuna sandwich is *a popular lunch.*

Verb phrases

A main verb and its auxiliary verbs make up a verb phrase, which can function only one way in a sentence: as a predicate.

> ▶ I *can swim* for a long time.
> ▶ His problem *might have been caused* by tension between his parents.

Prepositional phrases

A prepositional phrase includes a preposition, a noun or pronoun (called the object of the preposition), and any modifiers of the object. Prepositional phrases function as either adjectives or adverbs.

ADJECTIVE   Our house *in Maine* is a cabin.

ADVERB   *From Cadillac Mountain,* you can see the northern lights.

Verbal phrases

Verbals are verb forms that do not function as verbs. Instead, they function as nouns, adjectives, or adverbs. There are three kinds of verbals: participles, gerunds, and infinitives. A verbal phrase is made up of a verbal and any modifiers, objects, or complements.

PARTICIPIAL PHRASES

Participial phrases always function as adjectives. They can include a present participle (the *crying* child) or a past participle (the *spoken* word).

▶ A dog *howling at the moon* kept me awake.

▶ *Irritated by the delay,* Louise complained.

GERUND PHRASES

Gerunds have the same form as present participles, ending in *-ing*; gerund phrases always function as nouns.

                       SUBJECT
▶ *Opening their eyes to the problem* was not easy.

                       DIRECT OBJECT
▶ They suddenly heard *a loud wailing from the sandbox.*

INFINITIVE PHRASES

Infinitive phrases can function as nouns, adjectives, or adverbs. The infinitive is the *to*-form of a verb: *to be, to write.*

                    ADJECTIVE
▶ A vote would be a good way *to end the meeting.*

    ADVERB
▶ *To perfect a draft,* always proofread carefully.

    NOUN
▶ *To know him* is a pleasure.

Absolute phrases

Absolute phrases usually include a noun or pronoun and a participle. They modify an entire sentence rather than a particular word.

Absolutes may appear almost anywhere in a sentence and are usually set off from the rest of the sentence with commas (29a).

▶ **I stood on the deck,** *the wind whipping my hair.*

▶ *My fears laid to rest,* **I climbed into the plane for my first solo flight.**

Appositive phrases

A noun phrase that renames the noun or pronoun immediately preceding it is called an appositive phrase.

▶ **The report,** *a hefty three-volume work,* **included forty-five recommendations.**

▶ **A single desire,** *to change the corporation's policies,* **guided our actions.**

16m Clauses

A clause is a group of words containing a subject and a predicate. There are two kinds of clauses: independent and dependent.

Independent clauses (also known as main clauses) can stand alone as complete sentences: *The window is open.* Pairs of independent clauses may be joined with a coordinating conjunction (*and, but, for, or, nor, so,* or *yet*) and a comma.

▶ **The window is open,** *so* **we'd better be quiet.**

Like independent clauses, dependent clauses (also known as subordinate clauses) contain a subject and a predicate. They cannot stand alone as complete sentences, however, for they begin with a subordinating word. Dependent clauses function as nouns, adjectives, or adverbs (10b).

▶ *Because the window is open,* **the room feels cool.**

In this combination, the subordinating conjunction *because* transforms the independent clause *the window is open* into a dependent adverb clause. In doing so, it indicates a causal relationship between the two clauses.

Noun clauses

Noun clauses can function as subjects, direct objects, subject complements, or objects of prepositions. Thus a noun clause does not stand apart but is always contained within another clause. Noun clauses usually begin with a relative pronoun (*that, which, what, who, whom, whose, whatever, whoever, whomever, whichever*) or with *when, where, whether, why*, or *how*.

▶ *That she had a good job* was important to him.

▶ He asked *where she went to college.*

▶ The real question was *why he wanted to know.*

▶ He was looking for *whatever information was available.*

Notice that in each of these sentences the noun clause is an integral part of the independent clause that makes up the sentence. For example, in the second sentence the independent clause is not just *he asked* but *he asked where she went to college.*

Adjective clauses

Adjective clauses modify nouns and pronouns in other clauses. Usually adjective clauses immediately follow the words they modify. Most of these clauses begin with the relative pronouns *who, whom, whose, that*, or *which*. Some begin with *when, where*, or *why*.

▶ The surgery, *which took three hours*, was a complete success.

▶ It was performed by the surgeon *who had developed the procedure.*

▶ The hospital was the one *where I was born.*

Sometimes the relative pronoun introducing an adjective clause may be omitted.

▶ That is one book *[that] I intend to read.*

Adverb clauses

Adverb clauses modify verbs, adjectives, or other adverbs. They begin with a subordinating conjunction (*after, although, as, as if, because, before, even though, if, in order that, once, since, so that, than, that, though, unless, until, when, where, whether, while*).

▶ We hiked *where there were few other hikers.*

▶ My backpack felt heavier *than it ever had.*

▶ I climbed as swiftly *as I could under the weight of my backpack.*

TYPES OF SENTENCES

Like words, sentences can be classified in different ways: grammatically or functionally.

16n Classifying sentences grammatically

Grammatically, sentences may be classified as *simple, compound, complex,* and *compound-complex*.

Simple sentences

A simple sentence consists of one independent clause and no dependent clause.

INDEPENDENT CLAUSE
▶ **The trailer is surrounded by a wooden deck.**

Compound sentences

A compound sentence consists of two or more independent clauses and no dependent clause. The clauses may be joined by a comma and a coordinating conjunction (*and, but, or, nor, for, so, yet*) or by a semicolon.

IND CLAUSE   IND CLAUSE
▶ **Occasionally a car goes up the dirt trail, and dust flies everywhere.**

Complex sentences

A complex sentence consists of one independent clause and at least one dependent clause.

┌──── IND CLAUSE ────┐┌──── DEP CLAUSE────────┐
▶ **Many people believe that anyone can earn a living.**

Compound-complex sentences

A compound-complex sentence consists of two or more independent clauses and at least one dependent clause.

┌──── IND CLAUSE────┐┌──── DEP CLAUSE────────┐┌──── IND CLAUSE ────┐
▶ **I complimented Joe when he finished the job, and he seemed pleased.**

┌──────────── IND CLAUSE ────────────┐┌──── IND CLAUSE────────┐
▶ **Sister Lucy tried her best to help Martin, but he was an undisciplined**
┌─────────── DEP CLAUSE ──────────┐
boy who drove many teachers to despair.

16o **Classifying sentences functionally**

In terms of function, sentences can be classified as declarative (making a statement), interrogative (asking a question), imperative (giving a command), or exclamatory (expressing strong feeling).

DECLARATIVE	He sings with the Grace Church Boys Choir.
INTERROGATIVE	How long has he sung with them?
IMPERATIVE	Comb his hair before the performance starts.
EXCLAMATORY	What voices those boys have!

17
Verbs

Restaurant menus are often a good source of verbs in action. One famous place in Boston, for instance, offers to bake, broil, pan-fry, deep-fry, poach, sauté, fricassee, blacken, or scallop any of the fish entrees on its menu. To someone ordering—or cooking—at this restaurant, the important distinctions lie entirely in the verbs.

When used skillfully, verbs can be the heartbeat of prose, moving it along, enlivening it, carrying its action. This chapter aims to help you use verbs in all these ways.

Editing the Verbs in Your Own Writing

- Circle all forms of *be*, *do*, and *have* that you used as main verbs. Try in each case to substitute a stronger, more specific verb. (17a, b)
- If you have trouble with verb endings, review the rules for using them in 17a and c.
- Double-check forms of *lie* and *lay*, *sit* and *set*, *rise* and *raise*. See that the words you use are appropriate for your meaning. (17d)
- If you have problems with verb tenses, use the guidelines on p. 115 to check your verbs.
- If you are writing about a literary work, you should refer to the action in the work in the present tense. (17e)
- Check all uses of the passive voice for appropriateness. (17g)
- Check all verbs used to introduce quotations, paraphrases, and summaries. If you rely on *say*, *write*, and other very general verbs, try substituting more vivid, specific verbs (*claim*, *insist*, *wonder*, for instance). (44c)

17a The five forms of verbs

Except for *be*, all English verbs have five forms.

BASE FORM	PAST TENSE	PAST PARTICIPLE	PRESENT PARTICIPLE	-s FORM
talk	talked	talked	talking	talks
adore	adored	adored	adoring	adores

BASE FORM	We often *go* to Legal Seafood.
PAST TENSE	Grandpa always *ordered* bluefish.
PAST PARTICIPLE	Have you *tried* their oyster stew?
PRESENT PARTICIPLE	Juanita is *getting* the shrimp platter.
-s FORM	The chowder *needs* salt and pepper.

-s *and* -es *endings*

Except with *be* and *have*, the -s form consists of the base form plus -s or -es. This form indicates action in the present for third-person singular subjects. All singular nouns; the words *he, she,* and *it*; and many indefinite pronouns (such as *anyone* or *someone*) are third-person singular.

	SINGULAR	PLURAL
FIRST PERSON	I wish	we wish
SECOND PERSON	you wish	you wish
THIRD PERSON	he/she/it wishes Joe wishes someone wishes	they wish children wish

The third-person singular form of *have* is *has*.

Forms of be

Be has eight forms, including three forms in the present tense and two in the past tense.

BASE FORM	be
PAST PARTICIPLE	been
PRESENT PARTICIPLE	being
PRESENT TENSE	I am, he/she/it is, we/you/they are
PAST TENSE	I/he/she/it was, we/you/they were

A Matter of Style: Be

> My sister at work. She be there every day 'til five.

These sentences illustrate two common usages of *be*. The first shows the absence of *be*; the same sentence in standard academic English would read "My sister's at work." The second shows the use of "habitual *be*," indicating that something is always the case. The same sentence in standard academic English would read "She's there every day until five."

These usages of *be* are common in the discourse of many African American speakers and some southern white speakers. You may well have occasion to quote dialogue featuring these patterns in your own writing; doing so can be a good way to evoke particular regions or communities. See Chapter 26 on using varieties of English appropriately.

17b Use the appropriate auxiliary verbs.

Auxiliary verbs are used with a base form, present participle, or past participle to form verb tenses, questions, and negatives. The most common auxiliaries are forms of *be, do,* and *have.*

▶ We *have considered* all viewpoints.
▶ The problem *is ranking* them fairly.
▶ *Do* you *have* a solution? No, I *do* not *have* one yet.

Modal auxiliaries—*can, could, might, may, must, ought to, shall, will, should, would*—indicate future actions, possibility, necessity, obligation, and so on.

▶ You *can see* three states from the top of the mountain.
▶ She *should visit* this spot more often.

❖ **For Multilingual Writers: Using Modal Auxiliaries**

Why do we not say "Alice can to read Latin"? For discussion of *can* and other modal auxiliaries, see 56a.

17c Regular and irregular verb forms

A verb is regular when its past tense and past participle are formed by adding *-ed* or *-d* to the base form.

BASE FORM	PAST TENSE	PAST PARTICIPLE
love	loved	loved
honor	honored	honored
obey	obeyed	obeyed

A verb is irregular when it does not follow the *-ed* or *-d* pattern. If you are unsure about whether a verb form is regular or irregular, or what the correct form is, consult the following list or a dictionary. Dictionaries list any irregular forms under the entry for the base form.

Some common irregular verbs

BASE FORM	PAST TENSE	PAST PARTICIPLE
arise	arose	arisen
be	was/were	been
bear	bore	borne, born
beat	beat	beaten
become	became	become
begin	began	begun
bite	bit	bitten, bit
blow	blew	blown
break	broke	broken
bring	brought	brought
broadcast	broadcast	broadcast
build	built	built
burn	burned, burnt	burned, burnt
burst	burst	burst
buy	bought	bought
catch	caught	caught
choose	chose	chosen
come	came	come
cost	cost	cost
cut	cut	cut
dig	dug	dug
dive	dived, dove	dived
do	did	done
draw	drew	drawn
dream	dreamed, dreamt	dreamed, dreamt
drink	drank	drunk
drive	drove	driven
eat	ate	eaten
fall	fell	fallen
feel	felt	felt
fight	fought	fought
find	found	found
fly	flew	flown

BASE FORM	PAST TENSE	PAST PARTICIPLE
forget	forgot	forgotten, forgot
freeze	froze	frozen
get	got	gotten, got
give	gave	given
go	went	gone
grow	grew	grown
hang (suspend)[1]	hung	hung
have	had	had
hear	heard	heard
hide	hid	hidden
hit	hit	hit
keep	kept	kept
know	knew	known
lay	laid	laid
lead	led	led
leave	left	left
lend	lent	lent
let	let	let
lie (recline)[2]	lay	lain
lose	lost	lost
make	made	made
mean	meant	meant
meet	met	met
pay	paid	paid
prove	proved	proved, proven
put	put	put
read	read	read
ride	rode	ridden
ring	rang	rung

---

[1]*Hang* meaning "execute by hanging" is regular: *hang, hanged, hanged.*

[2]*Lie* meaning "tell a falsehood" is regular: *lie, lied, lied.*

BASE FORM	PAST TENSE	PAST PARTICIPLE
rise	rose	risen
run	ran	run
say	said	said
see	saw	seen
send	sent	sent
set	set	set
shake	shook	shaken
shoot	shot	shot
show	showed	showed, shown
shrink	shrank	shrunk
sing	sang	sung
sink	sank	sunk
sit	sat	sat
sleep	slept	slept
speak	spoke	spoken
spend	spent	spent
spread	spread	spread
spring	sprang, sprung	sprung
stand	stood	stood
steal	stole	stolen
strike	struck	struck, stricken
swim	swam	swum
swing	swung	swung
take	took	taken
teach	taught	taught
tear	tore	torn
tell	told	told
think	thought	thought
throw	threw	thrown
wake	woke, waked	waked, woken
wear	wore	worn
win	won	won
wind	wound	wound
write	wrote	written

17d Distinguish between *lie* and *lay*, *sit* and *set*, *rise* and *raise*.

These pairs of verbs cause confusion because both verbs in each pair have similar-sounding forms and somewhat related meanings. In each pair, one of the verbs is transitive, meaning that it takes a direct object (*I lay the package on the counter*). The other is intransitive, meaning that it does not take an object (*He lies on the floor unable to move*). The best way to avoid confusing these verbs is to memorize their forms and meanings.

BASE FORM	PAST TENSE	PAST PARTICIPLE	PRESENT PARTICIPLE	–S FORM
lie (recline)	lay	lain	lying	lies
lay (put)	laid	laid	laying	lays
sit (be seated)	sat	sat	sitting	sits
set (put)	set	set	setting	sets
rise (get up)	rose	risen	rising	rises
raise (lift)	raised	raised	raising	raises

▶ The doctor asked the patient to ~~lay~~ *lie* on his side.

▶ She ~~sat~~ *set* the vase on the table.

▶ He ~~rose~~ *raised* himself to a sitting position.

17e Verb tenses

Tenses show when the action expressed by a verb takes place. The three simple tenses are the present tense, the past tense, and the future tense.

PRESENT TENSE	I use
PAST TENSE	I used
FUTURE TENSE	I will use

More complex aspects of time, such as ongoing or completed actions or conditions, are expressed through progressive, perfect, and perfect progressive forms of the simple tenses.

PRESENT PROGRESSIVE	she *is asking, writing*
PAST PROGRESSIVE	she *was asking, writing*
FUTURE PROGRESSIVE	she *will be asking, writing*
PRESENT PERFECT	she *has asked, written*
PAST PERFECT	she *had asked, written*
FUTURE PERFECT	she *will have asked, written*
PRESENT PERFECT PROGRESSIVE	she *has been asking, writing*
PAST PERFECT PROGRESSIVE	she *had been asking, writing*
FUTURE PERFECT PROGRESSIVE	she *will have been asking, writing*

The simple tenses locate an action only within the three basic time frames of present, past, and future. Progressive forms express continuing actions; perfect forms express completed actions; perfect progressive forms express actions that continue up to some point in the present, past, or future.

Present tense

SIMPLE PRESENT

Use the simple present to indicate actions occurring now and those occurring habitually.

▶ They *are* very angry about the decision.
▶ I *eat* breakfast every day at 8:00 A.M.
▶ Love *conquers* all.

When writing about action in literary works, use the simple present.

▶ Ishmael slowly ~~came~~ *comes* to realize all that ~~was~~ *is* at stake in the search for the white whale.

General truths or scientific facts should be in the simple present, even when the predicate of the sentence is in the past tense.

▶ Pasteur demonstrated that his boiling process ~~made~~ *makes* milk safe.

When you are quoting, summarizing, or paraphrasing a work, use the present tense.

▶ Keith Walters ~~wrote~~ *writes* that the "reputed consequences and promised blessings of literacy are legion."

Note that documenting an essay using APA (American Psychological Association) style and reporting the results of your experiments or another researcher's work calls for using the past tense (*wrote, noted*) or the present perfect (*has reported*). (See Chapter 49.)

▶ Comer (1995) ~~notes~~ *noted* that protesters who deprive themselves of food (for example, Gandhi and Dick Gregory) are seen not as dysfunctional but rather as "caring, sacrificing, even heroic" (p. 5).

PRESENT PROGRESSIVE

Use the present progressive to indicate actions that are ongoing in the present: *You are driving too fast.*

PRESENT PERFECT

Use the present perfect to indicate actions begun in the past and either completed at some unspecified time in the past or continuing into the present: *Uncontrolled logging has destroyed many forests.*

PRESENT PERFECT PROGRESSIVE

Use the present perfect progressive to indicate an ongoing action begun in the past and continuing into the present: *The two sides have been trying to settle the case out of court.*

Past tense

SIMPLE PAST

Use the simple past to indicate actions that occurred at a specific time and do not extend into the present: *Germany invaded Poland on September 1, 1939.*

PAST PROGRESSIVE

Use the past progressive to indicate continuing actions in the past: *Lenin was living in exile in Zurich when the tsar was overthrown.*

PAST PERFECT

Use the past perfect to indicate actions that were completed by a specific time in the past or before some other past action occurred: *By the fourth century, Christianity had become the state religion.*

PAST PERFECT PROGRESSIVE

Use the past perfect progressive to indicate continuing actions in the past that began before a specific time or before some other past action began: *Carter had been planning a naval career until his father died.*

Future tense

SIMPLE FUTURE

Use the simple future to indicate actions that have yet to begin: *The Vermeer show will come to Washington in September.*

FUTURE PROGRESSIVE

Use the future progressive to indicate continuing actions in the future: *The loans will be coming due in the next two years.*

FUTURE PERFECT

Use the future perfect to indicate actions that will be completed by a specified time in the future: *In ten years, your investment will have doubled.*

FUTURE PERFECT PROGRESSIVE

Use the future perfect progressive to indicate continuing actions that will be completed by some specified time in the future: *In May, I will have been working at IBM for five years.*

Editing Verb Tenses

If you have trouble with verb tenses, make a point of checking for these common errors as you proofread.

- Errors of verb form: writing *seen* for *saw*, for example, which is an instance of confusing the past participle and past-tense forms. (17e)
- Errors in tense: using the simple past (*Uncle Charlie arrived*) when meaning requires the present perfect (*Uncle Charlie has arrived*). (17f)
- Other errors result from using a regional or ethnic variety of English (*she nervous*) in situations calling for standard academic English (*she is nervous*). (See p. 107 and Chapter 26.)

17f Sequence verb tenses accurately.

Careful and accurate use of tenses is important to clear writing. Even the simplest narrative describes actions that take place at different times. When you use the appropriate tense for each action, readers can follow such time changes easily.

▶ By the time he lent her the money, she *had* declared bankruptcy.

> The original sentence suggests that the two events occurred at the same time; the revised sentence makes clear that the bankruptcy occurred first.

Use an infinitive (*to* plus a base form: *to go*) to indicate actions occurring at the same time as or later than the action of the predicate verb.

▶ We had hoped ~~to have planted~~ *to plant* our garden by now.

> The action of the infinitive *to plant* follows that of the sentence's main verb (*had hoped*).

Use a present participle (base form plus *-ing*) to indicate actions occurring at the same time as that of the predicate verb.

▶ **Seeking to relieve unemployment, Roosevelt established several public works programs.**

> The seeking and establishment of the programs occurred simultaneously.

A past participle or a present perfect participle (*having* plus a past participle) indicates actions occurring before that of the predicate verb.

▶ ~~Flying~~ *Flown* **to the front, the troops joined their hard-pressed comrades.**

> The past participle *flown* shows that the flying occurred before the joining.

▶ ~~Crushing~~ *Having crushed* **all opposition at home, he launched a war of conquest.**

> He launched the war after he crushed the opposition.

17g Use active voice and passive voice appropriately.

Voice tells whether a subject is acting (*He questions us*) or being acted upon (*He is questioned*). When the subject is acting, the verb is in the active voice; when the subject is being acted upon, the verb is in the passive voice. Most contemporary writers use the active voice as much as possible because it livens up their prose.

PASSIVE   Huge pine trees *were uprooted* by the storm.

ACTIVE   The storm *uprooted* huge pine trees.

The passive voice can work to good advantage in some situations. Newspaper reporters often use the passive voice to protect the confidentiality of their sources, as in the familiar phrase *it is reported that*. You can also use the passive voice when you want to emphasize the recipient of an action rather than the performer of the action.

DALLAS, Nov. 22—President John Fitzgerald Kennedy was shot and killed by an assassin today.   – TOM WICKER, *New York Times*

Wicker uses the passive voice with good reason: to focus on Kennedy, not on who killed him.

To shift a sentence from passive to active voice, make the performer of the action the subject of the sentence.

> *Researchers told the*
> ▶ ~~The~~ test administrator ~~was told~~ to give students an electric shock
>   ^   *they gave*
> each time a wrong answer. ~~was given.~~
>   ^   ^

A Matter of Style: Technical and Scientific Writing

Much technical and scientific writing uses the passive voice effectively to highlight what is being studied rather than who is doing the studying. Look at the following example, from a description of geological movement:

The Earth's plates are created where they separate and are recycled where they collide, in a continuous process of creation and destruction.
– FRANK PRESS AND RAYMOND SIEVER, *Understanding Earth*

17h   Select the appropriate mood.

The mood of a verb indicates the attitude of the writer toward what he or she is saying. The indicative mood is used for stating facts or opinions and for asking questions: *I did the right thing*. The imperative mood is used for giving commands and instructions: <u>*Do* the right thing</u>. The subjunctive mood (used primarily in dependent clauses beginning with *that* or *if*) expresses wishes and conditions that are contrary to fact: *If I <u>had done</u> the right thing, I would not be in trouble now.*

Forming and using the subjunctive

The present subjunctive uses the base form of the verb with all subjects.

▶ It is important that children *be* psychologically ready for a new sibling.

The past subjunctive is the same as the simple past except for the verb *be*, which uses *were* for all subjects.

▶ He spent money as if he *had* infinite credit.
▶ If the store *were* better located, it would attract more customers.

Because the subjunctive creates a rather formal tone, many people today tend to substitute the indicative mood in informal conversation.

▶ If the store *was* better located, it would attract more customers.

For academic or professional writing, use the subjunctive in the following contexts:

CLAUSES EXPRESSING A WISH

▶ He wished that his mother ~~was~~ still living nearby.
       were

IF-CLAUSES EXPRESSING A CONDITION THAT DOES NOT EXIST

▶ If the federal government ~~was~~ to ban the sale of tobacco, tobacco
      were
companies and distributors would suffer a great loss.

One common error is to use *would* in both clauses. Use the subjunctive in the *if*-clause and *would* in the independent clause.

▶ If I ~~would have~~ played harder, I would have won.
   had

THAT-CLAUSES EXPRESSING A REQUEST OR DEMAND

▶ The job demands that employees ~~are~~ in good physical condition.
      be

<table>
<tr><td>✻</td><td>For Multilingual Writers: Using the Subjunctive</td></tr>
</table>

✻ **For Multilingual Writers: Using the Subjunctive**

"If you practiced writing every day, it would eventually seem much easier to you." For a discussion of this and other uses of the subjunctive, see 58g.

18

Subject-Verb Agreement

In everyday terms, the word *agreement* refers to an accord of some sort: you reach an agreement with your boss about salary; friends agree to go to a movie; the members of a family agree to share household chores. This meaning covers grammatical agreement as well. In the present tense, verbs agree with their subjects in number (singular or plural) and in person (first, second, or third). This chapter will take a closer look at subject-verb agreement.

Editing for Subject-Verb Agreement

- Check your drafts verb by verb, and identify the subject that goes with each verb.

  ▶ The players on our side ~~is sure~~ to win.

  are

  Because the simple subject here is *players*, the verb needs to be *are*. When you take away the words between the subject and the verb, it is easier to identify agreement problems. (18b)

- Check compound subjects. Those joined by *and* usually take a plural verb. With those subjects joined by *or* or *nor*, however, the verb agrees with the part of the subject closest to the verb. *Neither Claire's parents nor Claire plans to vote.* (18c)

- Check collective-noun subjects. These nouns take a singular verb when they refer to a group as a single unit, but they take a plural verb when they refer to the multiple members of a group. *The crowd screams its support.* (18d)

- Check indefinite-pronoun subjects. Most take a singular verb. (*Both, few, many, others,* and *several* take a plural verb.) *Each of the singers rehearses for three hours daily.* (18e)

18a Make verbs agree with third-person singular subjects.

To make a verb in the present tense agree with a third-person singular subject, add *-s* or *-es* to the base form.

▶ **A vegetarian diet *lowers* the risk of heart disease.**

To make a verb in the present tense agree with any other subject, use the base form of the verb.

▶ **I *miss* my family.**
▶ **They *live* in another state.**

Have and *be* do not follow the *-s* or *-es* pattern with third-person singular subjects. *Have* changes to *has*; *be* has irregular forms in both the present and past tenses (17a).

▶ **War *is* hell.**
▶ **The soldier *was* brave beyond the call of duty.**

18b Make subjects and verbs agree, even when separated by other words.

Sometimes the simple subject is separated from the verb by other words. Make sure the verb agrees with the subject and not with another noun that falls in between.

▶ **A vase of flowers makes a room attractive.**
▶ **Many books on the best-seller list has little literary value.**

> have

The simple subject is *books*, not *list*.

The phrases as well as, along with, in addition to, together with

Be careful when you use these and other similar phrases. They do not make a singular subject plural.

▶ **The president, along with many senators, oppose the bill.**

> opposes

▶ **A passenger, as well as the driver, were injured in the accident.**

> was

Though this sentence has a grammatically singular subject, it suggests the idea of a plural subject. The sentence makes better sense with a compound subject: *The driver and a passenger were injured in the accident.*

18c Compound subjects generally take plural verbs.

> ► A backpack, a canteen, and a rifle ~~was~~ issued to each recruit.
> ^{were}

When subjects joined by *and* are considered a single unit or refer to the same person or thing, they take a singular verb form.

> ► John Kennedy's closest friend and political ally *was* his brother.
> ► Drinking and driving ~~remain~~ a major cause of highway fatalities.
> ^{remains}

In this sentence, *drinking and driving* is considered a single activity, and a singular verb is used.

If the word *each* or *every* precedes subjects joined by *and*, the verb form is singular.

> ► Each boy and girl *chooses* one gift to take home.

With subjects joined by *or* or *nor*, the verb agrees with the part closest to the verb.

> ► Neither my roommate nor my neighbors *like* my loud music.
> ► Either the witnesses or the defendant *is* lying.

In this sentence If you find this sentence awkward, put the plural noun closest to the verb: *Either the defendant or the witnesses are lying.*

> ► Either you or I ~~are~~ wrong.
> ^{am}

18d Collective nouns can be singular or plural, depending on meaning.

Collective nouns—such as *family, team, audience, group, jury, crowd, band, class,* and *committee*—refer to a group. Collective nouns can take either singular or plural verbs, depending on whether they refer to the group as a single unit or to the multiple members of the group. The meaning of a sentence as a whole is your guide to whether a collective noun refers to a unit or to the multiple parts of a unit.

▶ **After deliberating, the jury *reports* its verdict.**

The jury acts as a single unit.

▶ **The jury still *disagree* on a number of counts.**

The members of the jury act as multiple individuals.

▶ **The family of ducklings ~~scatters~~ when the cat approaches.**
   scatter

Family here refers to the many ducks; they cannot scatter as one.

▶ **Two-thirds of the park ~~have~~ burned.**
   has

Two-thirds refers to the single unit of the park that burned.

▶ **Two-thirds of the students ~~was~~ commuters.**
   were

Two-thirds here refers to the students who commuted as many individuals.

The phrases the number of, a number of

Treat phrases starting with *the number of* as singular and with *a number of* as plural.

SINGULAR   The number of applicants for the internship *was* unbelievable.

PLURAL   A number of applicants *were* put on the waiting list.

18e   Most indefinite pronouns take singular verbs.

Indefinite pronouns are those that do not refer to specific persons or things. Most take singular verb forms.

SOME COMMON INDEFINITE PRONOUNS

another	each	much	one
any	either	neither	other
anybody	everybody	nobody	somebody
anyone	everyone	no one	someone
anything	everything	nothing	something

▶ Of the two jobs, neither *holds* much appeal.

▶ Each of the plays ~~depict~~ *depicts* a hero undone by a tragic flaw.

Both, few, many, others, and *several* are plural.

▶ Though many *apply,* few *are* chosen.

▶ Several articles in today's newspaper ~~contains~~ *contain* references to the deficit.

All, any, enough, more, most, none, and *some* can be singular or plural, depending on the noun they refer to.

▶ All of the cake *was* eaten.

▶ All of the candidates *promise* to improve the schools.

18f ## Make verbs agree with the antecedents of *who, which,* and *that.*

When the relative pronouns *who, which,* and *that* are used as a subject, the verb agrees with the antecedent of the pronoun.

▶ Fear is an ingredient that *goes* into creating stereotypes.

▶ Guilt, jealousy, and fear are ingredients that *go* into creating stereotypes.

Problems often occur with the words *one of the*. In general, *one of the* takes a plural verb, while *only one of the* takes a singular verb.

▶ Carla is one of the employees who always ~~works~~ *work* overtime.

Some employees always work overtime. Carla is among them. Thus *who* refers to *employees*, and the verb is plural.

▶ Sam is the only one of the employees who always ~~work~~ *works* overtime.

Only one employee always works overtime, and that employee is Sam. Thus *one*, and not *employees*, is the antecedent of *who*, and the verb form must be singular.

18g Make linking verbs agree with their subjects, not with their complements.

A linking verb should agree with its subject, which usually precedes the verb, not with the subject complement, which follows it.

> The signings of three key treaties ~~is~~ the topic of my talk.
>
> *are*

The subject is *signings*, not *topic*.

> Nero Wolfe's passion ~~were~~ orchids.
>
> *was*

The subject is *passion*, not *orchids*.

18h Words such as *physics* and *news* take singular verbs.

Some words that end in *-s* seem to be plural but are singular in meaning and thus take singular verbs.

> Measles still ~~strike~~ many Americans.
>
> *strikes*

Some nouns of this kind (such as *statistics* and *politics*) may be either singular or plural, depending on context.

SINGULAR   Statistics *is* a course I really dread.

PLURAL   The statistics in that study *are* highly questionable.

18i Make verbs agree with subjects that follow them.

In English, verbs usually follow subjects. When this order is reversed, it is easy to become confused. Make the verb agree with the subject, not with a noun that happens to precede it.

> Beside the barn ~~stands~~ silos filled with grain.
>
> *stand*

The subject is *silos*; it is plural, so the verb must be *stand*.

In sentences beginning with *there is* or *there are* (or *there was* or *were*), *there* serves only as an introductory word; the subject follows the verb.

▶ There *are* five basic positions in classical ballet.

The subject, *positions*, is plural, so the verb must also be plural.

18j Titles and words used as words take singular verbs.

               describes
▶ *One Writer's Beginnings* ~~describe~~ Eudora Welty's childhood.
               ^

      is
▶ *Steroids* ~~are~~ a little word that packs a big punch in the world of sports.
     ^

A Matter of Style: -s and -es Endings

> She go to work seven days a week.
> He don't take it to heart.

These two sentences are typical of some varieties of African American English and of some regional white English, in which third-person singular verbs do not end with -*s* or -*es*. (In standard academic English, these verb forms are *she goes* and *he doesn't*.) You will often see verb forms such as those in the sentences above in African American literature, especially in dialogue, and you may well quote passages using these varieties of English in your own writing. In most academic and professional writing, however, add -*s* or -*es* to third-person singular verb forms.

19

Adjectives and Adverbs

Adjectives and adverbs often bring indispensable differences in meaning to the words they modify. In basketball, for example, there is an important difference between a *flagrant* foul and a *technical* foul, a layup and a *reverse* layup, and an *angry* coach and a *really angry* coach. In each instance, the modifiers are crucial to accurate communication.

    Adjectives modify nouns and pronouns, answering the questions which? how many? and what kind? Adverbs modify verbs, adjectives, and other adverbs; they answer the questions how? when? where? and to what extent? Many adverbs are formed by adding *-ly* to adjectives (*slight, slightly*), but many adverbs are formed in other ways (*outdoors*) or have forms of their own (*very*).

Editing Adjectives and Adverbs

- Carefully scrutinize each adjective and adverb in your writing to see whether it's the best word possible. Considering one or two synonyms for each adjective or adverb should help you decide.

- Is each adjective necessary? Would a more specific noun eliminate the need for an adjective (*mansion* rather than *enormous house*, for instance)? Follow this same line of inquiry with the verbs and adverbs in your writing.

- Look for places where you might make your writing more specific or vivid by adding an adjective or adverb.

- Are all comparisons complete? (19c)

- If English is not your first language, check that adjectives are in the right order. (56e)

19a Use adjectives after linking verbs.

When adjectives come after linking verbs, they usually serve as a subject complement, to describe the subject: *I am patient*. Note that in specific sentences, some verbs may or may not be linking verbs—*look, appear, sound, feel, smell, taste, grow,* and *prove*, for instance. When a word following one of these verbs modifies the subject, use an adjective; when it modifies the verb, use an adverb.

ADJECTIVE **Otis Thorpe looked *angry*.**

ADVERB **He looked *angrily* at the referee.**

Linking verbs suggest a state of being, not an action. In the preceding examples, *looked angry* suggests the state of being angry; *looked angrily* suggests an angry action.

✳ **For Multilingual Writers: Determining Adjective Sequence**

Should you write *these beautiful old-fashioned kitchen tiles* or *these old-fashioned beautiful kitchen tiles*? See 55e for guidelines on adjective sequence.

19b Use adverbs to modify verbs, adjectives, and adverbs.

In everyday conversation, you will often hear (and perhaps use) adjectives in place of adverbs. For example, people often say *go quick* instead of *go quickly*. When you write in standard academic English, however, use adverbs to modify verbs, adjectives, and other adverbs.

▶ You can feel the song's meter if you listen ~~careful.~~ *carefully.*

▶ The audience was ~~real~~ *really* disappointed by the show.

The modifiers *good, well, bad,* and *badly* cause problems for many writers because the distinctions between *good* and *well* and between *bad* and *badly* are often not observed in conversation. Problems also arise because *well* can function as either an adjective or an adverb.

Good *and* well

▶ I look ~~well~~ *good* in blue.

▶ Now that the fever has broken, I feel ~~good~~ *well* again.

▶ He plays the trumpet ~~good.~~ *well.*

Bad *and* badly

▶ I feel ~~badly~~ *bad* for the Toronto fans.

▶ Their team played ~~bad.~~ *badly.*

19c   Comparatives and superlatives

Most adjectives and adverbs have three forms: positive, comparative, and superlative.

POSITIVE	COMPARATIVE	SUPERLATIVE
large	larger	largest
early	earlier	earliest
careful	more careful	most careful
happily	more happily	most happily

▶ Canada is *larger* than the United States.
▶ My son needs to be *more careful* with his money.
▶ They are the *most happily* married couple I know.

As these examples show, you usually form the comparative and superlative of one- or two-syllable adjectives by adding *-er* and *-est*: *short, shorter, shortest*. With longer adjectives and with most adverbs, use *more* and *most*: *scientific, more scientific, most scientific; elegantly, more elegantly, most elegantly.*

Irregular adjectives and adverbs

Some short adjectives and adverbs have irregular comparative and superlative forms.

POSITIVE	COMPARATIVE	SUPERLATIVE
good	better	best
well	better	best
bad, badly	worse	worst
little (quantity)	less	least
many, much	more	most

Comparatives vs. superlatives

Use the comparative to compare two things; use the superlative to compare three or more things.

▶ Rome is a much *older* city than New York.
▶ Damascus is one of the *oldest* cities in the world.

In conversation, you will often hear the superlative form used even when only two things are being compared: *Of the two paintings, the one by Klee is the most interesting.* When you write standard academic English, however, use the comparative: *Of the two paintings, the one by Klee is the more interesting.*

Double comparatives and superlatives

Double comparatives and superlatives are those that unnecessarily use both the *-er* or *-est* ending and *more* or *most.* Occasionally, these forms can act to build a special emphasis, as in the title of Spike Lee's movie *Mo' Better Blues.* In academic and professional writing, however, do not use *more* or *most* before adjectives or adverbs ending in *-er* or *-est.*

▶ Paris is the ~~most~~ loveliest city in the world.

▶ Rome lasted ~~more~~ longer than Carthage.
  much

A Matter of Style: Multiple Negation

Speakers of English sometimes use more than one negative at a time — saying, for instance, "I can't hardly see you." Multiple negatives, in fact, have a long history in English (and can be found in the works of Chaucer and Shakespeare, for example). It was only in the eighteenth century, in an effort to make English more "logical," that double negatives came to be seen as incorrect.

In fact, the use of double negatives for emphasis is very popular in many areas of the South. Someone might say, for example, "Can't nothing be done." Emphatic double negatives — and triple, quadruple, and more — are used by many speakers of African American vernacular English, who may say, for instance, "Don't none of my people come from up North."

Even though they occur in many varieties of English (and in many other languages, including French and Russian), multiple negatives are not characteristic of standard academic English. In academic or professional writing, you may well have reason to quote passages that include multiple negatives, whether you're quoting Shakespeare, Toni Morrison, or your grandmother, but you will play it safe if you avoid other uses of multiple negatives.

Incomplete comparisons

In speaking, we sometimes state only part of a comparison because the context makes the meaning clear. For example, after comparing your car with a friend's, you might say "Yours is better," but the context makes it clear that you mean "Yours is better *than mine.*" In writing, such a context may not exist. So when editing, take the time to check for incomplete comparisons—and to complete them if they are unclear.

▶ The patients taking the drug appeared healthier/ *than those receiving a placebo.*

Absolute concepts

Some adjectives and adverbs—such as *perfect, final,* and *unique*—are absolute concepts, so it is illogical to form comparatives or superlatives of these words.

▶ The patient felt compelled to have ~~more~~ perfect control over his thoughts.

▶ Anne has ~~the most~~ *a* unique sense of humor.

20

Modifier Placement

Modifiers enrich writing by making it more concrete or vivid, often adding important or even essential details. To be effective, modifiers should refer clearly to the words they modify and be positioned close to those words. Consider, for example, a sign seen recently in a hotel:

DO NOT USE THE ELEVATORS IN CASE OF FIRE.

Should we really avoid the elevators altogether, in case there is ever a fire? Repositioning the modifier *in case of fire* eliminates such confusion—and makes clear that we are to avoid the elevators only if there is a fire: IN CASE OF FIRE, DO NOT USE THE ELEVATORS. This chapter reviews the conventions of accurate modifier placement.

Editing Misplaced or Dangling Modifiers

1. Identify all the modifiers in each sentence, and draw an arrow from each modifier to the word it modifies.

2. If a modifier is far from the word it modifies, try to move the two closer together. (20a)

3. Does any modifier seem to refer to a word other than the one it is intended to modify? If so, move the modifier so that it refers clearly to only the intended word. (20a, c)

4. If you cannot find the word to which a modifier refers, revise the sentence: supply such a word, or revise the modifier itself so that it clearly refers to a word already in the sentence. (20d)

20a Position modifiers close to the words they modify.

Modifiers can cause confusion or ambiguity if they are not close enough to the words they modify or if they seem to modify more than one word in the sentence.

▶ She teaches a seminar ~~this term~~ on voodoo *this term* at Skyline College.

Surely the voodoo was not at the college.

▶ ~~Billowing from every window,~~ H̶e saw clouds of smoke *billowing from every window.*

People cannot billow from windows.

▶ *After he lost the 1962 gubernatorial race,* Nixon told reporters that he planned to get out of politics. ~~after he lost the 1962 gubernatorial race.~~

The unedited sentence implies that Nixon planned to lose the race.

Limiting modifiers

Be especially careful with the placement of limiting modifiers such as *almost, even, just, merely,* and *only.* In general, these modifiers should be placed right before or after the words they modify. Putting them in other positions may produce not just ambiguity but a completely different meaning.

AMBIGUOUS	The court only hears civil cases on Tuesdays.
CLEAR	The court hears *only* civil cases on Tuesdays.
CLEAR	The court hears civil cases on Tuesdays *only*.

Placing *only* before *hears* makes the meaning ambiguous. Does the writer mean that civil cases are the only cases heard on Tuesdays or that those are the only days when civil cases are heard?

▶ The city ~~almost~~ spent *almost* twenty million dollars on the new stadium.

The original sentence suggests the money was almost spent; moving *almost* makes clear that the amount spent was almost twenty million dollars.

Squinting modifiers

If a modifier could refer to the word before it and the word after it, it is called a squinting modifier. Put the modifier where it clearly relates to only a single word.

SQUINTING	Students who practice writing *often* will benefit.
REVISED	Students who *often practice* writing will benefit.
REVISED	Students who practice writing will *often benefit*.

20b Move disruptive modifiers.

Disruptive modifiers interrupt the connections between parts of a grammatical structure or a sentence, making it hard for readers to follow the progress of the thought. Be careful that modifiers do not disrupt the flow of a sentence.

▶ ~~Vegetables will if they are cooked too long,~~ *If they are cooked too long, vegetables will* lose most of their nutritional value.

20c Move modifiers that unnecessarily split an infinitive.

In general, do not place a modifier between the *to* and the verb of an infinitive (*to often complain*). Doing so makes it hard for readers to recognize that the two go together.

> *surrender*
> ► Hitler expected the British to fairly quickly. ~~surrender.~~
>   ^   ^

In some sentences, however, a modifier sounds awkward if it does not split the infinitive. In such cases, it may be best to reword the sentence to eliminate the infinitive altogether.

SPLIT   I hope *to* almost *equal* my last year's income.

REVISED   I hope that I will earn almost as much as I did last year.

20d Revise dangling modifiers.

Dangling modifiers are words that modify nothing in particular in the rest of a sentence. They often *seem* to modify something that is implied but not actually present in the sentence. Dangling modifiers frequently appear at the beginnings or ends of sentences.

DANGLING   Driving nonstop, Salishan Lodge is located two hours from Portland.

REVISED   Driving nonstop from Portland, you can reach Salishan Lodge in two hours.

To revise a dangling modifier, often you need to add a subject that the modifier clearly refers to; sometimes you have to revise the modifier itself, turning it into a phrase or a clause.

> *our family gave away*
> ► Reluctantly, the hound ~~was given away~~ to a neighbor.
>   ^

In the original sentence, was the dog reluctant, or was someone else who is not mentioned?

> *When he was*
> ► ~~As~~ a young boy, his grandmother told stories of her years as a country
>   ^
> schoolteacher.

His grandmother was never a young boy.

> ► ~~Thumbing through the magazine,~~ my eyes automatically noticed the
>   M
> perfume ads.
>   *as I was thumbing through the magazine.*
>   ^

Eyes cannot thumb through a magazine.

21

Pronouns

As words that stand in for nouns, pronouns carry a lot of weight in everyday discourse. For example:

> Take the Interstate until you come to Exit 3 and then Route 313. Go past it, and take the next exit, which will be Broadway.

These directions, intended to lead an out-of-towner to her friend's house, provide a good example of why it's important for a pronoun to refer clearly to a specific noun or pronoun antecedent. The little word *it* in this example could mean either Exit 3 or Route 313 — or are they the same thing? If Exit 3 and Route 313 aren't clearly marked, she could have difficulty finding her way. This chapter aims to help you use pronouns accurately.

Editing Pronouns

- Are all pronouns after forms of the verb *be* in the subjective case? *It's me* is common in spoken English, but in writing it should be *It is I*. (21a)

- To check for correct use of *who* and *whom* (and *whoever* and *whomever*), try substituting *he* or *him*. If *he* is correct, use *who* (or *whoever*); if *him*, use *whom* or *whomever*. (21b)

- In compound structures, make sure any pronouns are in the same case they would be in if used alone. (*She and Jake were living in Spain*.) (21c)

- When a pronoun follows *than* or *as*, complete the sentence mentally. If the pronoun is the subject of an unstated verb, it should be subjective. (*I like her better than he [likes her]*.) If it is the object of an unstated verb, make it objective. (*I like her better than [I like] him*.) (21d)

- Check any use of *anyone, each, everybody, many*, and other indefinite pronouns (see list in 18e) to be sure they are treated as singular or plural as appropriate. (21f)

- If you find *he, his*, or *him* used to refer to persons of either sex, revise the pronouns, or recast the sentences altogether. (21f)

- For each pronoun, identify a specific word that it refers to. If you cannot find one specific word, supply one. If the pronoun refers to more than one word, revise the sentence. (21g)

- Check any use of *it, this, that*, and *which* to be sure each pronoun refers to some specific word elsewhere in the sentence. (21g)

- Be sure that any use of *you* refers to your specific reader or readers.

21a Pronoun case

Most speakers of English know intuitively when to use *I*, when to use *me*, and when to use *my*. Our choices reflect differences in case, the form a pronoun takes to indicate its function in a sentence. Pronouns functioning as subjects are in the subjective case (*I*); those functioning as objects are in the objective case (*me*); those functioning as possessives are in the possessive case (*my*).

SUBJECTIVE PRONOUNS	OBJECTIVE PRONOUNS	POSSESSIVE PRONOUNS
I	me	my/mine
we	us	our/ours
you	you	your/yours
he/she/it	him/her/it	his/her/its
they	them	their/theirs
who/whoever	whom/whomever	whose

Subjective case

A pronoun should be in the subjective case (*I, you, he/she/it, we, they*) when it is a subject, a subject complement, or an appositive renaming a subject or subject complement.

SUBJECT

She was passionate about recycling.

SUBJECT COMPLEMENT

The main supporter of the recycling program was *she*.

APPOSITIVE RENAMING A SUBJECT OR SUBJECT COMPLEMENT

Three colleagues—Peter, John, and *she*—worked on the program.

Many Americans routinely use the objective case for subject complements, especially in conversation: *Who's there? It's me*. If the subjective case for a subject complement sounds stilted or awkward (*It's I*), try rewriting the sentence using the pronoun as the subject (*I'm here*).

▶ The first person to see Monty after the awards ~~was she.~~
   She was the

Objective case

A pronoun should be in the objective case (*me, you, him/her/it, us, them*) when it functions as a direct or indirect object, an object of a preposition, an appositive renaming an object, or a subject of an infinitive.

DIRECT OBJECT
The boss surprised *her* with a big raise.

INDIRECT OBJECT
The owner gave *him* a reward.

OBJECT OF A PREPOSITION
Several friends went with *me.*

APPOSITIVE RENAMING AN OBJECT
We elected two representatives, Joan and *me.*

SUBJECT OF AN INFINITIVE
The students convinced *him* to vote for the school bond.

Possessive case

A pronoun should be in the possessive case when it shows possession or ownership. Notice that there are two forms of possessive pronouns: adjective forms, which are used before nouns or gerunds (*my, your, his/her/its, our, their, whose*), and noun forms, which take the place of a possessive noun (*mine, yours, his/hers/its, ours, theirs, whose*).

BEFORE A NOUN
The sound of *her* voice came right through the walls.

SUBSTITUTE FOR A POSSESSIVE NOUN
The responsibility is *hers.*

Pronouns before a gerund should be in the possessive case.

▶ I remember *his* singing.

21b Use *who, whoever, whom,* and *whomever* appropriately.

A common problem with pronoun case is deciding whether to use *who* or *whom.* Use *who* and *whoever,* which are subjective-case pronouns, for subjects or subject complements. Use *whom* and *whomever*, which are objective-case pronouns, for objects. Two particular situations lead to confusion with *who* and *whom*: when they begin a question and when they introduce a dependent clause.

In questions

You can determine whether to use *who* or *whom* at the beginning of a question by answering the question using a personal pronoun. If the answer is in the subjective case, use *who*; if it is in the objective case, use *whom*.

▶ *Whom*
Who did you visit?
   ∧

   I visited *them*. *Them* is objective; thus *whom* is correct.

▶ *Who*
Whom do you think wrote the story?
   ∧

   I think *she* wrote the story. *She* is subjective; thus *who* is correct.

In dependent clauses

The case of a pronoun in a dependent clause is determined by its function in the clause, no matter how that clause functions in the sentence. If the pronoun acts as a subject or subject complement in the clause, use *who* or *whoever*. If the pronoun acts as an object in the clause, use *whom* or *whomever*.

▶   *who*
Anyone can hypnotize someone whom wants to be hypnotized.
                                     ∧

   The verb of the clause is *wants*, and its subject is *who*.

▶ *Whomever*
Whoever the party suspected of disloyalty was executed.
   ∧

   Whomever is the object of *suspected* in the clause *whomever the party suspected of disloyalty*.

If you are not sure which case to use, try separating the dependent clause from the rest of the sentence and looking at it in isolation. Then rewrite the clause as a new sentence, and substitute a personal pronoun for *who(ever)* or *whom(ever)*. If the personal pronoun you substitute is in the subjective case, use *who* or *whoever*; if it is in the objective case, use *whom* or *whomever*.

▶ **The minister grimaced at (*whoever/whomever*) made any noise.**

Isolate the clause *whoever/whomever made any noise*. Substituting a personal pronoun gives you *they made any noise*. *They* is in the subjective case; therefore, *The minister grimaced at* <u>whoever</u> *made any noise.*

▶ **The minister smiled at (*whoever/whomever*) she greeted.**

Isolate and transpose the clause to get *she greeted whoever/whomever*. Substituting a personal pronoun gives you *she greeted them*. *Them* is in the objective case; therefore, *The minister smiled at* <u>whomever</u> *she greeted.*

21c Use the appropriate case in compound structures.

When a pronoun is part of a compound subject, complement, or object, put it in the same case you would use if the pronoun were alone.

▶ When ~~him~~ *he* and Zelda were first married, they lived in New York.
▶ The boss invited ~~she~~ *her* and her family to dinner.
▶ This morning saw yet another conflict between my sister and ~~I.~~ *me.*

To decide whether to use the subjective or objective case in a compound structure, use each part of the compound alone in the sentence.

▶ Come to the park with Carlotta and ~~I.~~ *me.*

Separating the compound structure gives you *Come to the park with Carlotta* and *Come to the park with me*; thus *Come to the park with Carlotta and* <u>me</u>.

21d Use the correct case in elliptical constructions.

Elliptical constructions are those in which some words are understood but left out. When an elliptical construction ends in a pronoun, put the pronoun in the case it would be in if the construction were complete.

▶ His sister has always been more athletic than *he* [is].

In some elliptical constructions, the case of the pronoun depends on the meaning intended.

▶ **Willie likes Lily more than** *she* **[likes Lily].**

She is the subject of the omitted verb *likes.*

▶ **Willie likes Lily more than [he likes]** *her.*

Her is the object of the omitted verb *likes.*

21e Use *we* and *us* appropriately before a noun.

If you are unsure about whether to use *we* or *us* before a noun, recasting the sentence without the noun will give you the answer. Use whichever pronoun would be correct if the noun were omitted.

    We
▶ **U̶s̶ fans never give up hope.**
    ^

Fans is the subject, so the subjective *we* is used.

                 us
▶ **The Rangers depend on w̶e̶ fans.**
                     ^

Fans is the object of a preposition, so the objective *us* is used.

21f Make pronouns agree with their antecedents.

The antecedent of a pronoun is the noun or other pronoun the pronoun refers to. Pronouns and antecedents are said to "agree" when they match up in person, number, and gender.

SINGULAR   **The *choirmaster* raised *his* baton.**

PLURAL   **The *boys* picked up *their* music.**

Compound antecedents

Compound antecedents joined by *and* require plural pronouns.

▶ **My parents and I tried to resolve *our* disagreement.**

When a compound antecedent is preceded by *each* or *every*, however, it takes a singular pronoun.

▶ Every *plant* and *animal* has *its* own ecological niche.

With a compound antecedent joined by *or* or *nor*, the pronoun agrees with the nearest antecedent. If the parts of the antecedent are of different genders or persons, however, this kind of sentence can be awkward and may need to be revised.

▶ **Neither *Annie* nor *Astrid* got *her* work done.**

AWKWARD   Neither Annie nor Barry got his work done.

REVISED   Annie didn't get her work done, and neither did Barry.

When a compound antecedent contains both singular and plural parts, the sentence may sound awkward unless the plural part comes last.

▶ **Neither the newspaper nor the radio stations would reveal *their* sources.**

Collective-noun antecedents

A collective noun that refers to a single unit (*herd, team, audience*) requires a singular pronoun.

▶ **The *audience* fixed *its* attention on center stage.**

When such an antecedent refers to the multiple parts of a unit, however, it requires a plural pronoun.

▶ **The director chose this cast because *they* had experience in the roles.**

Indefinite-pronoun antecedents

Indefinite pronouns are those that do not refer to specific persons or things. Most indefinite pronouns are always singular; a few are always plural. Some can be singular or plural depending on the context.

▶ **None of the ballerinas lost *her* balance.**

▶ **Many in the audience jumped to *their* feet.**

SINGULAR   **Some of the furniture was showing *its* age.**

PLURAL   **Some of the farmers abandoned *their* land.**

Sexist pronouns

Indefinite pronouns often refer to antecedents that may be either male or female. Writers used to use a masculine pronoun, known as the generic *he*, to refer to such indefinite pronouns. In recent decades, however, many people have pointed out that such wording ignores or even excludes females — and thus should not be used.

Ways of Editing for the Generic Use of *He, His,* or *Him*

Look at the following sentence:

> Every citizen should know *his* rights under the law.

Now consider three ways to express the same idea without *his*.

1. Revise to make the antecedent plural.
   All citizens should know their *rights under the law.*
2. Revise the sentence altogether.
   Every citizen should have some knowledge of basic legal rights.
3. Use both masculine and feminine pronouns.
   Every citizen should know his *or* her *rights under the law.*

This third option, using both masculine and feminine pronouns, can be awkward, especially when repeated several times in a passage.

21g Maintain clear pronoun reference.

The antecedent of a pronoun is the word the pronoun substitutes for. If a pronoun is too far from its antecedent, readers will have trouble making the connection between the two.

Ambiguous antecedents

Readers have trouble when a pronoun can refer to more than one antecedent.

▶ The meeting between Bowman and Sonny makes ~~him~~ **Bowman** compare his own unsatisfying domestic life with one that is emotionally secure.

Who is the antecedent of *him* and *his*: Bowman or Sonny? The revision makes the reference clear by replacing a pronoun (*him*) with a noun (*Bowman*).

▶ Kerry told Ellen, ~~she~~ should be ready soon."

(handwritten above: "I)

Reporting Kerry's words directly, in quotation marks, eliminates the ambiguity.

Vague use of it, this, that, *and* which

The words *it, this, that,* and *which* are often used as a shortcut for referring to something mentioned earlier. Like other pronouns, each of these words must refer to a specific antecedent.

▶ When the senators realized the bill would be defeated, they tried to
postpone the vote but failed. ~~It~~ was a fiasco.

(handwritten above: The entire effort)

▶ Nancy just found out that she won the lottery, which explains her
sudden resignation from her job.

(handwritten above: an event)

Indefinite use of you, it, *and* they

In conversation, we frequently use *you, it,* and *they* in an indefinite sense, in such expressions as *you never know* and *in the paper, it said.* In academic and professional writing, however, use *you* only to mean "you, the reader," and *they* or *it* only to refer to a clear antecedent.

▶ In Texas, ~~you~~ often ~~hear~~ about the influence of big oil corporations/

(handwritten above: one ... hears ... on state and local politics.)

▶ ~~On~~ the Weather Channel/ ~~it~~ said that Hurricane Fran will hit Virginia

Beach tomorrow morning.

(handwritten above: T)

▶ ~~In France, they~~ allow dogs. ~~in most restaurants.~~

(handwritten above: Most restaurants in France)

Implied antecedents

A pronoun must refer to a specific antecedent. Sometimes a possessive may clearly *imply* a noun antecedent, but it does not serve as a clear antecedent.

▶ In ~~Welty's~~ story, ~~she~~ characterizes Bowman as a man unaware of his
own isolation.

(handwritten above: her ... Welty)

✻ For Multilingual Writers: Using Pronoun Subjects

In some languages, such as Arabic, personal pronouns are added to the verbs as suffixes or prefixes. Native speakers of these languages sometimes tend to overcorrect in English by doubling the subject: *Jaime he lives next door.* If you are using a pronoun as a subject, make sure that you have not used a proper noun subject as well: *He lives next door.*

22

Comma Splices and Fused Sentences

A comma splice occurs when two independent clauses are joined with only a comma. We often see comma splices in advertising, where they can give slogans a catchy rhythm.

> It's not just a job, it's an adventure.
> – U.S. Army recruiting slogan

> Life's short, play hard.
> – Nike advertisement

Another common error is a fused, or run-on, sentence, which occurs when two independent clauses are joined with no punctuation or no connecting word between them. The Army slogan as a fused sentence would be "It's not just a job it's an adventure."

You will seldom if ever profit from using comma splices or fused sentences in academic or professional writing. In fact, doing so will almost always be identified as an error. This chapter will guide you in recognizing and revising comma splices and fused sentences.

Editing for Comma Splices and Fused Sentences

Look for independent clauses—groups of words that can stand alone as a sentence—coming one after another. If you find no punctuation between two independent clauses, you have identified a fused sentence. If you find two such clauses joined only by a comma, you have identified a comma splice. Here are five methods of editing comma splices and fused sentences.

(Continues)

1. Separate the clauses into two sentences. (22a)

    ▶ *Education* is an elusive word͵ˌ It it often means different

    things to different people.

2. Link the clauses with a comma and a coordinating conjunction (*and, but, or, nor, for, so,* or *yet*). (22b)

    ▶ *Education* is an elusive word, for it often means different things

    to different people.

3. Link the clauses with a semicolon. (22c)

    ▶ *Education* is an elusive word͵; it often means different

    things to different people.

    If the clauses are linked only with a comma and a conjunctive adverb—a word like *however, then, therefore*—add a semicolon.

    ▶ *Education* is an elusive word͵; indeed, it often means

    different things to different people.

4. Recast the two clauses as one independent clause. (22d)

    An elusive word, education
    ▶ ~~*Education* is an elusive word, it~~ often means

    different things to different people.

5. Recast one independent clause as a dependent clause. (22e)

    because
    ▶ *Education* is an elusive word, it often means different

    things to different people.

    To choose among these methods, you need to look at the sentences before and after the ones you are revising. Doing so will help you determine how a particular method will affect the rhythm of the passage. It may help to read the passage aloud to see how the revision sounds.

22a Separate the clauses into two sentences.

The simplest way to revise comma splices or fused sentences is to separate them into two sentences.

COMMA
SPLICE
My mother spends long hours every spring tilling the
soil and moving manure⁄ ʇhis part of gardening is
nauseating.

FUSED
SENTENCE
My mother spends long hours every spring tilling the
soil and moving manure. ʇhis part of gardening is
nauseating.

If the two clauses are very short, making them two sentences may sound abrupt and terse, and some other method of revision would probably be preferable.

22b Link the clauses with a comma and a coordinating conjunction.

If the two clauses are closely related and equally important, join them with a comma and a coordinating conjunction (*and, but, or, nor, for, so*, or *yet*).

COMMA
SPLICE
                                    but
I should pay my tuition, I need a new car.

FUSED
SENTENCE
                                    but
I should pay my tuition‚ I need a new car.

22c Link the clauses with a semicolon.

If the ideas in the two clauses are closely related and you want to give them equal emphasis, link them with a semicolon.

COMMA
SPLICE
This photograph is not at all realistic⁄; it even uses
dreamlike images to convey its message.

FUSED SENTENCE — **This photograph is not at all realistic; it even uses dreamlike images to convey its message.**

Be careful when you link clauses with a conjunctive adverb or a transitional phrase. You must use such words and phrases with a semicolon, with a period, or with a comma combined with a coordinating conjunction (16h).

SOME CONJUNCTIVE ADVERBS AND TRANSITIONAL PHRASES

also	indeed	now
anyway	instead	otherwise
besides	likewise	similarly
certainly	meanwhile	still
finally	moreover	then
furthermore	namely	therefore
however	nevertheless	thus
incidentally	next	undoubtedly
in fact	in contrast	in addition

Conjunctive adverbs and transitional phrases can appear in various positions in a clause. These words and expressions are usually set off from the rest of the clause by commas (29a, e).

COMMA SPLICE — **Many Third World countries have very high birthrates; therefore, most of their citizens are young.**

FUSED SENTENCE — *and,* **Many Third World countries have very high birthrates, therefore, most of their citizens are young.**

✻ **For Multilingual Writers: Judging Sentence Length**

If you speak a language that uses and values very long sentences, you may string together sentences in English in a way that results in comma-splice errors. (Arabic, Farsi, and Chinese are three such languages.) Note that in standard academic and professional English, a sentence should contain only one independent clause, *unless* the clauses are joined by a comma and a coordinating conjunction, or by a semicolon. (See Chapter 58.)

22d Recast the two clauses as one independent clause.

Sometimes you can reduce two independent clauses that are spliced or fused to a single independent clause.

COMMA
SPLICE

Many people complain that ~~a large part~~ **most** of their mail
is advertisements~~/~~ **and** ~~most of the rest is~~ bills.

FUSED
SENTENCE

Many people complain that ~~a large part~~ **most** of their mail
is advertisements **and** ~~most of the rest is~~ bills.

22e Recast one independent clause as a dependent clause.

When one independent clause is more important than the other, try converting one to a dependent clause (10b).

COMMA
SPLICE

Although Zora Neale Hurston is regarded as one of America's
major novelists, she died in obscurity.

FUSED
SENTENCE

Although Zora Neale Hurston is regarded as one of America's
major novelists**,** she died in obscurity.

The first clause stands in contrast to the second one: in contrast to Hurston's importance today (she is held in high esteem) are the circumstances of her death (obscurity). In the revision, the writer chose to emphasize the second clause and to make the first one into a dependent clause by adding the subordinating conjunction *although.*

COMMA
SPLICE

The arts and crafts movement called for handmade
objects~~/.~~ **, which reacted against mass production,** ~~it reacted against mass production.~~

FUSED
SENTENCE

The arts and crafts movement called for handmade
objects~~.~~ **, which reacted against mass production,** ~~it reacted against mass production.~~

Both clauses discuss related aspects of the arts and crafts movement. In the revision, the writer chose to emphasize the first clause, the one describing what the movement advocated, and to make the second clause, the one describing what it reacted against, into a dependent clause.

23

Sentence Fragments

If you pay close attention to advertisements, you will find sentence fragments in frequent use. For example:

Our Lifetime Guarantee may come as a shock.

Or a strut. Or a muffler. Because once you pay to replace them, Toyota's Lifetime Guarantee covers parts and labor on any dealer-installed muffler, shock, or strut for as long as you own your Toyota! So if anything should ever go wrong, your Toyota dealer will fix it. *Absolutely free.*

– TOYOTA ADVERTISEMENT

The three fragments (italicized here) grab our attention, the first two by creating a play on words and the third one by emphasizing that something is absolutely free. As complete sentences, the information would be less clever and far less memorable.

As this ad illustrates, sentence fragments are groups of words that are punctuated as sentences but lack some element grammatically necessary to a sentence, usually either a subject or a verb. Though you will see fragments in literature, hear them in conversation, and see them everywhere in advertising, you will seldom if ever want to use them in academic or professional writing (where some readers might regard them as errors).

Editing for Sentence Fragments

A group of words must meet three criteria to form a complete sentence. If it does not meet all three, it is a fragment. Revise a fragment by combining it with a nearby sentence or by rewriting it as a complete sentence.

1. A sentence must have a subject. (16j)
2. A sentence must have a verb, not just a verbal. A verbal cannot function as a sentence's verb without an auxiliary verb. (see 16l)

   VERB   **The terrier *is barking*.**

   VERBAL   **The terrier *barking*.**

3. Unless it is a question, a sentence must have at least one clause that does not begin with a subordinating word. Following are some common subordinating words:

although	if	when
as	since	where
because	that	whether
before	though	who
how	unless	why

23a Combine phrase fragments with an independent clause, or make them into sentences.

Phrases are groups of words that lack a subject, a verb, or both. When verbal phrases, prepositional phrases, noun phrases, and appositive phrases are punctuated like a sentence, they become fragments. To revise these fragments, attach them to an independent clause, or make them a separate sentence.

▶ NBC is broadcasting the debates. With discussions afterward.

> The second word group is a prepositional phrase, not a sentence. The editing combines the phrase with an independent clause.

▶ One of our nation's most cherished ideals , may be in danger. The
ideal of a good education for every child. may be in danger.

> *The ideal of a good education for every child* is an appositive phrase renaming the noun *ideals*. The editing attaches the fragment to the sentence containing the noun to which the appositive refers.

▶ Vivian stayed out of school for three months after Linda was born.
She did so to
To recuperate and to take care of her.

> *To recuperate and to take care of her* includes verbals, not verbs. The revision — adding a subject (*she*) and a verb (*did*) — turns the fragment into a separate sentence.

Fragments beginning with transitions

Transitional expressions sometimes lead to fragments. If you introduce an example or explanation with one of the following transitions, be certain you write a sentence, not a fragment. Transitional words and phrases include:

again	but	like
also	finally	or
and	for example	specifically
as a result	for instance	such as
besides	instead	that is

▶ Joan Didion has written on many subjects,/, ~~Such~~ *such* as the Hoover Dam and migraine headaches.

The second word group is a phrase, not a sentence. The editing combines it with an independent clause.

23b Combine compound-predicate fragments with independent clauses.

A compound predicate consists of two or more verbs, along with their modifiers and objects, that have the same subject. Fragments occur when one part of a compound predicate is punctuated as a separate sentence although it lacks a subject. These fragments usually begin with *and, but,* or *or.* You can revise them by attaching them to the independent clause that contains the rest of the predicate.

▶ They sold their house./*a*nd moved into an apartment.

23c Combine dependent-clause fragments with independent clauses, or delete opening words.

Dependent clauses contain both a subject and a verb, but they cannot stand alone as sentences because they depend on an independent clause to complete their meaning. Dependent clauses usually begin with words such as *after, because, before, if, since, though, unless, until, when, where, while, who, which,* and *that.* You can usually combine dependent-clause fragments with a nearby independent clause.

▶ When I decided to work part-time./, I gave up some earning potential.

If you cannot smoothly attach a clause to a nearby independent clause, try deleting the opening subordinating word and turning the dependent clause into a sentence.

▶ Injuries in automobile accidents occur in two ways. ~~When~~ *A*n occupant either is hurt by something inside the car or is thrown from the car.

A Matter of Style: Fragments

We often find sentence fragments in narrative writing, where they call up the rhythms of speech. For example:

> On Sundays, for religion, we went up on the hill. Skipping along the hexagon-shaped tile in Colonial Park. Darting up the steps to Edgecomb Avenue. Stopping in the candy store on St. Nicholas to load up. Leaning forward for leverage to finish the climb up to the church. I was always impressed by this particular house of the Lord.
>
> – KEITH GILYARD, *Voices of the Self*

Here Gilyard uses fragments to move the narrative—and the reader—up the hill. He could have strung the fragments together into one long sentence, but the series of fragments (as well as the parallelism of *skipping, darting, stopping,* and *leaning*) is more effective: he creates a rhythm and a sense of movement that take us as readers to the "house of the Lord."

WORDS/GLOSSARY

A word is dead
When it is said,
Some say.
I say it just
Begins to live
That day.

– EMILY DICKINSON

WORDS/GLOSSARY

24

Using Appropriate and Precise Language

One restaurant's "down-home beef stew with spuds" may be similar to another restaurant's "boeuf bourguignonne with butter-creamed potatoes." Both describe beef dishes, but in each case the language aims to say something about how the beef is prepared as well as something about the restaurant serving it. This chapter will help you to choose words that are clear and appropriate for your purpose, topic, and audience.

Editing to Make Your Language Appropriate and Precise

- Check to see that your language reflects the appropriate level of formality for your audience, purpose, and topic. If you use slang or colloquial language (such as *yeah*), is it appropriate? Is your language sufficiently courteous? (24a)
- Check to be sure your audience will understand any necessary jargon or technical language. If not, either define the jargon, or replace it with words that will be understood. (24a)
- Consider the connotations of words carefully to be sure they convey your intended meaning. If you say someone is *pushy*, be sure you mean to be critical; otherwise, use a word like *assertive*. (24b)
- Be sure to use both general and concrete words. If you are writing about the general category of beds, for example, do you give enough concrete detail (*an antique four-poster bed*)? (24c)
- Look for clichés, and replace them with fresher language. (24d)

24a Use the appropriate level of formality.

In writing, as in speaking, you need to choose a level of formality that matches your audience and purpose. In an email or letter to a friend or close associate, informal language is often appropriate. For most academic and professional writing, however, more formal language is appropriate as you address people you do not know well. Compare the following responses to a request for information about a job candidate:

EMAIL TO SOMEONE YOU KNOW WELL

Iris is great—hire her if you can!

155

LETTER OF RECOMMENDATION TO SOMEONE YOU DO NOT KNOW

I am pleased to recommend Iris Young. She will bring good ideas and extraordinary energy to your organization.

Slang and colloquial language

Slang, extremely informal language, is often confined to a relatively small group and usually becomes obsolete rather quickly, though some slang gains wide use (*yuppie, bummer*). Colloquial language, such as *a lot, in a bind*, or *snooze*, is less informal, more widely used, and longer lasting than most slang.

Writers who use slang and colloquial language run the risk of not being understood or of not being taken seriously. If you are writing for a general audience about arms-control negotiations, for example, and you use the term *nukes* to refer to nuclear missiles, some readers may not know what you mean, and others may be irritated by what they see as a frivolous reference to a deadly serious subject.

Jargon

Jargon is the special vocabulary of a trade or profession, enabling members to speak and write concisely to one another. It should be reserved as much as possible for a specific technical audience.

JARGON

The VDTs in composition were down last week, so we had to lay out on dummies and crop and size the art with a wheel.

REVISED FOR A GENERAL AUDIENCE

The video display terminals were not working last week in the composing room, where models of the newspaper pages are made up for printing, so we had to arrange the contents of each page on a large cardboard sheet and use a wheel, a kind of circular slide rule, to figure out the size and shape of the pictures and other illustrations.

Stuffy language and euphemisms

Stuffy or pompous language is unnecessarily formal for the purpose, audience, or topic. Hence it often gives writing an insincere or unintentionally humorous tone, making a writer's ideas seem insignificant, or even unbelievable.

A Matter of Style: Jargon

Many fields create special vocabularies or give common words special meanings. Businesspeople talk about *greenmail* and *upside movement*, biologists about *nucleotides* and *immuno-destruction*, and baseball fans about a *fielder's choice* and *suicide bunts*. Such terms can be confusing to those who are unfamiliar with the particular field. You need, then, to judge your use of technical language very carefully, making sure that your audience will understand your terms and replacing or defining those that they will not.

STUFFY

Pursuant to the August 9 memorandum regarding petroleum supply exigencies, it is incumbent upon us to endeavor to make maximal utilization of telephonic communication in lieu of personal visitation.

REVISED

As of August 9, petroleum shortages require us to use the telephone whenever possible, rather than make personal visits.

Euphemisms are words and phrases that make unpleasant ideas seem less harsh. *Your position is being eliminated* seeks to soften the blow of being fired or laid off; the British call this employment situation being *declared redundant*, while Canadians refer to being *made surplus*. Other euphemisms include *pass on* for *die* and *sanitation engineer* for *garbage collector*. Use euphemisms with great care. Although they can sometimes appeal to an audience by showing that you are considerate of people's feelings, euphemisms can also sound insincere or evasive.

24b Be alert to a word's denotation and connotation.

Denotation signals the general, or dictionary, meaning of a word, connotation the associations that accompany the word. Words with similar denotations may have connotations that vary widely. The words *maxim, epigram, proverb, saw, saying,* and *motto* all carry roughly the same denotation. Because of their different connotations, however, *proverb* would be the appropriate word to use in reference to a saying from the Bible, *saw* in reference to the kind of wisdom handed down anonymously, *epigram* in reference to a witty statement by someone like Dave Barry.

Be sensitive to the connotations of the words you hear and use. Note the differences in connotation among the following three statements:

▶ **Students Against Racism erected a barrier on the campus oval, saying it symbolizes "the many barriers to those discriminated against by university policies."**

▶ **Left-wing agitators threw up an eyesore right on the oval to try to stampede the university into giving in to their demands.**

▶ **Supporters of human rights challenged the university's investment in racism by erecting a protest barrier on campus.**

The first statement is the most neutral, merely stating facts (and quoting the assertion about university policy to represent it as someone's words rather than as "facts"); the second, by using words with negative connotations (*agitators, eyesore, stampede*), is strongly critical; the third, by using words with positive connotations (*supporters of human rights*) and presenting assertions as facts (*the university's investment in racism*), gives a favorable slant to the story.

24c Balance general and specific diction.

Effective writers balance general words (those that name groups or classes) with specific words (those that identify individual and particular things). Abstractions, which are types of general words, refer to things we cannot perceive through our five senses. Specific words are often concrete, naming things we can see, hear, touch, taste, or smell.

GENERAL	LESS GENERAL	SPECIFIC	MORE SPECIFIC
book	dictionary	unabridged dictionary	my 1988 edition of *Webster's Dictionary*

ABSTRACT	LESS ABSTRACT	CONCRETE	MORE CONCRETE
culture	visual art	painting	Van Gogh's *Starry Night*

Passages that contain mostly general terms or abstractions are often hard to read. But writing that is full of specifics can also be hard to follow if the main point is not made clear or is lost amid a flood of details. In the following passage, the author might have simply made a general statement — *their breakfast was always liberal and good* — or simply given the details of the breakfast. Instead, he is both general and specific.

There would be a brisk fire crackling in the hearth, the old smoke-gold of morning and the smell of fog, the crisp cheerful voices of the people and their ruddy competent morning look, and the cheerful smells of breakfast, which was always liberal and good, the best meal that they had: kidneys and ham and eggs and sausages and toast and marmalade and tea.

– THOMAS WOLFE, *Of Time and the River*

24d Use figurative language to create vivid pictures.

One good way to communicate is by using figurative language, or figures of speech. Such language paints pictures in readers' minds, allowing them to "see" a point and hence understand more readily and clearly.

Similes, metaphors, and analogies

Similes use *like, as, as if,* or *as though* to make explicit the comparison between two seemingly different things.

▶ **The Digital Revolution is whipping through our lives like a Bengali typhoon.** – LOUIS ROSSETTO

▶ **The comb felt as if it was raking my skin off.**
– MALCOLM X, "My First Conk"

Metaphors are implicit comparisons, omitting the *like, as, as if,* or *as though* of similes.

▶ **Today, America Online might be called the Carnival Cruise Lines of interactivity, but in the spring of 1985 it was a tiny start-up called Quantum Computer Services, Inc.** – *Wired Style*

Analogies compare similar features of two dissimilar things; they explain something unfamiliar by relating it to something familiar.

▶ **Unix is the Swiss Army Knife of the Net.** – THOMAS MANDEL

▶ **One Hundred and Twenty-fifth Street was to Harlem what the Mississippi was to the South, a long traveling river always going somewhere, carrying something.** – MAYA ANGELOU, *The Heart of a Woman*

Clichés and mixed metaphors

Ineffective figures of speech can bore, irritate, or unintentionally amuse readers. Clichés and mixed metaphors are two common kinds of ineffective figurative language. A cliché is an overused expression such as *busy as a bee*. By definition, we use clichés all the time, especially in

---

A Matter of Style: Signifying

One distinctive use of figurative language found extensively in African American English is signifying, in which a speaker cleverly and often humorously needles or insults the listener. In the following passage, two African American men (Grave Digger and Coffin Ed) signify on their white supervisor (Anderson), who ordered them to find the originators of a riot:

> "I take it you've discovered who started the riot," Anderson said.
> "We knew who he was all along," Grave Digger said.
> "It's just nothing we can do to him," Coffin Ed echoed.
> "Why not, for God's sake?"
> "He's dead," Coffin Ed said.
> "Who?"
> "Lincoln," Grave Digger said.
> "He hadn't ought to have freed us if he didn't want to make provisions to feed us," Coffin Ed said. "Anyone could have told him that."
> – CHESTER HIMES, *Hot Day, Hot Night*

Coffin Ed and Grave Digger demonstrate the major characteristics of effective signifying: indirection, ironic humor, fluid rhythm—and a surprising twist at the end. Rather than insulting Anderson directly by pointing out that he's asked a dumb question, they criticize the question indirectly by ultimately blaming a white man (and one they're all supposed to revere). This twist leaves the supervisor speechless, teaching him something *and* giving Grave Digger and Coffin Ed the last word.

You will find examples of signifying in the work of many African American writers. You may also hear signifying in NBA basketball, for it is an important element of trash talking; what Grave Digger and Coffin Ed do to Anderson, Charles Barkley regularly does to his opponents on the court. As with all figurative language, it is important to recognize this verbal strategy—and to understand the meaning it adds.

speech, and many serve quite usefully as shorthand for familiar ideas. But if you use such paint-by-numbers language to excess in your writing, readers are likely to conclude that what you are saying is not very new or interesting — or true.

Mixed metaphors make comparisons that are inconsistent.

▶ The lectures were like brilliant comets streaking through the night sky,
dazzling   *flashes*
~~showering~~ listeners with ~~a torrential rain~~ of insights.
  ^   ^

The images of streaking light and heavy precipitation were inconsistent; in the revised sentence, all of the images relate to light.

25

Using Language to Build Common Ground

The supervisor who carefully and consistently refers to her staff as "team members" (rather than as "my staff" or as "subordinates") is choosing language intended to establish common ground with people who are important to her. This chapter will help you think about how your own language can work to build common ground with others.

Editing for Language That Builds Common Ground

- What unstated assumptions might come between you and your readers? Look, for instance, for language implying approval or disapproval and for the ways you use *we, you*, and *they*. (25b)

- Does any language used to describe others carry offensive stereotypes or connotations? (25b)

- Have you checked for use of masculine pronouns to refer to members of both sexes and for any other uses of potentially sexist language? (25c)

- Are your references to race, religion, gender, sexual orientation, and so on relevant or necessary to your discussion? If not, consider leaving them out. (25d, e)

- Are the terms you use to refer to groups accurate and acceptable? Because group labels and preferences are always changing, take care to use the most widely accepted terms. (25d)

25a   Remember the golden rule.

As a child, you may have learned to "do to others what you would have them do to you." To that golden rule, we could add "say to others what you would have them say to you." For the language we use has power: it can praise, delight, inspire—and also hurt, offend, or even destroy. Language that offends breaks the golden rule of language use, preventing others from identifying with you and thus damaging your credibility as a writer.

Few absolute guidelines exist for using language that respects differences and builds common ground. Two rules, however, can help: consider carefully the sensitivities and preferences of others, and watch for words that carry stereotypes and betray assumptions not directly stated.

25b   Watch for stereotypes and other assumptions.

Children like to play; U.S. citizens value freedom; people who do not finish high school fare less well in the job market than those who graduate. These broad statements contain stereotypes, standardized or fixed ideas about a group. To some extent, we all think in terms of stereotypes, and sometimes they can be helpful in making generalizations. Stereotyping any individual on the basis of generalizations about a group, however, can sometimes lead to inaccurate and even hurtful conclusions.

Stereotyping becomes especially evident in the words we choose to refer to others. Stereotyped language can break the links between writers and readers—or between speakers and listeners.

Because stereotypes are often based on half-truths, misunderstandings, and hand-me-down prejudices, they can lead to bias, bigotry, and intolerance. Even positive or neutral stereotypes can hurt, for they inevitably ignore the uniqueness of an individual. Careful writers will want to make sure that language doesn't stereotype any group *or* individual.

Other kinds of unstated assumptions that enter into thinking and writing can destroy common ground by ignoring differences between others and ourselves. For example, a student in a religion seminar who uses *we* to refer to Christians and *they* to refer to members of other religions had better be sure that everyone in the class is Christian, or some of them may feel left out of this discussion. Similarly, a letter to the editor that uses language implying that liberals are all bad and conservatives all good is likely to alienate some readers and prevent them from even considering the writer's argument.

Sometimes stereotypes even lead writers to call special attention to a group affiliation when it is not necessary or relevant to the point, as in "a woman bus driver" or "a Jewish doctor." Nevertheless, deciding whether to describe an individual as a member of a group is often difficult. The following sections invite you to think about how your language can build — rather than destroy — common ground.

25c Consider assumptions about gender.

Powerful and often invisible gender-related elements of language affect our thinking and our behavior. At one time, for instance, speakers always referred to hypothetical doctors or engineers as *he* and to nurses and secretaries as *she* (and then labeled any woman who worked as a doctor a *woman doctor* or any man who worked as a nurse a *male nurse*, as if to say, "they're exceptions"). Equally problematic was the traditional use of *man* and *mankind* to refer to people of both sexes and the use of *he, him, his,* and *himself* to refer to people of unknown sex. Because such usage ignores half the human race — or at least seems to assume that the male half is more important — it hardly helps a writer build common ground.

Sexist language, those words and phrases that stereotype or ignore members of either sex or that unnecessarily call attention to gender, can usually be revised fairly easily. There are several alternatives to using masculine pronouns to refer to persons of unknown sex. One option is to recast the sentence using plural forms.

▶ *Lawyers*
A lawyer must pass the bar exam before ~~he~~ *they* can begin to practice.

Another option is to substitute pairs of pronouns such as *he or she, him or her,* and so on.

▶ A lawyer must pass the bar exam before he *or she* can begin to practice.

Yet another way to revise the sentence is to eliminate the pronouns.

▶ A lawyer must pass the bar exam before ~~he can begin~~ *beginning* to practice.

INSTEAD OF	TRY USING
anchorman, anchorwoman	anchor
chairman, chairwoman	chair, chairperson
coed	student
congressman	member of Congress, representative
mailman	mail carrier
male nurse	nurse
man, mankind	humans, human beings, humanity, the human race, humankind
manpower	workers, personnel
mothering	parenting
policeman, policewoman	police officer
steward, stewardess	flight attendant
woman engineer	engineer

Editing for Sexist Language

- Have you used *man* or *men* or words containing one of them to refer to people who may be female? If so, consider substituting another word—instead of *fireman*, for instance, try *firefighter*.

- If you have mentioned someone's gender, is it necessary to do so? If you identify someone as a female architect, for example, do you (or would you) refer to someone else as a *male architect*? And if you then note that the female is an attractive blond mother of two, do you mention that the male is a muscular, square-jawed father of three? Unless gender and related matters—looks, clothes, parenthood—are relevant to your point, leave them unmentioned.

- Do you use any occupational stereotypes? Watch for the use of female pronouns for nurses and male ones for engineers, for example.

- Do you use language that in any way patronizes either sex? Do you refer to a wife as *the little woman*, for instance, or to a husband as *her old man*?

- Have you used *he, him, his,* or *himself* to refer to people who may be female?

- Have you overused *he and she, him and her,* and so on? Frequent use of these pronoun pairs can irritate readers.

25d Consider assumptions about race and ethnicity.

As we all know only too well, generalizations about racial and ethnic groups can result in especially harmful stereotyping. Such assumptions underlie statements that suggest, for instance, that all Asian Americans excel in math and science, or that all Germans are efficient. In building common ground, writers must watch for any language that ignores differences not only among individual members of a race or ethnic group but also among subgroups. Writers must be aware, for instance, of the many nations to which Native Americans belong and of the diverse places from which Americans of Spanish-speaking ancestry have emigrated.

Preferred terms

Avoiding stereotypes and other assumptions based on race or ethnicity is only a first step. Beyond that is the responsibility to refer to any group in terms that its members actually desire. Identifying those terms is sometimes not an easy task, for preferences change and even vary widely.

The word *colored*, for example, was once widely used in the United States to refer to Americans of African ancestry. By the 1950s, the preferred term had become *Negro*; in the 1960s, however, *black* came to be preferred by most, though certainly not all, members of that community. Then, in the late 1980s, some leaders of the American black community urged that *black* be replaced by *African American*.

The word *Oriental*, once used to refer to people of East Asian descent, is now often considered offensive. At the University of California at Berkeley, the Oriental Languages Department is now known as the East Asian Languages Department. One advocate of the change explained that *Oriental* is appropriate for objects like rugs, but not for people.

Many of those U.S. citizens once referred to as *American Indians* now prefer *Native Americans*. In Alaska and Canada, many of the native peoples once referred to as *Eskimos* now prefer *Inuit* (which is the official designated term in Canada).

Among Americans of Spanish-speaking descent, the preferred terms are many: *Chicano/Chicana, Hispanic, Latin American, Latino/Latina, Mexican American, Dominican,* and *Puerto Rican,* to name but a few.

Clearly, then, ethnic terminology changes often enough to challenge even the most careful writers. The best advice may be to consider your words carefully, to *listen* for the way members of groups refer to themselves (or *ask* their preferences), and to check any term you're unsure of in a current dictionary.

25e Consider other kinds of difference.

Age

Mention age if it is relevant, but be aware that age-related terms can carry derogatory connotations (*matronly, well-preserved,* and so on). Describing Mr. Fry as *elderly but still active* may sound polite to you, but chances are Mr. Fry would prefer being called *an active seventy-eight-year-old* — or just *a seventy-eight-year-old*, which eliminates the unstated assumption of surprise that he is active "at his age."

Class

Since you may not think about class distinctions as often as you do about age or race, take special care to examine your words for stereotypes or assumptions about class. As a writer, do not assume that all your readers share your background or values — that the members of your audience are all homeowners, for instance. And avoid using any words — *redneck, blue blood,* and the like — that might alienate members of an audience.

Geographical areas

Stereotypes about geographical areas are very often clichéd and exaggerated. New Englanders are not all thrifty and tight-lipped; Florida offers more than retirement and tourism; midwesterners are not all hardworking; not all Californians care about the latest trends. Be careful not to make these kinds of simplistic assumptions.

Check also that you use geographical terms accurately.

AMERICA, AMERICAN Although many people use these words to refer to the United States *alone*, such usage is not accurate — and will not necessarily be acceptable to people from Canada, Mexico, and Central or South America.

BRITISH, ENGLISH Use *British* to refer to the island of Great Britain, which includes England, Scotland, and Wales, or to the United Kingdom of Great Britain and Northern Ireland. In general, do not use *English* for these broader senses.

ARAB This term refers only to people of Arabic-speaking descent. Note that Iran is not an Arab nation; its people speak Farsi, not Arabic. Note also that *Arab* is not synonymous with *Muslim* or *Moslem* (a believer in Islam). Most (but not all) Arabs are Muslim, but many Muslims (those in Pakistan, for example) are not Arab.

Physical ability or health

When writing about a person with a serious illness or physical disability, ask yourself whether mentioning the disability is relevant to your discussion, and whether the words you use carry negative connotations. You might choose, for example, to say someone *uses* a wheelchair rather than to say he or she *is confined to* one. Similarly, you might note a subtle but meaningful difference in calling someone a *person with AIDS* rather than an *AIDS victim*. Mentioning the person first and the disability second, such as referring to a *child with diabetes* rather than a *diabetic child* or a *diabetic*, is always a good idea.

Religion

Religious stereotypes are very often inaccurate and unfair. For example, Roman Catholics hold a wide spectrum of views on abortion, Muslim women do not all wear veils, and many Baptists are not fundamentalists. In fact, many people do not believe in or practice a religion at all, so be careful of such assumptions. As in other cases, do not use religious labels without considering their relevance to your point, and make every effort to be accurate — for example, *Reformed* churches but *Reform* synagogues.

Sexual orientation

Partly because sexual orientation is a topic that was "erased" from most public discourse until recent decades, the stereotypes and assumptions that surround it are particularly deep-seated and, often, unconscious. Writers who wish to build common ground, therefore, should not assume that readers all share one sexual orientation.

As with any label, reference to sexual orientation should be governed by context. Someone writing about Representative Barney Frank's economic views would probably have little if any reason to refer to his sexual orientation. On the other hand, someone writing about diversity in U.S. government might find it important to note that Frank is a representative who has made his homosexuality public.

26

Language Variety

English comes in many dialects—varieties of language that differ from one another in pronunciation, vocabulary, rhetoric, and grammar. Whether you order a hero, a poor boy, a hoagie, a submarine, a grinder, or a *cubano* reflects such differences. In addition to numerous varieties of English, many other languages are spoken in the United States. This chapter focuses on how you can appropriately use different dialects of English and different languages.

> ### Editing for Language Variety
>
> You can use different varieties of language to good effect for the following purposes:
> - To repeat someone's exact words
> - To evoke a person, place, or activity
> - To establish your credibility and build common ground with your readers
> - To make a strong point
> - To get your audience's attention

26a Standard varieties of English

One variety of English, often referred to as the "standard," is that taught prescriptively in schools, represented in this and all other textbooks, used in the national media, and written and spoken widely by those wielding the most social and economic power. As the language used in business and most public institutions, standard English is a variety you will want to be completely familiar with. Standard English, however, is only one of many effective varieties of English and itself varies according to purpose and audience, from the very formal style used in academic writing to the informal style characteristic of casual conversation.

26b Ethnic varieties of English

Whether you are a Native American or trace your ancestry to Europe, Asia, Africa, Latin America, or elsewhere, you have an ethnic heritage that probably lives on in the English language. See how one Hawaiian writer uses an ethnic variety of English to paint a picture of young teens hearing a scary "chicken-skin" story about sharks from their grandmother.

> "—So, rather dan being rid of da shark, da people were stuck with many little ones, for dere mistake."
>
> Then Grandma Wong wen' pause, for dramatic effect, I guess, and she wen' add, "Dis is one of dose times. . . . Da time of da sharks."
>
> Those words ended another of Grandma's chicken skin stories. The stories she told us had been passed on to her by her grandmother, who had heard them from her grandmother. Always skipping a generation.
>
> – RODNEY MORALES, "When the Shark Bites"

Notice how the narrator uses both standard and ethnic varieties of English—presenting information necessary to the story line mostly in standard English and using a local, ethnic variety to represent spoken language, which helps us "hear" the characters talk.

Zora Neale Hurston often mixes African American vernacular with standard English. In the following passage, she recounts how as a child she used to hail passing strangers and offer to ride down the road with them for a bit:

> My grandmother worried about my forward ways a great deal. She had known slavery and to her my brazenness was unthinkable.
>
> "Git down offa dat gate-post! You li'l sow, you! Git down! Setting up dere looking dem white folks right in de face! They's gowine to lynch you, yet. And don't stand in dat doorway gazing out at 'em neither. Youse too brazen to live long."
>
> Nevertheless, I kept right on gazing at them, and "going a piece of the way" whenever I could make it.
>
> – ZORA NEALE HURSTON, *Dust Tracks on a Road*

Hurston shifts from standard to vernacular in order to represent the pronunciation (*git, offa, dere*), the diction (*piece of the way*), and the syntax (*youse, don't . . . neither*) of her grandmother and to emphasize the ways in which what lay beyond her small home town seemed very different to her young eyes.

In both of these examples, the writers choose to shift from standard English to other varieties. In each case, one important reason for the shift is to demonstrate that the writer is a member of the community whose language he or she is representing and thus to build credibility with others in the community.

Take care, however, in using the language of communities other than your own. Used inappropriately, such language can have an opposite effect, perhaps destroying credibility and alienating your audience.

26c Occupational varieties of English

From the fast-food business to taxi driving, from architecture to zoology, every job has its own special variety of English. Examples abound, from specialized words (*hermeneutics* in literary studies) to invented words (*quark* in physics). Here is an example from the computer world about a problem plaguing the World Wide Web.

> Right now, even if you're using a fully stocked Pentium and have a T1 line running into your bedroom, the Web can seem overloaded and painfully slow. Conventional wisdom says the solution lies in new network technologies like AIM and fiber optics. But researchers are investigating how to change the way computers communicate to minimize pauses, stutters, and false starts. After all, using the Internet isn't just a matter of shouting, "Hey, *www.hotwired.com*, shoot me that GIF!"   – STEVE G. STEINBERG, *Wired*

The columnist writing here uses technical abbreviations (*T1*) and acronyms (*AIM, GIF*), as well as ordinary words that have special meanings, such as "pauses" and "stutters." He also uses a quotation to capture the sound and rhythm of speech and to help make his point: the Internet is governed by specific rules that can speed up—or slow down—communication.

The language that sportscasters use also varies, depending on whether the announcer is giving play-by-play commentary or color commentary. The following excerpt, from a conversation between Pat Summerall (play-by-play) and John Madden (color) as they announce an Eagles-Giants football game, illustrates such variation:

Summerall: Second and nine. Cunningham to throw it. Giles ducks to about a foot short of first. It looks like Cooks and Taylor on the stop.

Madden: Jimmie Giles says, "I've been in a lot of big games" (he's a thirteen-year veteran), and the bad news for the Eagles was that they lost Keith Jackson, of course, but the good news is that they have Jimmie Giles. I'll tell you, Randall Cunningham feels very, very comfortable with Jimmie Giles.

Notice that the play-by-play announcer strings together words in ways not found in ordinary syntax but that here are visually and semantically meaningful to those watching the game. In addition, the play-by-play announcer provides specific technical information (*a first down*) and uses technical vocabulary (*second and nine, on the stop*). The color commentator, on the other hand, speaks in nearly complete sentences, provides interesting but not essential information, and uses technical vocabulary only occasionally. These differences reflect the different purposes of each announcer: one tries to sketch in exactly what is happening on the field; the other to color that sketch by commenting on it.

26d Regional varieties of English

Using regional language is an effective way to evoke a character or place. Look, for example, at the following piece of dialogue from an essay about Vermont:

> "There'll be some fine music on the green tonight, don't ya know?"
> "Well, I sure do want to go."
> "So don't I!"

Here the regional English creates a homespun effect and captures some of the language used in a particular place.

See how an anthropologist weaves together regional and standard academic English in writing about one Carolina community.

> For Roadville, schooling is something most folks have not gotten enough of, but everybody believes will do something toward helping an individual "get on." In the words of one oldtime resident, "Folks that ain't got no schooling don't get to be nobody nowadays."
> –SHIRLEY BRICE HEATH, *Ways with Words*

Notice that the researcher takes care to let a resident of Roadville speak her mind — and in her own words. She does so to be faithful to the person she is quoting as well as to capture some of the flavor of the spoken language.

26e Bringing in other languages

You might use a language other than English for the same reasons you might use different varieties of English: to represent the actual words of a speaker, to make a point, to connect with your audience, to get their attention. See how Gerald Haslam uses Spanish to capture his great-grandmother's words and to make a point about his relationship to her.

> "*Expectoran su sangre!*" exclaimed Great-grandma when I showed her the small horned toad I had removed from my breast pocket. I turned toward my mother, who translated: "They spit blood."
>
> "*De los ojos*," Grandma added. "From their eyes," mother explained, herself uncomfortable in the presence of the small beast.
>
> I grinned, "Awwwwwww."
>
> But my Great-grandmother did not smile. "*Son muy toxicos*," she nodded with finality. Mother moved back an involuntary step, her hands suddenly busy at her breast. "Put that thing down," she ordered.
>
> "His name's John," I said.   – GERALD HASLAM, *California Childhood*

You may also use a particularly apt foreign phrase that seems more appropriate untranslated. See how the novelist Michele Herman uses Yiddish to evoke her grandmother's world.

> "Skip *shabes*?" Rivke chuckled. "I don't think this is possible. Once a week comes *shabes*. About this a person doesn't have a choice."
>
> "What I mean"—Myra's impatience was plain—"is skip the preparation. It's too much for you, it tires you out."
>
> "*Ach*," Rivke said. "Too much for me it isn't."
>
> – MICHELE HERMAN, *Missing*

Rivke's syntax—the inversion of word order ("Once a week comes *shabes*," "Too much for me it isn't")—reflects Yiddish rhythms. In addition, the use of the Yiddish *shabes* carries a strong association with a religious institution, one that would be lost if it were translated to "sabbath." It is not "sabbath" to Rivke; it is *shabes*.

✻ **For Multilingual Writers: Global English**

English is used in many countries around the world, resulting in many global varieties. You may, for example, have learned a British variety. British English differs somewhat from U.S. English in certain vocabulary (*bonnet* for *hood* of a car), syntax (*to hospital* rather than *to the hospital*), spelling (*centre* rather than *center*), and of course pronunciation. If you have learned a British variety of English, you will want to recognize the ways in which it differs from the U.S. standard.

27

Spelling

Drive down any commercial street, and you are sure to see many intentionally misspelled words—from a "Kountry Kitchen" restaurant to a "drive-thru" bank. Such fanciful or playful spelling will get you no points, however, in academic or professional writing. This chapter provides some fairly straightforward rules and guidelines that answer the most common questions about English spelling. And keep in mind: research shows that writers who use spell checkers make fewer than half as many spelling errors as those who do not.

27a Learn the most commonly misspelled words.

The three thousand college essays used in the research for this book revealed a fairly small number of persistently misspelled words. Look over the fifty words most commonly misspelled. If you have trouble with any of them, take a moment to create a special memory device, such as the following, to help you remember them correctly: *They're certain their coats were over there.*

The fifty most commonly misspelled words

1. their/there/they're
2. too/to
3. a lot
4. noticeable
5. receive/-d/-s
6. lose
7. you're/your
8. an/and
9. develop/-s
10. definitely
11. than/then
12. believe/-d/-s
13. occurred
14. affect/-s
15. cannot
16. separate
17. success
18. through
19. until
20. where
21. successful/-ly
22. truly
23. argument/-s
24. experience/-s
25. environment
26. exercise/-s/-ing
27. necessary
28. sense
29. therefore
30. accept/-ed
31. heroes
32. professor
33. whether
34. without
35. business/-es
36. dependent
37. every day
38. may be
39. occasion/-s
40. occurrences
41. woman
42. all right
43. apparent/-ly
44. categories
45. final/-ly
46. immediate/-ly
47. roommate/-s
48. against
49. before
50. beginning

Guidelines for Using a Spell Checker

- Keep a dictionary near your computer, and look up any word the spell checker highlights that you are not absolutely sure of.
- If your program has a "learn" option, enter into your spell-checker dictionary any proper names, non-English words, or specialized language you use regularly and have trouble spelling.
- Because spell checkers do not recognize homonym errors, use the search function to identify homonyms for you to double-check. (27b)
- Spell checkers will not catch missing capital letters, so be sure to proofread carefully for capitalization.

27b   Learn to distinguish among homonyms.

English has many homonyms, words that sound alike but have different spellings and meanings. But a relatively small number of them — just eight groups — cause writers frequent trouble. Here are the eight groups, from the most commonly confused on down.

The most troublesome homonyms

their (possessive form of *they*)
there (in that place)
they're (contraction of *they are*)

to (in the direction of)
too (in addition; excessive)
two (number between *one* and *three*)

weather (climatic conditions)
whether (if)

accept (take or receive)
except (leave out)

who's (contraction of *who is* or *who has*)
whose (possessive form of *who*)

its (possessive form of *it*)
it's (contraction of *it is* or *it has*)

your (possessive form of *you*)
you're (contraction of *you are*)

affect (an emotion; to have an influence)
effect (a result; to cause to happen)

Other homonyms and frequently confused words

advice (suggestion)
advise (suggest [to])

all ready (fully prepared)
already (previously)

allude (refer [to])
elude (avoid or escape)

allusion (reference)
illusion (false idea or appearance)

all ways (by every means)
always (at all times)

altar (sacred platform or table)
alter (change)

bare (uncovered; to uncover)
bear (animal; to carry or endure)

brake (device for stopping; to stop)
break (fracture; to fragment)

buy (purchase)
by (near; beside; through)

capital (principal city)
capitol (legislators' building)

cite (refer to)
sight (seeing; something seen)
site (location)

coarse (rough or crude)
course (plan of study; path)

complement (something that completes; to complete)
compliment (praise; to praise)

conscience (moral sense)
conscious (mentally aware)

council (leadership group)
counsel (advice; to advise)

desert (dry area; to abandon)
dessert (sweet course at end of a meal)

elicit (draw forth)
illicit (illegal)

eminent (distinguished)
imminent (expected in the immediate future)

every day (each day)
everyday (daily, ordinary)

forth (forward)
fourth (between *third* and *fifth*)

gorilla (ape)
guerrilla (irregular soldier)

hear (perceive with the ears)
here (in this place)

hoarse (sounding rough)
horse (animal)

know (understand)
no (opposite of *yes*)

lead (a metal; to go before)
led (past tense of *lead*)

loose (not tight; not confined)
lose (misplace; fail to win)

may be (might be)
maybe (perhaps)

passed (went by; received a passing grade)
past (beyond; events that have already occurred)

patience (quality of being patient)
patients (persons under medical care)

personal (private or individual)
personnel (employees)

plain (simple, not fancy; flat land)
plane (airplane; tool; flat surface)

presence (condition of being)
presents (gifts; gives)

principal (most important; head of a school)
principle (fundamental truth)

rain (precipitation)
rein (strap; to control)
reign (period of rule; to rule)

right (correct; opposite of *left*)
rite (ceremony)
write (produce words on a surface)

scene (setting; view)
seen (past participle of *see*)

stationary (unmoving)
stationery (writing paper)

than (as compared with)
then (at that time; therefore)

threw (past tense of *throw*)
thorough (complete)
through (in one side of and out the other; by means of)

waist (part of the body)
waste (squander)

weak (feeble)
week (seven days)

which (what; that)
witch (woman with supernatural power)

✳ **For Multilingual Writers: Recognizing British Spellings**

The following are some words that are spelled differently in American and British English.

AMERICAN	BRITISH
center	centre
check	cheque
civilization	civilisation
color	colour
criticize	criticise
judgment	judgement
realize	realise
theater	theatre

27c Take advantage of spelling rules.

i *before* e *except after* c

Use *i* before *e* except after *c*, when pronounced "ay" (as in *weigh*), or in *weird* exceptions.

I BEFORE *E*	achieve, brief, field, friend
EXCEPT AFTER *C*	ceiling, receipt, perceive
OR WHEN PRONOUNCED "AY"	eighth, reign, neighbor, weigh
OR IN WEIRD EXCEPTIONS	either, foreign, height, neither, leisure, seize

Prefixes

A prefix does not change the spelling of the word it is added to, even when the last letter of the prefix and the first letter of the base word are the same. (See 38e on using hyphens with some prefixes and suffixes.)

> dis- + service = disservice   over- + rate = overrate

Suffixes

A suffix may change the spelling of the word it is added to.

FINAL SILENT *E*

Drop the final silent *e* when adding a suffix to a word that starts with a vowel.

> imagine + -able = imaginable   exercise + -ing = exercising
> future + -istic = futuristic   continue + -ous = continuous

Keep the final *e* if the suffix starts with a consonant.

> force + -ful = forceful   state + -ly = stately
>
> EXCEPTIONS   changeable, noticeable, argument, truly, judgment

FINAL *Y*

If adding an ending to a word that ends in *y*, change the *y* to an *i* if it is preceded by a consonant.

> try, tried   busy, busily

Keep the *y* if it follows a vowel, if it is part of a proper name, or if the suffix begins with *i*.

> employ, employed   Kennedy, Kennedyesque   dry, drying

FINAL CONSONANTS

When adding a suffix to a word that ends in a consonant, the consonant is sometimes doubled. If the word ends in a vowel + consonant, double the final consonant if the word contains only one syllable or ends in an accented syllable.

> stop, stopping   begin, beginner   occur, occurrence

Do not double the final consonant if it is preceded by more than one vowel or by a vowel and another consonant, or if the new word is not accented on the last syllable.

bait, baiting   infer, inference
benefit, benefiting   refer, reference
fight, fighter

Plurals

ADDING -S OR -ES

For most words, add -s. For words ending in s, *ch,* *sh,* x, or z, add -es.

pencil, pencils   church, churches   bus, buses

Add -s to words ending in *o* if the *o* is preceded by a vowel. Add -es if the *o* is preceded by a consonant.

rodeo, rodeos   patio, patios   veto, vetoes
potato, potatoes   hero, heroes

EXCEPTIONS   memo, memos; piano, pianos; solo, solos

OTHER PLURALS

For words ending in *y,* change *y* to *i* and add -es if the *y* is preceded by a consonant. Keep the *y* and add -s if the *y* is preceded by a vowel or if it ends a proper name.

theory, theories   eighty, eighties   Kennedy, Kennedys
attorney, attorneys   guy, guys

Memorize irregular plurals.

bacterium, bacteria   datum, data   criterion, criteria
series, series   basis, bases   thesis, theses

For compound nouns written as separate or hyphenated words, make the most important part plural.

brother-in-law, brothers-in-law
lieutenant governor, lieutenant governors

28

Glossary of Usage

Conventions of usage might be called the "good manners" of discourse. And just as our notions of good manners vary from culture to culture and time to time, so do conventions of usage. The word *ain't*, for instance, now considered inappropriate in academic and professional discourse, was once widely used by the most proper British speakers and is still commonly used in some spoken U.S. dialects. In short, matters of usage, like other language choices you must make, depend on what your purpose is and on what is appropriate for a particular audience at a particular time. This glossary provides usage guidelines for some commonly confused words and phrases.

a, an   Use *a* with a word that begins with a consonant (*a* book), with a consonant sound such as "y" or "w" (*a euphoric moment, a one-sided match*), and with a sounded *h* (*a hemisphere*). Use *an* with a word that begins with a vowel (*an umbrella*), with a vowel sound (*an X-ray*), and with a silent *h* (*an honor*).

accept, except   The verb *accept* means "receive" or "agree to." Used as a preposition, *except* means "aside from" or "excluding." *All the plaintiffs except Mr. Kim decided to accept the settlement.*

advice, advise   The noun *advice* means an "opinion" or "suggestion"; the verb *advise* means "offer or provide advice." *Charlotte's mother advised her to become a secretary, but Charlotte, who intended to become a dancer, ignored the advice.*

affect, effect   As a verb, *affect* means "influence" or "move the emotions of"; as a noun, it means "emotions" or "feelings." *Effect* is a noun meaning "result"; less commonly, it is a verb meaning "bring about." *Many people are affected by the realization that a nuclear war would have far-reaching effects.*

aggravate   The formal meaning is "make worse." *Having another mouth to feed aggravated their poverty.* In academic and professional writing, avoid using *aggravate* to mean "irritate" or "annoy."

all ready, already   *All ready* means "fully prepared." *Already* means "previously." *We were all ready for Lucy's party when we learned that she had already left.*

all right   *All right* means "acceptable" or signals agreement. *Alright*, a less common variant of the term, is not the preferred spelling.

all together, altogether   *All together* means "all in a group" or "gathered in one place." *Altogether* means "completely" or "everything considered." *When the union members were all together in the room, their consensus was altogether obvious.*

allude, elude   *Allude* means "refer indirectly." *Elude* means "avoid" or "escape from." *The candidate alludes to his parents who had eluded political oppression.*

allusion, illusion An *allusion* is an indirect reference, as when a writer hints at a well-known event, person, or quotation, assuming the reader will recognize it (*a literary allusion*). An *illusion* is a false or misleading appearance (*an optical illusion*).

already See *all ready, already*.

alright See *all right*.

altogether See *all together, altogether*.

among, between In referring to two things or people, use *between*. In referring to three or more, use *among*. *The relationship between the twins is different from that among the other three children.*

amount, number Use *amount* with quantities you cannot count; use *number* for quantities you can count. *A small number of volunteers cleared a large amount of brush within a few hours.*

an See *a, an*.

and/or Avoid this term except in business or legal writing, where it is a short way of saying that one or both of two terms apply.

any body, anybody, any one, anyone *Anybody* and *anyone* are indefinite pronouns. *Anyone* [or *anybody*] *could enjoy carving wood. Any body* is two words, an adjective modifying a noun. *Any body of water has its own ecology. Any one* is two adjectives or a pronoun modified by an adjective. *Customers could buy only two sale items at any one time.*

anyplace, anywhere In academic and professional discourse, use *anywhere*, not *anyplace*.

anyway, anyways In writing, use *anyway*, not *anyways*.

anywhere See *anyplace, anywhere*.

apt, liable, likely *Likely to* means "probably will," and *apt to* means "inclines or tends to." Either will do in many instances. *Liable to* often carries a more negative sense and is also a legal term meaning "obligated" or "responsible for."

as Avoid sentences in which it is not clear if *as* means "because" or means "when." For example, does *Carl left town as his father was arriving* mean "at the same time as his father was arriving" or "because his father was arriving"?

as, as if, like Use *as* to identify equivalent terms in a description. *Gary served as moderator at the meeting.* Use *like* as a preposition to indicate similarity but not equivalency. *Hugo, like Jane, was a detailed observer. Like* cannot act as a conjunction introducing a clause. *The dog howled like a wolf, just as if* [not *like*] *she were a wild animal.*

assure, ensure, insure *Assure* means "convince" or "promise"; its direct object is usually a person or persons. *She assured voters she would not raise taxes. Ensure* and *insure* both mean "make certain," but *insure* carries the sense of protection against financial loss. *When the city rationed water to ensure that the supply would last, the Browns could no longer afford to insure their car-wash business.*

as to Do not use *as to* as a substitute for *about*. *Karen was unsure about* [not *as to*] *Bruce's intentions.*

at, where See *where*.

awful, awfully *Awful* and *awfully* mean "awe-inspiring" and "in an awe-inspiring way." Casual usage dilutes *awful* to mean "bad" (*I had an awful day*) and *awfully* to mean "very" (*It was awfully cold*). Avoid these casual usages in academic and professional writing.

awhile, a while Always use *a while* after a preposition such as *for, in,* or *after*. *We drove awhile and then stopped for a while.*

bad, badly Use *bad* after a linking verb such as *be, feel,* or *seem*. Use *badly* to modify an action verb, an adjective, or another verb. *The hostess felt bad because the dinner was badly prepared.*

because of, due to Use *due to* when the effect, stated as a noun, appears before the verb *be*. *His illness was due to malnutrition.* (*Illness*, a noun, is the effect.) Use *because of* when the effect is stated as a clause. *He was sick because of malnutrition.* (*He was sick*, a clause, is the effect.)

being as, being that Do not use these expressions in academic or professional writing; use *because* or *since* instead. *Because* [not *being as*] *Romeo killed Tybalt, he was banished to Padua.*

beside, besides *Beside* is only a preposition, meaning "next to." *Besides* can be a preposition meaning "other than" or an adverb meaning "moreover." *No one besides Francesca knows whether the tree is still growing beside the house.*

between See *among, between*.

breath, breathe *Breath* is a noun; *breathe*, a verb. *"Breathe,"* said the nurse, so *June took a deep breath of laughing gas.*

bring, take Use *bring* when an object is moved from a farther to a nearer place; use *take* when the opposite is true. *Take the box to the post office; bring back my mail.*

but, yet Don't use these words together. *He is strong but* [not *but yet*] *gentle.*

but that, but what Avoid using these as substitutes for *that* in expressions of doubt. *Hercule Poirot never doubted that* [not *but that*] *he would solve the case.*

can, may *Can* refers to ability and *may* to possibility or permission. *Since I can ski the slalom well, I may win the race.*

can't hardly, can't scarcely *Hardly* and *scarcely* are negatives; therefore, *can't hardly* and *can't scarcely* are double negatives. These expressions are commonly used in some regional and ethnic varieties of English but are not used in standard academic English. *Tim can* [not *can't*] *hardly wait.*

can't help but This expression is redundant. Use the more formal *I cannot but go* or the less formal *I can't help going* rather than *I can't help but go.*

can't scarcely See *can't hardly, can't scarcely*.

censor, censure   *Censor* means "remove that which is considered offensive." *Censure* means "formally reprimand." *The public censured the newspaper for censoring letters to the editor.*

complement, compliment   *Complement* means "go well with." *Compliment* means "praise." *Guests complimented her on how her earrings complemented her gown.*

comprise, compose   *Comprise* means "contain." *Compose* means "make up." *The class comprises twenty students. Twenty students compose the class.*

conscience, conscious   *Conscience* means "a sense of right and wrong." *Conscious* means "awake" or "aware." *After lying, Lisa was conscious of a guilty conscience.*

consensus of opinion   Use *consensus* instead of this redundant phrase. *The family consensus was to sell the old house.*

consequently, subsequently   *Consequently* means "as a result"; *subsequently* means "then." *He quit, and subsequently his wife lost her job; consequently, they panicked.*

continual, continuous   *Continual* refers to an activity repeated at regular or frequent intervals. *Continuous* describes an ongoing activity or an object connected without break. *The damage done by continuous erosion was increased by the continual storms.*

could of   See *have, of.*

criteria, criterion   *Criterion* means "standard of judgment" or "necessary qualification." *Criteria* is the plural form. *Image is the wrong criterion for choosing a president.*

data   *Data* is the plural form of the Latin word *datum*, meaning "fact." Although *data* is used informally as either singular or plural, in academic or professional writing, treat *data* as plural. *These data indicate that fewer people smoke today than ten years ago.*

different from, different than   *Different from* is generally preferred in academic and professional writing, although both phrases are used widely. *Her lab results were no different from [not than] his.*

discreet, discrete   *Discreet* means "tactful" or "prudent." *Discrete* means "separate" or "distinct." *The manager's discreet words calmed all the discrete factions.*

disinterested, uninterested   *Disinterested* means "unbiased." *Uninterested* means "indifferent." *I'm uninterested in the problem of finding disinterested jurors.*

distinct, distinctive   *Distinct* means "separate" or "well defined." *Distinctive* means "characteristic." *Each of the distinct elements has its own distinctive properties.*

doesn't, don't   *Doesn't* is the contraction for *does not.* Use it with *he, she, it,* and singular nouns. *Don't* stands for *do not;* use it with *I, you, we, they,* and plural nouns.

due to   See *because of, due to.*

each other, one another   Use *each other* in sentences involving two subjects and *one another* in sentences involving more than two.

effect   See *affect, effect.*

elicit, illicit   The verb *elicit* means "draw out." The adjective *illicit* means "illegal." *The police elicited from the criminal the names of others involved in illicit activities.*

elude   See *allude, elude.*

emigrate from, immigrate to   *Emigrate from* means "move away from one's country." *Immigrate to* means "move to another country and settle there." *We emigrated from Norway in 1957. We immigrated to the United States.*

ensure   See *assure, ensure, insure.*

enthused, enthusiastic   Avoid the term *enthused* in academic and professional writing.

equally as good   Replace this redundant phrase with *equally good* or *as good as.*

every day, everyday   *Everyday* is an adjective meaning "ordinary." *Every day* is an adjective and a noun, specifying a particular day. *I wore everyday clothes. I wore a dress every day.*

every one, everyone   *Everyone* is an indefinite pronoun. *Every one* is an adjective and a noun, referring to each member of a group. *Because he began the assignment after everyone else, David knew he could not finish every one of the problems.*

except   See *accept, except.*

explicit, implicit   *Explicit* means "directly or openly expressed." *Implicit* means "indirectly expressed or implied." *The explicit message of the ad urged consumers to buy the product, while the implicit message promised popularity.*

farther, further   *Farther* refers to physical distance. *How much farther is it to Munich? Further* refers to time or degree. *I want to avoid further delays.*

fewer, less   Use *fewer* with nouns that can be counted. Use *less* with general amounts that you cannot count. *The world will be safer with fewer bombs and less hostility.*

finalize   *Finalize* is a pretentious way of saying "end" or "make final." *We closed* [not *finalized*] *the deal.*

firstly, secondly, thirdly   These are common in British English; *first, second,* and *third* are more common in U.S. English.

flaunt, flout   *Flaunt* means "show off." *Flout* means "mock" or "scorn." *The teens flouted convention by flaunting their multicolored wigs.*

former, latter   *Former* refers to the first and *latter* to the second of two things previously introduced. *Kathy and Anna are athletes; the former plays tennis, and the latter runs.*

further   See *farther, further.*

good, well   *Good* is an adjective and should not be used as a substitute for the adverb *well. Gabriel is a good host who cooks well.*

good and   *Good and* is colloquial for "very"; avoid it in academic and professional writing.

hanged, hung   *Hanged* refers to executions; *hung* is used for all other meanings. *The old woman hung her head as she passed the tree where the murderer was hanged.*

hardly   See *can't hardly, can't scarcely.*

have, of   *Have,* not *of,* should follow *could, would, should,* or *might. We should have [*not *of] invited them.*

herself, himself, myself, yourself   Do not use these reflexive pronouns as subjects or as objects unless they are necessary. Compare *John cut him* and *John cut himself. Jane and I [*not *myself] agree. They invited John and me [*not *myself].*

he/she, his/her   Better solutions for avoiding sexist language are to write out *he or she,* to eliminate pronouns entirely, or to make the subject plural (*they*). Instead of writing *Everyone should carry his/her driver's license,* try *Drivers should carry driver's licenses* or *People should carry their driver's licenses.*

himself   See *herself, himself, myself, yourself.*

his/her   See *he/she, his/her.*

hisself   Replace with *himself* in academic or professional writing.

hopefully   *Hopefully* is often misused to mean "it is hoped," but its correct meaning is "with hope." *Sam watched the roulette wheel hopefully [*not *Hopefully, Sam will win].*

hung   See *hanged, hung.*

if, whether   Use *whether* or *whether or not* for alternatives. *She was considering whether or not to go.* Reserve *if* for the conditional. *If it rains tomorrow, we will meet inside.*

illicit   See *elicit, illicit.*

illusion   See *allusion, illusion.*

immigrate to   See *emigrate from, immigrate to.*

impact   Avoid the colloquial use of *impact* or *impact on* as a verb meaning "affect." *Population control may reduce [*not *impact] world hunger.*

implicit   See *explicit, implicit.*

imply, infer   To *imply* is to suggest. To *infer* is to make an educated guess. *The note implied they were planning a small wedding; we inferred we would not be invited.*

infer   See *imply, infer.*

inside, inside of, outside, outside of   Drop *of* after the prepositions *inside* and *outside. The class regularly met outside [*not *outside of] the building.*

insure   See *assure, ensure, insure.*

interact with, interface with   *Interact with* is a vague phrase meaning "doing something that somehow involves another person." *Interface with* is computer jargon for "discuss" or "communicate." Avoid both expressions in academic and professional writing.

irregardless, regardless   *Irregardless* is a double negative. Use *regardless*.

is when, is where   These vague expressions are often incorrectly used in definitions. *Schizophrenia is a psychotic condition in which* [not *when* or *where*] *a person withdraws from reality.*

its, it's   *Its* is a possessive form, even though it, like *his* and *her*, does not have an apostrophe. *It's* is a contraction for *it is* or *it has*. *It's important to observe the rat before it has its meal.*

kind, sort, type   Modify these singular nouns with *this*, and follow them with other singular nouns. *Wear this kind of dress. Wear these kinds of hats.*

kind of, sort of   Avoid these colloquialisms. *Amy was somewhat* [not *kind of*] *tired.*

later, latter   *Later* means "after some time." *Latter* refers to the last of two items named. *Juan and Chad won early on, but the latter was injured later in the season.*

latter   See *former, latter* and *later, latter*.

lay, lie   *Lay* means "place" or "put." Its main forms are *lay, laid, laid*. It generally has a direct object, specifying what has been placed. *She laid her books on the desk. Lie* means "recline" or "be positioned" and does not take a direct object. Its main forms are *lie, lay, lain. She lay awake until two.*

leave, let   *Leave* means "go away." *Let* means "allow." *Leave alone* and *let alone* are interchangeable. *Let me leave now, and leave* [or *let*] *me alone from now on!*

lend, loan   *Loan* is a noun, and *lend* is a verb. *Please lend me your pen so that I may fill out this application for a loan.*

less   See *fewer, less*.

let   See *leave, let*.

liable   See *apt, liable, likely*.

lie   See *lay, lie*.

like   See *as, as if, like*.

like, such as   *Like* means "similar to"; use *like* when comparing a subject to examples. *A hurricane, like a flood or any other major disaster, may strain emergency resources.* Use *such as* when examples represent a general category; *such as* is often an alternative to *for example. A destructive hurricane, such as Gilbert in 1988, may drastically alter an area's economy.*

likely   See *apt, liable, likely*.

literally   *Literally* means "actually" or "exactly as written." Use it to stress the truth of a statement that might otherwise be understood as figurative. Do not use *literally* as an intensifier in a figurative statement. *Mirna was literally at the* *edge of her seat* may be accurate, but *Mirna is so hungry that she could* <u>literally</u> *eat a horse* is not.

loan See *lend, loan.*

loose, lose *Lose* is a verb meaning "misplace." *Loose* is an adjective that means "not securely attached." *Sew on that* <u>loose</u> *button before you* <u>lose</u> *it.*

lots, lots of These are informal expressions that mean "much" or "many"; avoid using them in academic or professional discourse.

man, mankind Many people consider these terms sexist because they do not mention women. Replace such words with *people, humans, humankind, men and women,* or similar phrases.

may See *can, may.*

may be, maybe *May be* is a verb phrase, whereas *maybe* is an adverb that means "perhaps." *He* <u>may be</u> *the president today, but* <u>maybe</u> *he will lose the next election.*

media *Media* is the plural form of the noun *medium* and takes a plural verb. *The* <u>media are</u> [not <u>is</u>] *consolidating.*

might have See *have, of.*

moral, morale A *moral* is a succinct lesson. *The* <u>moral</u> *of the story is that generosity is rewarded. Morale* means "spirit" or "mood." *Office* <u>morale</u> *was low.*

Ms. Use *Ms.* as a title before a woman's name unless the woman specifies another title (*Miss* or *Mrs.*). Use *Ms.* with a woman's first name, not with her husband's name: <u>Ms.</u> *Susan Hewitt* or <u>Ms.</u> *Hewitt* [not <u>Ms.</u> *Peter Hewitt*].

myself See *herself, himself, myself, yourself.*

nor, or Use *either* with *or* and *neither* with *nor.*

number See *amount, number.*

of See *have, of.*

off, off of Use *off* rather than *off of. The spaghetti slipped* <u>off</u> [not <u>off of</u>] *the plate.*

OK, O.K., okay All are acceptable spellings, but avoid them in academic and professional discourse.

on account of Use this substitute for *because of* sparingly or not at all.

one another See *each other, one another.*

or See *nor, or.*

outside, outside of See *inside, inside of, outside, outside of.*

owing to the fact that Avoid this and other wordy expressions for *because.*

per Use the Latin *per* only in standard technical phrases such as *miles per hour.* Otherwise, find English equivalents. *As mentioned in* [not <u>as per</u>] *the latest report, our town's average food expenses every week* [not <u>per week</u>] *are $40* <u>per capita</u>.

percent, percentage Both words indicate a fraction of one hundred. Use *percent* with a specific number; use *percentage* with an adjective such as *large* or *small*. *Last year, 80 percent of the club's members were female. A large percentage of the club's members are women.*

plenty *Plenty* means "enough" or "a great abundance." *They told us America was a land of plenty.* Colloquially, it is used to mean "very," a usage you should avoid in academic and professional writing. *He was very [not plenty] tired.*

plus *Plus* means "in addition to." *Your salary plus mine will cover our expenses.* Do not use *plus* to mean "besides" or "moreover." *That dress does not fit me. Besides [not Plus], it is the wrong color.*

precede, proceed *Precede* means "come before"; *proceed* means "go forward." *Despite the storm that preceded the flooding of the parking lot, we proceeded to our cars.*

pretty Avoid using *pretty* as a substitute for "rather," "somewhat," or "quite." *Bill was quite [not pretty] disagreeable.*

principal, principle When used as a noun, *principal* refers to a head official or an amount of money; when used as an adjective, it means "most significant." *Principle* means "fundamental law or belief." *Albert went to the principal and defended himself with the principle of free speech.*

proceed See *precede, proceed*.

quotation, quote *Quote* is a verb, and *quotation* is a noun. *He quoted the president, and the quotation [not quote] was preserved in history books.*

raise, rise *Raise* means "lift" or "move upward." (Referring to children, it means "bring up.") It takes a direct object; someone raises something. *The guests raised their glasses to toast. Rise* means "go upward." It does not take a direct object; something rises by itself. *She saw the steam rise from the pan.*

rarely ever Use *rarely* by itself, or use *hardly ever*. *When we were poor, we rarely went to the movies.*

real, really *Real* is an adjective, and *really* is an adverb. Do not substitute *real* for *really*. *The older man walked really [not real] slowly.*

reason is because Use either *the reason is that* or the word *because*—not both. *The reason the copier stopped is that [not is because] the paper jammed.*

reason why This expression is redundant. *The reason [not the reason why] this book is short is market demand.*

regardless See *irregardless, regardless*.

respectfully, respectively *Respectfully* means "with respect." *Respectively* means "in the order given." *Karen and David, respectively a juggler and an acrobat, respectfully greeted the audience.*

rise See *raise, rise*.

scarcely See *can't hardly, can't scarcely*.

secondly See *firstly, secondly, thirdly*.

set, sit *Set* means "put" or "place" and takes a direct object. *Sit* refers to taking a seat but does not take an object. *"Set your cup on the table, and sit down."*

should of   See *have, of.*

since   *Since* has two uses: (1) to show passage of time, as in *I have been home since Tuesday;* (2) to mean "because," as in *Since you are in a bad mood, I will leave.* Be careful not to use *since* ambiguously. In *Since I broke my leg, I've stayed home, since* might be understood to mean "because" or "ever since."

sit   See *set, sit.*

so, so that   In academic and professional writing, follow *so* with *that* to show how the intensified condition leads to a result. *Aaron was so tired that he fell asleep at the wheel.*

some body, somebody, some one, someone   *Somebody* and *someone* are indefinite pronouns. *When somebody comes walking down the hall, I always hope that it is someone I know. Some body* is an adjective modifying a noun. *Some one* is two adjectives or a pronoun modified by an adjective. *In dealing with some body like the senate, arrange to meet consistently some one person who can represent the group.*

someplace, somewhere   Use *somewhere* in academic and professional writing.

some time, sometime, sometimes   *Some time* refers to a length of time. *Please leave me some time to dress. Sometime* means "at some indefinite later time." *Sometime I will take you to London. Sometimes* means "occasionally." *Sometimes I eat sushi.*

somewhere   See *someplace, somewhere.*

sort   See *kind, sort, type.*

sort of   See *kind of, sort of.*

so that   See *so, so that.*

stationary, stationery   *Stationary* means "standing still"; *stationery* is writing paper. *When the bus was stationary, Pat took out stationery and wrote a note.*

subsequently   See *consequently, subsequently.*

such as   See *like, such as.*

supposed to, used to   Both expressions require the final *-d. He is supposed to sing.*

sure, surely   Avoid using *sure* as an intensifier. Instead use *surely* (or *certainly* or *without a doubt*). *Surely, the doctor will prescribe an antibiotic.*

take   See *bring, take.*

than, then   Use *than* in comparative statements. *The cat was bigger than the dog.* Use *then* when referring to a sequence of events. *I won, and then I cried.*

that, which   A clause beginning with *that* singles out the object being described. *The book that is on the table is a good one* specifies the book on the table as opposed to some other book. A clause beginning with *which* may or may not single out the object, although some writers use *which* clauses only to add more information about an object being described. *The book, which is on the table, is a good one* contains a *which* clause between the commas. The clause simply adds extra, nonessential information about the book; it does not specify which book.

theirselves, themselves Use *themselves* rather than *theirselves*.

then See *than, then*.

thirdly See *firstly, secondly, thirdly*.

to, too, two *To* generally shows direction. *Too* means "also." *Two* is the number. *We, too, are going to the meeting in two hours.* Avoid using *to* after *where*. *Where are you flying* [not *flying to*]?

to, where See *where*.

two See *to, too, two*.

type See *kind, sort, type*.

uninterested See *disinterested, uninterested*.

unique *Unique* means "the one and only." Do not use it with adjectives that suggest degree, such as *very* or *most*. *Mel's hands are unique* [not *very unique*].

used to See *supposed to, used to*.

very Avoid using *very* to intensify a weak adjective or adverb; instead, replace the adjective or adverb with a stronger, more precise, or more colorful word. Instead of *very nice*, for example, use *kind, warm, sensitive, endearing*, or *friendly*.

way, ways When referring to distance, use *way*. *May was a long way* [not *ways*] *off*.

well See *good, well*.

when, where See *is when, is where*.

where Use *where* alone, not with words such as *at* and *to*. *Where are you going?* [not *Where are you going to?*]

whether See *if, whether*.

which See *that, which*.

who, whom In adjective clauses, use *who* if the next word is a verb. *Liv, who smokes incessantly, is my godmother. Liv, who is my godmother, smokes incessantly.* Use *whom* if the following word is a noun or pronoun. *I heard that Liv, whom I have not seen for years, wears only purple.* Exception: ignore an expression such as *I think* within the clause. *Liv, who I think wears nothing but purple, is my godmother.* [Ignore *I think*; use *who* because the next word is a verb, *wears*.]

who's, whose *Who's* is the contraction of *who* and *is* or *has*. *Who's on the patio? Whose* is a possessive form. *Whose sculpture is in the garden? Whose is on the patio?*

would of See *have, of*.

yet See *but, yet*.

your, you're *Your* shows possession. *Bring your sleeping bag along. You're* is the contraction of *you* and *are*. *You're in the wrong sleeping bag.*

yourself See *herself, himself, myself, yourself*.

PUNCTUATION/ MECHANICS

"You can show a lot with a look. . . .
It's punctuation."

– CLINT EASTWOOD

PUNCTUATION/MECHANICS

29

Commas

It's hard to go through a day without encountering directions of some kind, and commas often play a crucial role in how you interpret instructions. See how important the comma is in the following directions for making hot cereal:

> Add Cream of Wheat slowly, stirring constantly.

The comma here tells the cook to *add the cereal slowly*. If the comma came before the word *slowly*, however, the cook might add all of the cereal at once and *stir slowly*—perhaps resulting in lumpy cereal. This chapter aims to help you use commas correctly and effectively.

Editing for Commas

Research has shown that five of the most common errors in college writing involve commas. Check your writing for these five errors.

1. Check every sentence that doesn't begin with the subject to see whether it opens with an introductory element (a word, phrase, or clause that tells when, where, how, or why the main action of the sentence occurs). An introductory element needs to be followed by a comma, separating the introduction from the main part of the sentence. (29a)

2. Look at every sentence that contains one of the conjunctions *and, but, or, nor, for, so,* and *yet*. If the group of words before and after the conjunction each functions as a complete sentence, you have a compound sentence. Make sure to use a comma before the conjunction. (29b)

3. Look at all adjective clauses beginning with *which, who, whom, whose, when,* or *where,* and at phrases and appositives (16l). Consider each element, and decide whether it is essential to the meaning of the sentence. If the rest of the sentence would be unclear without it, you should *not* set off the element with commas. (29c)

4. Identify all adjective clauses beginning with *that*, and make sure they are *not* set off with commas. (29c, j)

5. Check every *and* and *or* to see if it comes before the last item in a series of three or more words, phrases, or clauses. Be sure that each item in a series (except the last) is followed by a comma. (29d)

29a Use commas to set off introductory words, phrases, and clauses.

▶ Slowly, she became conscious of her predicament.
     ^

▶ In fact, only you can decide.
     ^

▶ Eventually, I wondered whether I should change careers.
     ^

▶ In Fitzgerald's novel, the color green takes on great symbolic qualities.
     ^

▶ Sporting a pair of specially made running shoes, Jamie prepared for
the race.
     ^

▶ To win the contest, Connor needed luck.
     ^

▶ Pens poised in anticipation, the interns waited for the test to be
distributed.
     ^

▶ Since my mind was not getting enough stimulation, I decided to read
some good literature.
     ^

Note that some writers omit the comma after an introductory element if it is short and does not seem to require a pause after it. However, you will never be wrong if you use a comma.

▶ At the racetrack, Jason lost nearly his entire paycheck.
     ^

In general, do *not* set off an adverb clause that follows a main clause unless it begins with *although, even though, while,* or another conjunction expressing the idea of contrast.

▶ He uses semicolons frequently, while she prefers periods and short
sentences.
     ^

29b Use commas to separate clauses in compound sentences.

A comma usually precedes a coordinating conjunction (*and, but, or, nor, for, so,* or *yet*) that joins two independent clauses in a compound sentence (16m).

▶ The title may sound important, but *administrative clerk* is only a
euphemism for *photocopier*.

▶ The climbers will reach the summit today, or they must turn back.

▶ The show started at last, and the crowd grew quiet.

With very short clauses, you can sometimes omit the comma.

▶ She saw her chance and she took it.

Always use the comma if there is any chance the sentence will be mis-
read without it.

▶ I opened the junk drawer, and the cabinet door jammed.

Use a semicolon rather than a comma when the clauses are long and
complex or contain their own commas.

▶ There is no royal path to good writing; and such paths as exist do not
lead through neat critical gardens, various as they are, but through the
jungles of self, the world, and of craft.   – JESSAMYN WEST

29c Use commas to set off nonrestrictive elements.

Nonrestrictive elements are clauses, phrases, and words that do not
limit, or restrict, the meaning of the words they modify. Since such elements are not essential to the meaning of a sentence, they should be set
off from the rest of the sentence with commas. Restrictive elements,
on the other hand, *do* limit meaning; they should *not* be set off with
commas.

RESTRICTIVE   Drivers *who have been convicted of drunken driving*
                     should lose their licenses.

In the preceding sentence, the clause *who have been convicted of drunken
driving* is essential to the meaning because it limits the word it modifies,
Drivers, to only those drivers who have been convicted of drunken
driving. Therefore, it is *not* set off by commas.

NONRESTRICTIVE   The two drivers involved in the accident, *who have
                     been convicted of drunken driving*, should lose their
                     licenses.

In this sentence, however, the clause *who have been convicted of drunken driving* is not essential to the meaning because it does not limit what it modifies, *The two drivers involved in the accident*, but merely provides additional information about these drivers. Therefore, the clause *is* set off with commas.

To decide whether an element is restrictive or nonrestrictive, mentally delete the element, and then see if the deletion changes the meaning of the rest of the sentence or makes it unclear. If the deletion does change the meaning, the element is probably restrictive, and you should not set it off with commas. If it does not change the meaning, the element is probably nonrestrictive and requires commas.

Adjective and adverb clauses

An adjective clause that begins with *that* is always restrictive; do not set it off with commas. An adjective clause beginning with *which* may be either restrictive or nonrestrictive; however, some writers prefer to use *which* only for nonrestrictive clauses, which they set off with commas. As noted earlier, an adverb clause that follows a main clause usually does *not* require a comma to set it off *unless* the adverb clause expresses contrast.

NONRESTRICTIVE CLAUSES

▶ **I borrowed books from the rental library of Shakespeare and Company,** *which was the library and bookstore of Sylvia Beach at 12 rue de l'Odeon.*   – ERNEST HEMINGWAY, *A Moveable Feast*

The adjective clause describing Shakespeare and Company is not necessary to the meaning of the independent clause and therefore is set off with a comma.

▶ **The park soon became a popular gathering place, although some**
nearby residents complained about the noise.
                                                                          ^

The adverb clause *although some nearby residents complained about the noise* expresses the idea of contrast; therefore, it is set off with a comma.

RESTRICTIVE CLAUSES

▶ **The claim** *that men like seriously to battle one another to some sort of finish* **is a myth.**   – JOHN MCMURTRY, "Kill 'Em! Crush 'Em! Eat 'Em Raw!"

The adjective clause is necessary to the meaning of the sentence because it explains which claim is a myth and therefore is not set off with a comma.

▶ The man͵/who rescued her puppy/won her eternal gratitude.

The adjective clause *who rescued her puppy* is necessary to the meaning because only the man who rescued the puppy won the gratitude; the clause is restrictive and so takes no commas.

Phrases

Participial phrases may be restrictive or nonrestrictive. Prepositional phrases are usually restrictive, but sometimes they are not essential to the meaning of a sentence and are therefore set off with commas (16l).

NONRESTRICTIVE PHRASES

▶ The bus drivers, rejecting the management offer, remained on strike.

Using commas around the phrase makes it nonrestrictive, telling us that all of the drivers remained on strike.

▶ Frédéric Chopin, in spite of poor health, composed prolifically.

The phrase *in spite of* does not limit the meaning of *Frédéric Chopin* and so is set off by commas.

RESTRICTIVE PHRASES

▶ The bus drivers/rejecting the management offer/remained on strike.

If the phrase *rejecting the management offer* limits the meaning of *The bus drivers*, the commas should be deleted. The revised sentence says that only some of the bus drivers, the ones who rejected the offer, remained on strike, implying that the other drivers went back to work.

Appositives

An appositive is a noun or noun phrase that renames a nearby noun. When an appositive is not essential to identify what it renames, it is set off with commas.

NONRESTRICTIVE APPOSITIVES

▶ Beethoven's only opera, *Fidelio*, includes the famous "Prisoner's Chorus."

Beethoven wrote only one opera, so its name is *not* essential to the meaning of the sentence and therefore is set off with commas.

RESTRICTIVE APPOSITIVES

▶ Mozart's opera/*The Marriage of Figaro*/was considered revolutionary.

The phrase *The Marriage of Figaro* is essential to the meaning of the sentence because Mozart wrote more than one opera. Therefore it is *not* set off with commas.

29d Use commas to separate three or more items in a series.

You may often see a series with no comma after the next-to-last item, particularly in newspaper writing. Omitting the comma can cause confusion, however, and you will never be wrong if you include it.

▶ He has plundered our seas, ravaged our coasts, burnt our towns, and destroyed the lives of our people.   – Declaration of Independence

▶ The long, twisting, muddy road led to a shack in the woods.

▶ Diners had a choice of broccoli, green beans, peas, and carrots.

Without the comma after *peas*, you wouldn't know if there were three choices (the third being a *mixture* of peas and carrots) or four.

A Matter of Style: Series Commas

Comma conventions are quite often a matter of style—and of what is called, in the publishing industry, "house style." Many newspapers, for example, follow the style of omitting the comma after the next-to-last item in a series of three or more. Here is such an example from the *New York Times*:

> Current alternative rockers like Courtney Love, P. J. Harvey and Alanis Morisette owe Patti Smith no small debt.
> — JON PARELES, "Return of the Godmother of Punk"

You may be required (by an instructor or by your company's house style) to follow this convention. But ordinarily you will never be wrong if you put a comma after each item in a series except the last: "Current alternative rockers like Courtney Love, P. J. Harvey, and Alanis Morisette owe Patti Smith no small debt."

29e   Use commas to set off parenthetical and transitional expressions.

Parenthetical expressions add comments or information. Because they often interrupt the flow of a sentence or digress, they are usually set off with commas.

▶ Some studies, incidentally, have shown that chocolate, of all things, helps to prevent tooth decay.

▶ Roald Dahl's stories, it turns out, were often inspired by his own childhood.

Transitional expressions are words such as *however* and *furthermore* and other words and phrases used to connect parts of sentences. They are usually set off with commas (16h, 23a).

▶ Ceiling fans are, moreover, less expensive than air conditioners.

▶ Ozone is a byproduct of dry cleaning, for example.

29f   Use commas to set off contrasting elements, interjections, direct address, and tag questions.

CONTRASTING ELEMENTS

▶ On official business it was she, *not my father*, one would usually hear on the phone or in stores.   – RICHARD RODRIGUEZ, "Aria: A Memoir of a Bilingual Childhood"

▶ The story is narrated objectively at first, *subjectively toward the end.*

INTERJECTIONS

▶ *My God*, who wouldn't want a wife?   – JUDY BRADY, "I Want a Wife"

DIRECT ADDRESS

▶ Remember, *sir*, that you are under oath.

TAG QUESTIONS

▶ The governor did not veto the unemployment bill, *did she*?

Use commas to set off parts of dates, addresses, titles, and numbers.

Dates

Use a comma between the day of the week and the month, between the day of the month and the year, and between the year and the rest of the sentence, if any.

▶ The war began on Thursday, January 17, 1991, with air strikes on Iraq.

Do not use commas with dates in inverted order or with dates consisting of only the month and the year.

▶ She dated the letter *26 October 1996*.

▶ Thousands of Germans swarmed over the wall in *November 1989*.

Addresses and place-names

Use a comma after each part of an address or place-name, including the state if there is no zip code. Do not precede a zip code with a comma.

▶ Forward my mail to the Department of English, The Ohio State University, Columbus, Ohio 43210.

▶ Portland, Oregon, is much larger than Portland, Maine.

Titles

Use commas to set off a title such as *M.D.*, *Ph.D.*, and so on, from the name preceding it and from the rest of the sentence.

▶ Oliver Sacks, M.D., has written about the way the mind works.

Numbers

In numerals of five digits or more, use a comma between each group of three, starting from the right.

▶ Danbury's population rose to *65,585* in the 1990 census.

The comma is optional within numerals of four digits but never occurs in four-digit dates, street addresses, or page numbers.

▶ The college had an enrollment of *1,789* [or *1789*] in the fall of *1994*.

▶ My grandparents live at *2428* Loring Place.

▶ Turn to page *1566*.

29h Use commas to set off most quotations.

Commas set off a quotation from words used to introduce or identify the source of the quotation. A comma following a quotation goes *inside* the closing quotation mark.

▶ A German proverb warns, "Go to law for a sheep, and lose your cow."

▶ "All I know about grammar," said Joan Didion, "is its infinite power."

Do not use a comma after a question mark or exclamation point.

▶ "What's a thousand dollars?" asks Groucho Marx in *Cocoanuts*. "Mere chicken feed. A poultry matter."

▶ "Out, out damned spot!" cries Lady Macbeth.

Do not use a comma when you introduce a quotation with *that*.

▶ The writer of Ecclesiastes concludes/that "all is vanity."

Do not use a comma before an indirect quotation, one that does not use the speaker's exact words.

▶ Patrick Henry declared/that he wanted either liberty or death.

29i Use commas to prevent confusion.

Sometimes commas are necessary to make sentences easier to read or understand.

▶ The members of the dance troupe strutted in, in matching costumes.

▶ Before, I had planned to major in biology.

29j Eliminate unnecessary commas.

Excessive use of commas can spoil an otherwise fine sentence.

Around restrictive elements

Do not use commas to set off restrictive elements — elements that limit, or define, the meaning of the words they modify or refer to. Such elements are essential to meaning, and therefore should not be set off with commas (29c).

▶ I don't let my children watch TV shows/that are violent.

> The *that* clause restricts the meaning of *TV shows,* so the comma should be omitted.

▶ A law/requiring the use of seat belts/was passed in 1987.

▶ My only defense/against my allergies/is to stay indoors.

▶ The actress/Rosemary Harris/has returned to Broadway.

Between subjects and verbs, verbs and objects or complements, and prepositions and objects

Do not use a comma between a subject and its verb, a verb and its object or complement, or a preposition and its object. This rule holds true even if the subject, object, or complement is a long phrase or clause.

▶ Watching movies late at night/has become an important way for me to relax.

▶ Parents must decide/how much TV their children may watch.

▶ The winner of/the trophy for outstanding community service stepped forward.

In compound constructions

In compound constructions (other than compound sentences), do not use a comma before or after a coordinating conjunction that joins the two parts (29b).

▶ **A buildup of the U.S. military/and deregulation of major industries were the Reagan administration's goals.**

The *and* here joins parts of a compound subject, which should not be separated by a comma.

▶ **Mark Twain trained as a printer/and worked as a steamboat pilot.**

The *and* here joins parts of a compound predicate, which should not be separated by a comma.

Before the first or after the last item in a series

▶ **The auction included/furniture, paintings, and china.**

▶ **The swimmer took slow, powerful/strokes.**

30

Semicolons

If you've ever pored over the fine print at the bottom of an ad for a big sale looking for the opening hours or the address of the store nearest you, then you've seen plenty of semicolons in action. Here's an example from a Bloomingdale's ad.

> Stores & Hours—
> *Short Hills*: SUN., 12–6; MON., 10–9:30; TUES., 10–5; WED. through FRI., 10–9:30; SAT., 10–8.

The semicolons separate the information for one day's hours from the next. Semicolons have the effect of creating a pause stronger than that of a comma but not as strong as the full pause of a period.

30a Use semicolons to link closely related independent clauses.

Though a comma and a coordinating conjunction often join independent clauses, semicolons provide writers with subtler ways of signaling closely related clauses. The clause following a semicolon often restates

> **Editing for Semicolons**
>
> - Check to see if you use any semicolons. If so, be sure they are used only between independent clauses—a group of words that can stand alone as a sentence (30a, b)—or between items in a series. (30c)
> - If you find few or no semicolons in your writing, determine if you should add some. Are there any closely related ideas in two sentences that might be better expressed in one sentence using a semicolon? (30a)

an idea expressed in the first clause, and it sometimes expands on or presents a contrast to the first.

▶ **Immigration acts were passed; newcomers had to prove, besides moral correctness and financial solvency, their ability to read.**
  – MARY GORDON, "More Than Just a Shrine"

Gordon uses a semicolon to join the two clauses, giving the sentence an abrupt rhythm that suits the topic: laws that imposed strict requirements.

▶ **Fuel oil, natural gas, and electricity are popular sources of energy for heating homes; The least polluting, however, is solar energy.**

If two independent clauses joined by a coordinating conjunction contain commas, you may use a semicolon instead of a comma before the conjunction to make the sentence easier to read.

▶ **Every year, whether the Republican or the Democratic party is in office, more and more power drains away from the individual to feed vast reservoirs in far-off places; and we have less and less say about the shape of events which shape our future.**
  – WILLIAM F. BUCKLEY JR., "Why Don't We Complain?"

30b Use semicolons to link independent clauses joined by conjunctive adverbs or transitional phrases.

A semicolon should link independent clauses joined by conjunctive adverbs or transitional phrases (see p. 206 for some examples).

▶ **Every kid should have access to a computer; furthermore, access to the Internet should be free.**

▶ **The circus comes as close to being the world in microcosm as anything I know; in a way, it puts all the rest of show business in the shade.**
– E. B. White, "The Ring of Time"

SOME CONJUNCTIVE ADVERBS

also	indeed	now
anyway	instead	otherwise
besides	likewise	similarly
certainly	meanwhile	still
finally	moreover	then
furthermore	namely	therefore
however	nevertheless	thus
incidentally	next	undoubtedly

SOME TRANSITIONAL PHRASES

as a result	granted that	in the meantime
as soon as	in addition	of course
even though	in conclusion	on the other hand
for example	in fact	on the whole
for instance	in other words	to summarize

When linking clauses with conjunctive adverbs or transitional phrases, be careful not to write fused sentences or comma splices (22c).

30c Use semicolons to separate items in a series containing other punctuation.

Ordinarily, commas separate items in a series (29d). But when the items themselves contain commas or other marks of punctuation, using semicolons to separate the items will make the sentence clearer and easier to read.

▶ **Anthropology encompasses archaeology, the study of ancient civilizations through artifacts; linguistics, the study of the structure and development of language; and cultural anthropology, the study of language, customs, and behavior.**

30d Eliminate misused semicolons.

A comma, not a semicolon, should separate an independent clause from a dependent clause or phrase.

▶ The police found fingerprints⁄, which they used to identify the thief.
                              ^

A colon, not a semicolon, should introduce a series or list.

▶ The tour includes visits to the following art museums⁄: the Prado, in
  Madrid; the Louvre, in Paris; and the Rijksmuseum, in^Amsterdam.

31

End Punctuation

Periods, question marks, and exclamation points often appear in advertising to create special effects or draw readers along from line to line. For example:

> The experts say America Online is a well-designed, easy-to-use service.
> So what are you waiting for?
> Get your hands on America Online today!

End punctuation tells us how to read each sentence — as a matter-of-fact statement, an ironic query, or an emphatic order. This chapter will guide you in using appropriate end punctuation in your own writing.

Editing for End Punctuation

- If you find that all or almost all of your sentences end with periods, see if any of them might be phrased more effectively as questions or exclamations. (31a, b, and c)
- Check to be sure you use question marks appropriately. (31b)
- Do you use exclamation points? If so, consider carefully whether they are justified. Does the sentence call for extra emphasis? If in doubt, use a period instead. (31c)

31a Periods

Use a period to close sentences that make statements, give mild commands, or make polite requests.

▶ **All books are either dreams or swords.**
        – AMY LOWELL

▶ **Never use a foreign phrase, a scientific word or a jargon word if you can think of an everyday English equivalent.**
        – GEORGE ORWELL, "Politics and the English Language"

▶ **Would you please close the door.**

A period also closes indirect questions, which report rather than ask questions.

▶ **I asked how old the child was.**

▶ **We all wonder who will win the election.**

In American English, periods are also used with most abbreviations.

Mr.	Jr.	Dr.
Ms.	B.C.	Ph.D.
Mrs.	B.C.E.	M.B.A.
A.M./a.m.	A.D.	R.N.
P.M./p.m.	ibid.	Sen.

Some abbreviations do not require periods. Among them are the postal abbreviations of state names, such as *FL* and *TN*, and most groups of initials (*GE, CIA, DOS, AIDS, YMCA, UNICEF*). If you are not sure whether a particular abbreviation should include periods, check a dictionary. (See Chapter 36 for more about abbreviations.)

Do not use an additional period when a sentence ends with an abbreviation that has its own period.

▶ **The social worker referred me to Evelyn Pintz, M.D./**

31b Question marks

Use question marks to close sentences that ask direct questions.

▶ **Who will be left to celebrate a victory made of blood and fire?**
        – THICH NHAT HANH, "Our Green Garden"

▶ **How is the human mind like a computer, and how is it different?**
        – KATHLEEN STASSEN BERGER AND ROSS A. THOMPSON, *The*
        Developing Person Through Childhood and Adolescence

Question marks do not close *indirect* questions, which report rather than ask questions.

▶ **She asked whether I opposed his nomination.**

Do not use a comma or a period after a question mark that ends a direct quotation.

▶ **"Am I my brother's keeper?" Cain asked.**

▶ **Cain asked, "Am I my brother's keeper?"**

Questions in a series may have question marks even when they are not separate sentences.

▶ **I often confront a difficult choice: should I go to practice? finish my homework? spend time with my friends?**

A question mark in parentheses indicates that a writer is unsure of a date, a figure, or a word.

▶ **Quintilian died in A.D. 96 (?).**

31c Exclamation points

Use an exclamation point to show surprise or strong emotion.

▶ **In those few moments of geologic time will be the story of all that has happened since we became a nation. And what a story it will be!**
        – JAMES RETTIE, "But a Watch in the Night"

Use exclamation points very sparingly because they can distract your readers or suggest that you are exaggerating.

▶ **This university is so large, so varied, that attempting to tell someone everything about it would take three years!.**

Do not use a comma or a period after an exclamation point that ends a direct quotation.

▶ **"Happiness hates the timid!" according to Eugene O'Neill, who went on to add, "So does Science!"/**

32

Apostrophes

The little apostrophe can sometimes make a big difference in meaning. A friend of ours found that out when he agreed to look after a neighbor's apartment while she was out of town. "I'll leave instructions on the kitchen counter," the neighbor said as she gave him her key. Here are the instructions he found: "The cat's food is on the counter. Once a day on the patio. Thanks. I'll see you Friday."

Because the note said *cat's*, our friend expected one cat—and when he saw one, he put it and the food outside on the patio. When the neighbor returned, she found one healthy cat—and a second, very weak one that had hidden under the bed. The difference between *cat's* and *cats'* in this instance almost cost his neighbor a cat.

Editing for Apostrophes

- Check all the nouns that end in -*s* with an apostrophe. Make sure each one shows ownership or possession. Then check that each one ends with an apostrophe in the right place: an apostrophe and -*s* for most singular nouns, including those that end in -*s*; an apostrophe and -*s* for plural nouns not ending in -*s*; and an apostrophe only for plural nouns ending in -*s*. (32a)
- Check indefinite pronouns such as *someone, nobody, one*, and *everything*. Any that end in -*s* should have an apostrophe before the -*s*.
- Check all contractions to make sure the apostrophe is used correctly. (32b)
- Check plural forms of numbers, letters, and symbols to ensure that the apostrophe is used correctly. (32c)

32a Use apostrophes to signal possessive case.

The possessive case denotes ownership or possession of one thing by another. Add an apostrophe and -*s* to form the possessive of most singular nouns, including those that end in -*s*, and of indefinite pronouns. The possessive forms of personal pronouns do not take apostrophes: *yours, his, hers, its, ours, theirs.*

▶ The *bus's* fumes overpowered her.
▶ Katharine *Hepburn's* first movies are considered classics.
▶ The reading list included *Dickinson's* poems and *Morrison's* novel.
▶ *Anyone's* guess is as good as mine.

Plural nouns

To form the possessive case of plural nouns not ending in -s, add an apostrophe and -s.

▶ Robert Bly helped to popularize the *men's* movement.
▶ The *children's* first Christmas was spent in Wales.

For plural nouns ending in -s, add only the apostrophe.

▶ The *clowns'* costumes were bright green and orange.
▶ *Fifty dollars'* worth of groceries filled only two shopping bags.

Compound nouns

To form the possessive case of compound nouns, make the last word in the group possessive.

▶ The *secretary of state's* speech was televised.
▶ Both her *daughters-in-law's* birthdays fall in July.
▶ My *in-laws'* disapproval dampened our enthusiasm for the new house.

Two or more nouns

To signal individual possession by two or more owners, make each noun possessive.

▶ Great differences exist between *John Wayne's and Henry Fonda's* films.

Wayne and Fonda appeared in different films.

To signal joint possession, make only the last noun possessive.

▶ *MacNeil and Lehrer's* television program focused on current issues.

MacNeil and Lehrer participated in the same program.

32b Use apostrophes to signal contractions.

Contractions are two-word combinations formed by leaving out certain letters, which are indicated by an apostrophe.

it is, it has/it's	I would/I'd	will not/won't
was not/wasn't	he would/he'd	let us/let's
I am/I'm	would not/wouldn't	who is, who has/who's
he is, he has/he's	do not/don't	cannot/can't
you will/you'll	does not/doesn't	

Contractions such as the preceding ones are common in conversation and informal writing. Academic and professional work, however, often calls for greater formality.

Apostrophes signal omissions in some common phrases.

rock and roll	class of 1997
rock 'n' roll	class of '97

Distinguishing it's *and* its

Do not confuse the possessive pronoun *its* with the contraction *it's*. *Its* is the possessive form of *it*. *It's* is a contraction for *it is* or *it has*.

▶ **This disease is unusual; *its* symptoms vary from person to person.**

▶ ***It's* a difficult disease to diagnose.**

32c Use apostrophes to form the plural of numbers, letters, symbols, and words used as terms.

Use an apostrophe and *-s* to form the plural of numbers, letters, symbols, and words referred to as terms.

▶ **The gymnasts need marks of *8*'s and *9*'s to qualify for the finals.**

▶ **The computer prints *e*'s whenever there is an error in the program.**

▶ **I marked special passages with a series of three *'s.**

▶ **The five *Shakespeare*'s in the essay were spelled five different ways.**

As in the above examples, italicize numbers, letters, and words referred to as words, but do not italicize the plural ending.

You can write the plural of years with or without the apostrophe (*1990's* or *1990s*). Whichever style you follow, be consistent.

33

Quotation Marks

"Hilarious!" "A great family movie!" "Two thumbs up!" Claims of this kind leap out from most movie ads, always set off by quotation marks. In fact, the quotation marks are a key component of such statements, indicating that the praise comes from people other than the movie promoter. In other words, it is praise that we should believe. This chapter provides tips for using quotation marks for many purposes.

Editing Quotation Marks

- Use quotation marks around direct quotations and titles of short works. (33a, c)
- Do not use quotation marks around set-off quotations of more than four lines of prose or three lines of poetry, or around titles of long works. (33b, c)
- Check other punctuation used with closing quotation marks. (33e)

  Periods and commas should be *inside* the quotation marks.

  Colons, semicolons, and footnote numbers should be *outside*.

  Question marks, exclamation points, and dashes should be *inside* if they are part of the quoted material, *outside* if they are not.
- Never use quotation marks around indirect quotations. (33f)

  ▶ Keith said that ⁄he was sorry.⁄
- Do not rely on quotation marks to add emphasis to words. (33f)

33a Use quotation marks to signal direct quotation.

▶ Bush called for a "kinder, gentler" country.

▶ She smiled and said, "Son, this is one incident that I will never forget."

Use quotation marks to enclose the words of each speaker within running dialogue. Mark each shift in speaker with a new paragraph.

> "But I can see you're bound to come," said the father. "Only we ain't going to catch us no fish, because there ain't no water left to catch 'em in."
> "The river!"
> "All but dry." — EUDORA WELTY, "Ladies in Spring"

Single quotation marks

Single quotation marks enclose a quotation within a quotation. Open and close the quoted passage with double quotation marks, and change any quotation marks that appear *within* the quotation to single quotation marks.

▶ **Baldwin says, "The title 'The Uses of the Blues' does not refer to music; I don't know anything about music."**

33b Use quotation marks to quote fewer than four lines of prose or poetry.

If the passage you wish to quote is four typed lines or more, set the quotation off by starting it on a new line and indenting it ten spaces from the left margin. This format, known as block quotation, does not require quotation marks.

> In *Winged Words: American Indian Writers Speak*, Leslie Marmon Silko describes her early education, saying:
>> I learned to love reading, and love books, and the printed page, and therefore was motivated to learn to write. The best thing . . . you can have in life is to have someone tell you a story . . . but in lieu of that . . . I learned at an early age to find comfort in a book, that a book would talk to me when no one else would. (145)

The page number in parentheses at the end of the quotation is a citation following the Modern Language Association's (MLA) style. The American Psychological Association (APA) has different guidelines for setting off block quotations. (See Chapters 45 and 49.)

When quoting poetry, if the quotation is brief (fewer than four lines), include it within your text. Separate the lines of the poem with slashes, each preceded and followed by a space, in order to tell the reader where one line of the poem ends and the next begins.

> In one of his best-known poems, Robert Frost remarks, "Two roads diverged in a yellow wood, and I— / I took the one less traveled by / And that has made all the difference."

To quote more than three lines of poetry, indent each line ten spaces from the left margin, and do not use quotation marks. When you quote poetry, take care to follow the indentation, spacing, capitalization, punctuation, and other features of the original passage.

The duke in Robert Browning's poem "My Last Duchess" is clearly a jealous, vain person, whose arrogance is illustrated through this statement:

> She thanked men, — good! but thanked
> Somehow — I know not how — as if she ranked
> My gift of a nine-hundred-years-old name
> With anybody's gift.

33c Use quotation marks around titles of short works.

Quotation marks enclose the titles of short poems, short stories, articles, essays, songs, sections of books, and episodes of television and radio programs.

- ▶ **"Dover Beach" moves from calmness to sadness.** [poem]
- ▶ **Alice Walker's "Everyday Use" is about more than just quilts.** [short story]
- ▶ **In "Photography," Susan Sontag considers the role of photography in our society.** [essay]
- ▶ **The *Atlantic* published an article entitled "Illiberal Education."** [article]
- ▶ **Nirvana's "Smells Like Teen Spirit" became an anthem for Generation X.** [song]
- ▶ **In the chapter "Complexion," Rodriguez describes his sensitivity about his skin color.** [section of book]
- ▶ **The *Nature* episode "Echo of the Elephants" portrays ivory hunters unfavorably.** [episode of television program]

33d Use quotation marks around definitions.

- ▶ **In social science, the term *sample size* means "the number of individuals being studied in a research project."**
  > – KATHLEEN STASSEN BERGER AND ROSS A. THOMPSON, *The Developing Person Through Childhood and Adolescence*

33e Check other punctuation used with quotation marks.

Periods and commas go *inside* closing quotation marks.

- ▶ **"Don't compromise yourself," said Janis Joplin. "You are all you've got."**

Colons, semicolons, and footnote numbers go *outside* closing quotation marks.

▶ I felt only one emotion after finishing "Eveline": pity.

▶ Everything is dark, and "a visionary light settles in her eyes"; this vision, this light, is her salvation.

▶ Tragedy is defined by Aristotle as "an imitation of an action that is serious and of a certain magnitude."[1]

Question marks, exclamation points, and dashes go *inside* if they are part of the quoted material, *outside* if they are not.

PART OF THE QUOTATION

▶ Gently shake the injured person while asking, "Are you all right?"

▶ "Jump!" one of the firefighters shouted.

NOT PART OF THE QUOTATION

▶ What is the theme of "The Birth-Mark"?

▶ "Break a leg"—that phrase is supposed to bring good luck.

A Matter of Style: Direct Quotation

As a way of bringing other people's words into our own, direct quotation can be a powerful writing tool. For example:

> Mrs. Macken urges parents to get books for their children, to read to them when they are "li'l," and when they start school to make certain they attend regularly. She holds herself up as an example of a "mill-hand's daughter who wanted to be a schoolteacher and did it through sheer hard work."   – SHIRLEY BRICE HEATH, *Ways with Words*

The writer could have paraphrased—and said, for example, that parents should read to their children when they are young. By quoting, however, she lets her subject speak for herself—and lets us as readers hear that person's voice. In fact, this writer is reporting from field research, which calls for the use of direct quotations. Thus the choice to quote directly is effective and appropriate to both the intended audience and the conventions of the field.

For information on using quotation marks with footnotes and in bibliographical references, see Chapters 46, 47, 49, and 51.

33f Check for misused quotation marks.

Do not use quotation marks for indirect quotations—those that do not use someone's exact words.

▶ Mother smiled and said that ⫽she would never forget the incident.⫽

Do not use quotation marks just to add emphasis to particular words or phrases.

▶ Michael said that his views may not be ⫽politically correct,⫽ but that he wasn't going to change them for anything.

▶ Much time was spent speculating about their ⫽relationship.⫽

Do not use quotation marks around slang or colloquial language; they create the impression that you are apologizing for using those words. If you have a good reason to use slang or a colloquial term, use it without quotation marks.

▶ After our twenty-mile hike, we were completely exhausted and ready to ⫽turn in.⫽

❋ **For Multilingual Writers: Quoting in American English**

American English and British English offer opposite conventions for double and single quotation marks. Writers of British English use single quotation marks first and, when necessary, double quotation marks for quotations within quotations. If you have studied British English, be careful to follow the U.S. conventions governing quotation marks: double quotation marks first and, when necessary, single quotation marks within double.

34

Other Punctuation

Parentheses, brackets, dashes, colons, slashes, and ellipses are all around us. Pick up the television listings, for instance, and you will find all these punctuation marks in abundance, helping viewers preview programs in the most clear and efficient way possible.

> **P.O.V.:** "A Litany for Survival—The Life and Work of Audre Lorde." 10 P.M. (13) An hour-long documentary about the poet who died of cancer in 1992 at 58. [Time approximate after pledge drive]

This chapter will guide you in deciding when you can use these marks of punctuation to signal relationships among sentence parts, to create particular rhythms, and to help readers follow your thoughts.

Editing for Effective Use of Punctuation

- Be sure that any material set off with dashes or enclosed in parentheses requires special treatment. Then check to see that the dashes or parentheses don't make the sentence difficult to follow. (34a, c)

- Decide whether the punctuation you have chosen creates the proper effect: parentheses tend to de-emphasize material they enclose; dashes add emphasis.

- Check to see that you use brackets to enclose parenthetical elements in material that is already within parentheses and to enclose words or comments inserted into a quotation. (34b)

- Check to see that you use colons to introduce explanations, series, lists, and quotations. Use dashes to mark off comments or to emphasize material at the end of a sentence. (34d)

- Check to be sure you've used slashes to mark line divisions in poetry quoted within text and to separate alternative terms. (34e)

- Make sure you've used ellipses (three equally spaced dots) to indicate omissions from quoted passages. (34f)

- If you are writing an online communication, check your use of asterisks to mark emphasis, underscore symbols before and after the titles of full-length works, and angle brackets to enclose email and World Wide Web addresses. Make sure you use emoticons sparingly. (34g)

34a Parentheses

Use parentheses to enclose material that is of minor or secondary importance in a sentence—material that supplements, clarifies, comments on, or illustrates what precedes or follows it.

▶ **Inventors and men of genius have almost always been regarded as fools at the beginning (and very often at the end) of their careers.**
                                                                    – FYODOR DOSTOYEVSKY

▶ **During my research, I found problems with the flat-rate income tax (a single-rate tax with no deductions).**

Enclosing textual citations

▶ **Freud and his followers have had a most significant impact on the ways abnormal functioning is understood and treated (Joseph, 1991).**
                                         – RONALD J. COMER, *Abnormal Psychology*

Enclosing numbers or letters in a list

▶ **Five distinct styles can be distinguished: (1) Old New England, (2) Deep South, (3) Middle American, (4) Wild West, and (5) Far West or Californian.**   **– ALISON LURIE,** *The Language of Clothes*

With other marks of punctuation

A period may be placed either inside or outside a closing parenthesis, depending on whether the parenthetical text is part of a larger sentence. A comma, if needed, is always placed *outside* a closing parenthesis (and never before an opening one).

▶ **Gene Tunney's single defeat in an eleven-year career was to a flamboyant and dangerous fighter named Harry Greb ("The Human Windmill"), who seems to have been, judging from boxing literature, the dirtiest fighter in history.**   **– JOYCE CAROL OATES, "On Boxing"**

Choosing among parentheses, commas, and dashes

In general, use commas when the material to be set off is least interruptive (29c, f), parentheses when it is more interruptive, and dashes when it is the most interruptive (34c).

34b Brackets

Use brackets to enclose parenthetical elements in material that is itself within parentheses. Also use brackets to enclose explanatory words or comments that you are inserting into a quotation. If your keyboard does not include keys for brackets, draw them in by hand.

Setting off material within parentheses

▶ Eventually the investigation had to examine the major agencies (including the previously sacrosanct National Security Agency [NSA]) that were conducting covert operations.

Inserting material within quotations

Use brackets to insert explanatory words or comments into quoted material.

▶ As Curtis argues, "[Johnson] saw [the war] as a game or wrestling match in which he would make Ho Chi Minh cry 'uncle.' "

The bracketed words replace the words *he* and *it* in the original quotation.

In the quotation in the following sentence, the artist Gauguin's name is misspelled. The bracketed word *sic*, which means "so," tells readers that the person being quoted — not the writer who has picked up the quotation — made the mistake.

▶ One admirer wrote, "She was the most striking woman I'd ever seen — a sort of wonderful combination of Mia Farrow and one of Gaugin's [*sic*] Polynesian nymphs."

34c Dashes

Use dashes to insert a comment or to highlight material in a sentence. Dashes give more emphasis than parentheses to the material they enclose. On most typewriters and with some word-processing software, a dash is made with two hyphens (- -) with no spaces before, between, or after. In some software, the solid dash can be typed — as it is in this book — by selecting it from the symbols menu.

▶ The pleasures of reading itself—who doesn't remember?—were like those of Christmas cake, a sweet devouring.
> — EUDORA WELTY, "A Sweet Devouring"

▶ Mr. Angell is addicted to dashes and parentheses—small pauses or digressions in a narrative like those moments when the umpire dusts off home plate or a pitcher rubs up a new ball—that serve to slow an already deliberate movement almost to a standstill.
> — JOEL CONARROE, *New York Times Book Review*

Emphasizing material at the end of a sentence

▶ In the twentieth century it has become almost impossible to moralize about epidemics—except those which are transmitted sexually.
> — SUSAN SONTAG, *AIDS and Its Metaphors*

Marking a sudden change in tone

▶ New York is a catastrophe—but a magnificent catastrophe.
> — LE CORBUSIER

Indicating hesitation in speech

▶ As the officer approached his car, the driver stammered, "What—what have I done?"

Introducing a summary or explanation

▶ In walking, the average adult person employs a motor mechanism that weighs about eighty pounds—sixty pounds of muscle and twenty pounds of bone.
> — EDWIN WAY TEALE

Use dashes carefully, not only because they are somewhat informal but also because they can cause an abrupt break in reading. Too many of them create a jerky, disconnected effect that can make it hard for readers to follow your thought.

34d Colons

Use a colon to introduce explanations or examples, and to separate elements from one another.

Introducing an explanation, an example, or an appositive

▶ The men may also wear the getup known as Sun Belt Cool: a pale beige suit, open-collared shirt (often in a darker shade than the suit), cream-colored loafers and aviator sunglasses.

– ALISON LURIE, *The Language of Clothes*

Introducing a series, a list, or a quotation

▶ At the baby's one-month birthday party, Ah Po gave him the Four Valuable Things: ink, inkslab, paper, and brush.

– MAXINE HONG KINGSTON, *China Men*

▶ We began a series of workshops on nonviolence, and we repeatedly asked ourselves: "Are you able to accept blows without retaliation?"

– MARTIN LUTHER KING JR., "Letter from Birmingham Jail"

Separating elements

SALUTATIONS IN FORMAL LETTERS

▶ Dear Dr. Chapman:

HOURS, MINUTES, AND SECONDS

▶ 4:59 P.M.

▶ 2:15:06

RATIOS

▶ a ratio of 5:1

BIBLICAL CHAPTERS AND VERSES

▶ I Corinthians 3:3–5

TITLES AND SUBTITLES

▶ *The Joy of Insight: Passions of a Physicist*

CITIES AND PUBLISHERS IN BIBLIOGRAPHIC ENTRIES

▶ New York: St. Martin's, 1997

Editing for colons

Do not put a colon between a verb and its object or complement — unless the object is a quotation.

▶ Some natural fibers are cotton, wool, silk, and linen.

Do not put a colon between a preposition and its object or after such expressions as *such as, especially*, and *including*.

▶ In poetry, additional power may come from devices such as simile, metaphor, and alliteration.

34e Slashes

Use slashes to mark line divisions between two or three lines of poetry quoted within text. When using a slash to separate lines of poetry, precede and follow it with a space (33b).

▶ In Sonnet 29, the persona states, "For thy sweet love rememb'red such wealth brings / That then I scorn to change my state with kings."

Use a slash to separate alternatives.

▶ Psychologists continue to study the male/female ratio for some personality disorders.

34f Ellipses

Ellipses, or ellipsis points, are three equally spaced dots. You usually use ellipses to indicate that you have omitted something from a quoted passage. Just as you should carefully use quotation marks around any material that you quote directly from a source, so you should carefully use ellipses to indicate that you have left out part of a quotation that otherwise appears to be a complete sentence. Ellipses have been used in the following example to indicate two omissions — one in the middle of the first sentence and one at the end of the second sentence.

ORIGINAL TEXT

Much male fear of feminism is the fear that, in becoming whole human beings, women will cease to mother men, to provide the breast, the lullaby, the continuous attention associated by the infant with the mother. Much male fear of feminism is infantilism — the longing to remain the mother's son, to possess a woman who exists purely for him.   – ADRIENNE RICH

WITH ELLIPSES

As Adrienne Rich argues, "Much male fear of feminism is the fear that . . . women will cease to mother men, to provide the breast, the lullaby, the continuous attention associated by the infant with the mother. Much male fear of feminism is infantilism—the longing to remain the mother's son. . . ."

When you omit the last part of a quoted sentence, add a period before the ellipsis—for a total of four dots. Be sure a complete sentence comes before and after the four points. If your shortened quotation ends with a source citation (such as a page number, a name, or a title), follow these steps:

1. Use three ellipsis points but no period after the quotation.
2. Add the closing quotation mark, closed up to the third ellipsis point.
3. Add the source of documentation in parentheses.
4. Use a period to indicate the end of the sentence.

▶ **Hawthorne writes, "My friend, whom I shall call Oberon—it was a name of fancy and friendship between him and me . . ." (575).**

You can also use ellipses to indicate a pause or a hesitation in speech in the same way that you can use a dash for that purpose (34c).

▶ **Then the voice, husky and familiar, came to wash over us—"The winnah, and still heavyweight champeen of the world . . . Joe Louis."**
    – MAYA ANGELOU, *I Know Why the Caged Bird Sings*

34g Online punctuation

If you participate in any computer bulletin boards, discussion groups, or other electronic communication, you are already familiar with some new uses of punctuation marks and other keyboard characters. These marks can add emphasis, set off the titles of works, and express something about the sender's mood. Limited by formatting constraints, online punctuation and mechanics reflect the informality of the Internet. (See Chapter 39.)

Emoticons, which are marks made with combinations of keyboard characters, commonly express humor or mood. Emoticons can show readers, for example, when you want your remarks to be considered humorous or ironic. (Look at them sideways.)

▶ **the smile: :-)**
▶ **the wink: ;-)**

When italics and underlining are unavailable, as they sometimes are in online communication, use asterisks to help create special emphasis.

▶ **Her homepage *must* be updated.**

Use the underscore symbol before and after the title of a full-length work.

▶ **Have you read Bill Gates's _The Road Ahead_?**

Generally use italics to set off email addresses and addresses on the World Wide Web from the rest of your text. If italics are unavailable, use angle brackets instead (39a).

▶ **Visit us on the Web at <www.smpcollege.com>.**

35
Capitalization

Capital letters are a key signal in everyday life. Look around any store to see their importance: you can shop for just Levi's or *any* blue jeans, for Coca-Cola or *any* cola, for Kleenex or *any* house brand. In each of these instances, the capital letter indicates a particular brand. This chapter will help you use capitals appropriately.

Editing for Capitalization

- Make sure to capitalize the first letter of each sentence. If you quote a poem, follow its original capitalization. (35a)
- Check to make sure you have appropriately capitalized proper nouns and proper adjectives. (35b)
- If you have used titles of people or of works, see that they are capitalized correctly. (35c, d)
- Double-check the capitalization of geographical directions (*north* or *North?*), family relationships (*dad* or *Dad?*), and seasons of the year (*spring*, never *Spring*). (35e, f, and g)

35a Capitalize the first word of a sentence.

The first word of a sentence is always capitalized. If you are quoting a full sentence, capitalize the first word of the quotation unless you are weaving the quotation into your sentence with *that*.

▶ **Getting everyone to the ceremony on time will present a challenge.**
▶ **I overheard Alex say, "Graduation will be traumatic."**
▶ **She said that graduation will be traumatic.**

Capitalization of a sentence following a colon is optional.

▶ **Gould cites the work of Darwin: The [*or* the] theory of natural selection incorporates the principle of evolutionary ties among all animals.**

Capitalize a sentence within parentheses unless the parenthetical sentence is inserted into another sentence.

▶ **Combining the best in Japanese engineering with the attitude of Evel Knievel (on a good day), the new MK9 is one bad hog. (It's also an ergonomically correct one.)** – *Wired*, **July 1996**

When citing poetry, follow the capitalization of the original poem. Though most poets capitalize the first word of each line in a poem, some poets do not.

▶ **Morning sun heats up the young beech tree**
leaves and almost lights them into fireflies
– JUNE JORDAN, **"Aftermath"**

35b Capitalize proper nouns and proper adjectives.

Capitalize proper nouns (those naming specific persons, places, and things) and most adjectives formed from proper nouns. All other nouns are common nouns and are not capitalized unless they are used as part of a proper noun: *a street*, but *Elm Street*.

PROPER	COMMON
Alfred Hitchcock, Hitchcockian	a director
Brazil, Brazilian	a nation
Golden Gate Bridge	a bridge

Some commonly capitalized terms

GEOGRAPHICAL NAMES

Pacific Ocean	an ocean
the South	the southern part of the island
Africa, African sculpture	a beautiful sculpture

STRUCTURES AND MONUMENTS

Washington Monument	a monument

SHIPS, TRAINS, AIRCRAFT, AND SPACECRAFT

SS *Titanic*	a luxury liner
Challenger	a spaceship

ORGANIZATIONS, BUSINESSES, AND GOVERNMENT INSTITUTIONS

Library of Congress	a federal agency
General Motors Corporation	a blue-chip company

ACADEMIC INSTITUTIONS AND COURSES

University of California	a state university
Political Science 102	a political science course

HISTORICAL EVENTS AND ERAS

Shays's Rebellion	a rebellion
the Renaissance	a renaissance of sorts

RELIGIONS AND RELIGIOUS TERMS

God	a god
the Koran	a prayer book
Catholicism, Catholics	a religion

NATIONALITIES AND THEIR LANGUAGES

Russia, Russian	a language

TRADE NAMES

Xerox copies	photocopies
Nike shoes	sneakers

35c Capitalize titles before a proper name.

When used alone or following a proper name, most titles are not capitalized. One common exception is the word *president*, which many writers capitalize when it refers to the President of the United States.

Justice O'Connor	Sandra Day O'Connor, the justice
Professor Lisa Ede	my history professor
Dr. W. A. Ueno	W. A. Ueno, our doctor

35d Capitalize titles of works.

Capitalize most words in titles of books, articles, speeches, stories, essays, plays, poems, documents, films, paintings, and musical compositions. Do not capitalize articles (*a, an, the*), short prepositions, conjunctions, and the *to* in an infinitive unless they are the first or last words in a title or subtitle.

Walt Whitman: A Life	Declaration of Independence
"As Time Goes By"	*Sense and Sensibility*

35e Capitalize compass directions only if the word designates a specific geographical region.

▶ John Muir headed west, motivated by the desire to explore.

▶ Ken divided the map into sections: the Northeast, the South, and the West.

A Matter of Style: Shouting

Some writers capitalize words or even passages to add special emphasis. Although you may see this use of capitals for emphasis in print, many listservs and discussion or news groups on the Internet ask participants to practice good "netiquette" by resisting the urge to use all capital letters, which can be irritating to readers who feel as if they are being SHOUTED AT.

> ❖ **For Multilingual Writers: Learning English Capitalization**
>
> English capitalization may pose challenges for speakers of other languages because capitalization systems vary considerably among languages. Arabic, Chinese, and Hebrew, for example, do not use capital letters at all. English may be the only language to capitalize the first-person singular pronoun (*I*), but Dutch and German capitalize some forms of the second-person pronoun (*you*). German capitalizes all nouns; and, in fact, English used to capitalize more nouns than it does now.

35f Capitalize family relationships only if the word is used as part of a name or as a substitute for the name.

▶ When she was a child, my mother shared a room with her aunt.

▶ The train on which Uncle Robert arrived spewed out thick black smoke.

▶ I could always tell when Mother was annoyed with Aunt Rose.

35g Do not capitalize seasons of the year or parts of the academic or financial year.

spring	fall semester
winter	winter term
autumn	third-quarter earnings

36
Abbreviations and Numbers

Any time you open up a telephone book, you see an abundance of abbreviations and numbers, as in the following movie theater listing from the Berkeley telephone book:

Oaks Theater   1875 Solano Av   Brk

Abbreviations and numbers allow writers to present detailed information in a small amount of space. This chapter explains the conventions for using abbreviations and figures in academic and professional writing.

Editing Abbreviations and Numbers

- Make sure you use abbreviations and numbers according to the conventions of a specific field (see p. 232): *57%* might be acceptable in a math paper but *57 percent* may be more appropriate in a sociology essay.
- If you use an abbreviation readers might not understand, make sure you spell out the term the first time you use it and give the abbreviation in parentheses.
- If you use an abbreviation more than once, make sure you use it consistently.

36a Abbreviate titles used before and after proper names.

Ms. Susanna Moller	Henry Louis Gates Jr.
Mr. Jason Bowen	Karen Lancry, M.D.
Dr. Edward Davies	Samuel Cohen, Ph.D.

Other titles, including religious, academic, and government titles, should be spelled out in academic writing. In other writing, they can be abbreviated before a full name but should be written out when used with a last name.

Rev. Fleming Rutledge	Reverend Rutledge
Prof. Jaime Mejia	Professor Mejia
Joan Krauskopf, LL.D.	
Juanita Comfort, C.P.A.	

Do not use both a title and an academic degree with a person's name. Use one or the other. Instead of *Dr. Beverly Moss, Ph.D.*, write *Dr. Beverly Moss* or *Beverly Moss, Ph.D.*

36b Use abbreviations with years and hours.

399 B.C. ("before Christ")

A.D. 49 (*anno Domini*, Latin for "year of our Lord")

210 B.C.E. ("before the common era")

11:15 A.M. (*or* a.m.)

9:00 P.M. (*or* p.m.)

36c Use abbreviations for familiar business, government, and science terms.

As long as you can be sure your readers will understand them, use common abbreviations such as PBS, NASA, DNA, and CIA. If an abbreviation may be unfamiliar, however, spell out the full term the first time you use it, and give the abbreviation in parentheses. After that, you can use the abbreviation by itself.

▶ **The Comprehensive Test Ban (CTB) Treaty was first proposed in the 1950s. For those nations signing it, the CTB would bring to a halt all nuclear weapons testing.**

36d Use abbreviations in official company names.

Use such abbreviations as *Co.*, *Inc.*, *Corp.*, and *&* if they are part of a company's official name. Do not, however, use these abbreviations in most other contexts.

▶ **Sears, Roebuck & Co. was the only large** ~~corp.~~ *corporation* **in town.**

36e Use abbreviations in notes and source citations.

cf.	compare (*confer*)
e.g.	for example (*exempli gratia*)
et al.	and others (*et alia*)
etc.	and so forth (*et cetera*)
i.e.	that is (*id est*)
N.B.	note well (*nota bene*)

These abbreviations are not generally appropriate except in notes and citations in most academic and professional writing.

▶ **Many firms have policies to help working parents,** *for example,* ~~e.g.,~~ **flexible hours, parental leave, day care.**

▶ **Before the conference began, Jean unpacked the name tags, programs, pens,** ~~etc.~~ *and so forth.*

A Matter of Style: Abbreviations and Numbers in Different Fields

Use of abbreviations and numbers varies in different fields. See a typical example from a biochemistry textbook.

> The energy of a green photon . . . is 57 kilocalories per mole (kcal/mol). An alternative unit of energy is the joule (J), which is equal to 0.239 calorie; 1 kcal/mol is equal to 4.184 kJ/mol.
>
> – LUBERT STRYER, *Biochemistry*

These two sentences demonstrate how useful figures and abbreviations can be; just imagine how difficult trying to read the same sentences would be if the numbers and units of measurement were all written out.

You should become familiar with the conventions governing abbreviations and numbers in your field. The following reference books provide guidelines:

MLA Handbook for Writers of Research Papers
for literature and the humanities

Publication Manual of the American Psychological Association
for the social sciences

Scientific Style and Format: The CBE Manual for Authors, Editors, and Publishers
for the natural sciences

The Chicago Manual of Style
for the humanities

AIP Style Manual
for physics and the applied sciences

36f Abbreviate units of measurement, and use symbols in charts and graphs.

Symbols such as %, +, $, and = are acceptable in charts and graphs. Dollar signs are acceptable with figures: *$11* (but not with words: *eleven dollars*). Units of measurement can be abbreviated in charts and graphs (*4 in.*) but not in the body of a paper (*four inches*).

36g Use other abbreviations according to convention.

Some abbreviations required in notes and in source citations are not appropriate in the body of a paper.

CHAPTER AND PAGES   chapter, page, pages, (*not* ch., p., pp.)

MONTHS   January, February (*not* Jan., Feb.)

STATES AND NATIONS   California, Mexico (*not* Calif., Mex.)
Two exceptions are Washington, D.C., and U.S., which is acceptable as an adjective but not as a noun: *U.S. borders* but *in the United States* (not *in the U.S.*).

36h Spell out numbers expressed in one or two words.

If you can write out a number in one or two words, do so. Use figures for longer numbers.

thirty-eight
▶ Her screams were heard by ~~38~~ people, none of whom called the police.

216
▶ A baseball is held together by ~~two hundred sixteen~~ red stitches.

If one of several numbers *of the same kind* in the same sentence requires a figure, you should use figures for all the numbers in that sentence.

$100
▶ An audio system can range in cost from ~~one hundred dollars~~ to $2,599.

36i Spell out numbers that begin sentences.

When a sentence begins with a number, either spell out the number or rewrite the sentence.

One hundred nineteen
▶ ~~119~~ years of CIA labor cost taxpayers sixteen million dollars.

Most readers find it easier to read figures than three-word numbers; thus the best solution may be to rewrite this sentence: *Taxpayers spent sixteen million dollars for 119 years of CIA labor.*

36j Use figures according to convention.

ADDRESSES	23 Main Street, 175 Fifth Avenue
DATES	September 17, 1951; 4 B.C.E.; the 1860s; the eighties
DECIMALS AND FRACTIONS	65.34, 8½
PERCENTAGES	77 percent (*or* 77%)
EXACT AMOUNTS OF MONEY	$7,348; $1.46 trillion; $2.50; thirty-five (*or* 35) cents
SCORES AND STATISTICS	an 8–3 Red Sox victory, a verbal score of 600, an average age of 22, a mean of 53
TIME OF DAY	6:00 A.M.

37

Italics

The slanted type known as italics is more than just a pretty typeface. Indeed, italics give words special meaning or emphasis. In the sentence "Many people read *People* on the subway every day," the italics tell us that *People* is a publication. You may have a word processor that produces italic type; if not, underline words that you would otherwise italicize.

Editing for Italics

- Check that all titles of long or complete works are italicized. (37a)
- If you use any words, letters, or numbers as terms, make sure they are in italics. (37b)
- Italicize any non-English words or phrases that are not in an English dictionary. (37c)
- When you use italics to emphasize words, check to be sure you use the italics sparingly. (37e)

37a Italicize titles of long or complete works.

In general, use italics for titles of long or complete works; use quotation marks for shorter works (33c).

BOOKS	*Beloved*
CHOREOGRAPHIC WORKS	Agnes de Mille's *Rodeo*
FILMS AND VIDEOS	*Schindler's List*
LONG POEMS	*The Bhagavadgita*
MAGAZINES AND JOURNALS	*Newsweek, New England Journal of Medicine*
LONG MUSICAL WORKS	*Brandenburg Concertos*
NEWSPAPERS	the Cleveland *Plain Dealer*
PAMPHLETS	Thomas Paine's *Common Sense*
PAINTINGS AND SCULPTURE	Georgia O'Keeffe's *Black Iris*
PLAYS	*Angels in America*
RADIO SERIES	*All Things Considered*
RECORDINGS	Public Enemy's *Fear of a Black Planet*
SOFTWARE	*Quicken*
TELEVISION SERIES	*Roseanne*

Do not use italics for sacred books, such as the Bible and the Koran; for public documents, such as the Constitution and the Magna Carta; or for the titles of your own papers.

37b Italicize words, letters, and numbers used as terms.

▶ On the back of his jersey was the famous 24.

▶ One characteristic of some New York speech is the absence of postvocalic *r*, for example, pronouncing the word *four* as "fouh."

37c Italicize non-English words and phrases.

Italicize words from other languages unless they have become part of English—the French "bourgeois" or the Russian "samovar," for example. If a word is in an English dictionary, it does not need italics.

▶ At last one of the phantom sleighs gliding along the street would come to a stop, and with gawky haste Mr. Burness in his fox-furred *shapka* would make for our door.   – VLADIMIR NABOKOV, *Speak, Memory*

Always italicize Latin genus and species names.

▶ The caterpillars of *Hapalia*, when attacked by the wasp *Apanteles machaeralis*, drop suddenly from their leaves and suspend themselves in air by a silken thread.   – STEPHEN JAY GOULD, "Nonmoral Nature"

37d   Italicize names of aircraft, spacecraft, ships, and trains.

Spirit of St. Louis   Amtrak's *Silver Star*
Discovery   USS *Iowa*

37e   Use italics for emphasis.

Italics can help to create emphasis in writing, but use them sparingly for this purpose. It is usually better to create emphasis with sentence structure and word choice.

▶ **Great literature and a class of literate readers are nothing new in India. What is new is the emergence of a gifted generation of Indian writers *working in English*.**   **– SALMAN RUSHDIE**

38

Hyphens

Hyphens show up every time you make a left-hand turn, wear a Chicago Bulls T-shirt, buy gasoline at a self-service station, visit a writing center for one-on-one tutoring, worry about a long-term relationship, listen to hip-hop, or eat Tex-Mex food. Sometimes the dictionary will tell you whether to hyphenate a word. Other times, you will have to apply some general rules, which you will find in this chapter.

Editing for Hyphens

- Check that words broken at the end of a line are divided at an appropriate point. (38a)
- Double-check compound words to be sure they are properly closed up, separated, or hyphenated. If in doubt, consult a dictionary. (38b, c, and d)
- Check all terms that have prefixes or suffixes to see if you need hyphens. (38e)

38a Use a hyphen to divide words at the end of a line.

Break words between syllables. The word *metaphor*, for instance, contains three syllables (*met-a-phor*), and you can break the word after either the *t* or the *a*. All dictionaries show syllable breaks, so the best advice for dividing words correctly is simply to look them up. In addition, you should follow certain other conventions.

- Never divide one-syllable words or abbreviations, contractions, or figures.
- Leave at least two letters on each line when dividing a word. Do not divide words such as *acorn* (*a-corn*) and *scratchy* (*scratch-y*) at all, and break a word such as *Americana* (*A-mer-i-can-a*) only after the *r* or the *i*.
- Divide compound words, such as *anklebone* or *mother-in-law*, only between their parts (*ankle-bone*) or after their hyphens.
- Divide words with prefixes or suffixes between the parts. Break the word *disappearance*, then, after its prefix (*dis-appearance*) or before its suffix (*disappear-ance*). Divide prefixed words that include a hyphen, such as *self-righteous*, only after the hyphen.

38b Check a dictionary to be certain when to use a hyphen with compound nouns and verbs.

Some compound nouns and verbs are one word, some are separate words, and some require hyphens. Consult a dictionary to be sure.

ONE WORD	rowboat, textbook, flowerpot, homepage
SEPARATE WORDS	high school, parking meter, shut up
WITH HYPHENS	city-state, sister-in-law, cross-fertilize

See 39e for more on spelling recently coined compound words.

38c Use a hyphen with compound adjectives before a noun.

Hyphenate most compound adjectives before a noun. Do not hyphenate compound adjectives that follow a noun.

a *worn-out* coat	The coat was *worn out*.
a *well-liked* boss	Our boss is *well liked*.
a *six-foot* plank	The plank is *six feet* long.

In general, the reason for hyphenating compound adjectives is to facilitate reading.

▶ **Designers often use potted palms as living‑room dividers.**

Without the hyphen, *living* may seem to modify *room dividers*.

Never hyphenate an *-ly* adverb and an adjective.

▶ **They used a widely distributed mailing list.**

Use suspended hyphens in a series of compound adjectives.

▶ **Each student did the work him- or herself.**

38d   Hyphenate fractions and compound numbers from *twenty-one* to *ninety-nine*.

two-sevenths   thirty-seven

38e   Use a hyphen with some prefixes and suffixes.

Most words containing prefixes or suffixes are written without hyphens: *antiwar, gorillalike*. Here are some exceptions.

BEFORE CAPITALIZED WORDS	pro-Democratic, non-Catholic
WITH FIGURES	pre-1960, post-1945
WITH *ALL-*, *EX-*, AND *SELF-*	all-state, ex-partner, self-possessed
WITH *-ELECT*	mayor-elect
FOR CLARITY	re-cover, anti-inflation, troll-like

Re-cover means "cover again"; the hyphen distinguishes it from *recover*, meaning "get well." In *anti-inflation* and *troll-like*, the hyphens separate double and triple letters.

WIRED STYLE/ DOCUMENT DESIGN

For writing to work online, it must
be pointed and must have a point of
view. It must grab attention and
hold it—or the reader will simply
click away to another page.

                          – *WIRED STYLE*

WIRED STYLE / DOCUMENT DESIGN

39

Wired Style

Should an email address be italicized? How do you quote an email message? For that matter, how do you even spell email: *email? E-mail? e-mail?* The computer revolution and the new modes of communication it has spawned raise these and many other questions for writers. Enter *Wired Style*, an offspring of the online and print magazine *Wired*.

This chapter presents information gleaned from *Wired Style*, providing help in using the language and style appropriate to the digital world. It may even raise some new questions for writers: Are all the new terms connected with electronic communication and technology really helpful and necessary? Does the electronic frontier reflect a new kind of macho cowboy, slinging not guns but geekspeak? How can you get your own voice into these electronic conversations and arenas?

Raising these and many other questions is, in fact, one of the goals of *Wired Style*, for language use in the electronic world is clearly still evolving, not yet bound by many rules. What follows, then, is *Wired's* current best advice, reflecting the usage of those most actively engaged in the language of technology and electronic communication. Read on—and feel free to send in your own questions and responses to *wiredstyle@wired.com* or visit *www.wiredstyle.com* on the World Wide Web.

39a Style FAQ

Wired's most frequently asked questions are collected here.

HOW DO YOU PRINT EMAIL ADDRESSES WHEN THEY APPEAR IN PROSE?
In text, email addresses should be italicized. This imparts the sense of the whole address as a discrete unit. When the email address is a parenthetical, make sure to also italicize the surrounding parentheses: "Send your rants, raves, and flames about this book to Constance Hale *(wiredstyle@wired.com)*." Some folks prefer angle brackets to parentheses: *<wiredstyle@wired.com>*. If you cannot italicize, just use angle brackets: <wiredstyle@wired.com>. [In works cited lists and bibliographies, however, email addresses are not italicized.]

When email addresses don't fit across one column and must be broken over two lines, never break them on a hyphen—this makes it unclear whether the hyphen is part of the address. Similarly, never break email addresses by adding hyphens into words.

Also, don't break them after a dot; it looks like a period ending the sentence. Instead, break email addresses just before the punctuation, pulling the dot, the at sign (@), or whatever down to the next line:

> *wiredstyle@wired*
>
> *.com.*

WHAT ARE YOUR GUIDELINES FOR PRINTING URLS, ESPECIALLY
THE LONG ONES?

Uniform resource locators (*not* universal resource locators), are the signposts of the World Wide Web, the directions you give your browser to navigate to a homepage or Web site.

- In text, the entire URL should be italicized. [If you cannot italicize, use angle brackets.] This gives it a kind of unity, which is important because so many are so long: "New Mexico's Monastery of Christ in the Desert is on the Web at *www.christdesert.org/pax.html.*"
- Like email addresses, URLs do not contain internal spaces.
- Punctuation marks in URLs act as critical separators and should never be dropped. They include:

  ~ [tilde]   - [hyphen]
  _ [underscore]   . [period or dot]
  / [forward slash]   \ [backslash]
  | [pipe]

- Domain names in URLs should be lowercase. Pathnames, which follow the first slash, *are* case-sensitive, so follow the style dictated by the site.
- Add a forward slash [/] at the end of a URL if the last item is a directory, but not if it is an actual HTML file. (You can easily check this by typing in the URL and leaving off the final slash. If your browser automatically adds it to the URL that appears in the location window, then the slash should be included when you reprint the URL. If not, leave it off. The overloaded servers of the world will thank you for doing this right.)

MANY URLS ARE HOPELESSLY LONG AND DON'T FIT ACROSS NARROW COLUMNS.
HOW DO YOU BREAK THEM OVER TWO LINES?

- Break a line before or after the discrete units that begin URLs—*http://*, *gopher://*, and *ftp://*—but do not force a break within these protocol tags.

- Don't break a URL at a hyphen. This may introduce confusion about whether or not the hyphen is part of the URL.
- Break URLs right before a punctuation mark, carrying the punctuation symbol to the next line. If this is impossible, break the URL with a soft return between syllables, as we had to do for this quote, pulled from an article on Thomas Paine and set as a headline:

> It's easy to imagine Paine as a citizen of
> the new culture, issuing fervent
> languages from his site *www.common
> sense.com*. He would be a cyber hell-raiser, a Net fiend.

- If a URL is at the end of a sentence, always add the requisite period.

DO EMAIL QUOTATIONS DIFFER FROM SPOKEN QUOTATIONS?

Email and online postings are a cross between print and conversation. They can be used much as spoken quotations would be used in a piece of writing, but because they are written, it is more important to reproduce them verbatim—spelling warts and all.

If email quotations are straightforward and indistinguishable from spoken quotations, they can be freely mixed in among quotations from a face-to-face interview. In this case, it's fine to style the email quotations according to print conventions and—go ahead—correct the typos.

If, on the other hand, the email quotation or online posting evokes the electronic medium—the mood and mores of online communication—leave all the idiosyncrasies, including:

- Odd spelling and syntax. Resist the urge to sanitize.
- The punctuation conventions of the font-free world of ASCII:

  asterisks (used for emphasis, like italics in print)

  /slashes/ (also used in place of italics)

  underscores (used especially for titles, or to indicate underlining)

  ALL CAPS (used to indicate shouting)

Don't use the bracketed word *sic* when you're citing emails—you might end up with as many *sic*'s as original words.

WHAT'S THE DEAL WITH ALL THE CAPITAL LETTERS IN THE MIDDLE OF WORDS?

Call 'em what you want—intercaps, incaps, midcaps, or BiCaps—these have become a fixture in the technology industry: in names like HotJava, QuarkXPress, QuickTime, and WordPerfect.

Follow company and product style for intercaps (BeBox, CU-SeeMe, RealAudio), but not for names that are all caps and five letters or longer, such as Siggraph, which just looks too ugly as SIGGRAPH.

WHAT'S THE PLURAL OF THAT SMALL, ROLLING, POINTING DEVICE INVENTED BY DOUGLAS ENGELBART IN 1964?
We prefer *mouses*. *Mice* is just too suggestive of furry little critters. But both terms are common, so take your pick.

By the way: mouseclick refers to the way mouses communicate to computers; mousepad is the mouse's turf.

IS PIN NUMBER REDUNDANT?
Yup. *PIN* stands for personal identification number. Put *PIN number* in a ballooning class of digital redundancies, most of them born of acronyms:

CD-ROM disc	Cobol language
DOS operating system	ISP providers
LCD display	RAM memory

Our all-time favorite might be this malapropism uttered by Senator Alfonse D'Amato: electronic email.

39b Transcend the technical.

True jargon—the argot of a special trade or community—is lucid language and can be as elegant as it is meaningful. What follows is a selection of the jargon we think essential to writing about technology.

@   The at sign is a fixture in every email address. It has also been adopted in trademarked names—@Home, *@times*—to signal a company's jones for digital cachet.

browser   Software that lets you travel the World Wide Web. Brand names include HotJava, NCSA Mosaic, Netscape Navigator, and Microsoft Explorer.

gopher   Named after the mascot of the University of Minnesota, where it was developed, gopher is a protocol that provides a seamless, menu-driven interface to transfer files, browse databases, and telnet to sites around the Internet, simply and easily. As with other Net tools like telnet, the term is treated as a generic term and styled all lowercase.

hypertext   A system of coding text that links electronic documents with each other. Elements in a hypertext document—words, pictures—are linked to elements in other documents. Click on a phrase and the screen will reload with a page of information about that idea; click on a picture of a seductive jungle river and you'll get info on how to travel there.

Hypertext is reminiscent of the links between a footnote and the main body of your high school theme papers, except that code is used instead of super-script numbers.

Internet　The Internet evolved from the small Arpanet into a worldwide net-work of computers communicating in a common language—TCP/IP—over telephone lines or microwave links. But the Net is more than that. It's a cultural watershed. It is home to the World Wide Web and to infinite numbers of news-groups, BBSes, and online forums. It is, as Julian Dibbell wrote, "the single most complex information entity since the emergence of the human brain."

Always capitalized; always preceded by *the* unless it's being used as a modifier (Internet service provider). Don't say "on Internet." The Net (also cap-italized), is synonymous with the Internet, though slightly more figurative.

listserv　Generic term for mail-handling software that lets people subscribe and unsubscribe to email lists.

operating system　The underlying software of a computer that mediates the hardware box and other hardware, and the software running on top of a ma-chine. OS/2, Unix, Windows 95, DOS, and other operating systems are more than just technical categories, though. They are cultures.

user　Overused term for a "he," a "she," or a "they" working at a computer.

telnet　Also known as "Remote Login," telnet allows you to connect to another computer on the Internet.

Web　Call it *the Web*, the *World Wide Web*, or *W3*, this is the place your money, phone calls, and email will soon live. A global online information repository, the Web is an application running on top of the Internet.

39c Capture the colloquial.

True colloquial writing doesn't just reflect the vernacular of your reader—it limns the lives and speech of the characters you write about. The digiculture has its own language:

cyber-　The terminally overused prefix for all things online and digital. (Go ahead, blame *Wired*.) Although it most often appears as a combining form—firmly attached to the root and without a hyphen (cyberbucks, cybercrats)—*cyber* can also stand alone as an adjective, especially to avoid clunky compounds (cyber rights, cyber cowboy, cyber pipe-dreams).

cyberspace　Information space. The ether. The place between phones, between computers, between you and me.

digital　The buzz adjective of the 90s, meaning in a wired state, as opposed to an analog one.

Digital Revolution   It's here. It gets capitalized, ranking it up there with its industrial predecessor. Think of this revolution as the radical reshaping and restructuring of social patterns caused by digital technology.

.   The period symbol is used in email addresses, URLs, and newsgroups to separate constituent parts. But in this context, it's called a "dot."

emoticons   Treacly expressions of emotion also known as *smileys*. Small graphical renderings composed of ASCII characters, which substitute for facial expressions and body language. Useful and appeasing in an online world where curt or hastily written emails and postings can easily offend. Be faithful to Net rendering, but use emoticons as sparingly as you would triple exclamation points. Tilt your head to the left to see a wink ;-), a smile :-), chagrin :-(, shock (:-o), and a touch of sarcasm (:/).

MUD   A multi-user dungeon, or domain, or dimension. (The word *dungeon* persists from the early 1970s, when the paper and pencil role-playing game Dungeons and Dragons swept the game culture.) Less literally, a MUD is virtual space, accessible via the Internet, where players participate in a new kind of social virtual reality. MUDs are organized around the metaphor of physical space and allow participants to create new, often anonymous, identities.

online   Possessed of a computer and a modem. Jacked in. Chances are the word started out as an adverb, but it is used today primarily as an adjective, as in online community. It also appears as a noun (synonymous with *cyberspace*) or an experience. Please, no hyphen. The solid spelling is not yet standard, especially in company names: America Online, Sierra On-line, Video On Line.

post   As a verb, to send a message to an online publication or community. As a noun, it is that message. As a gerund, it is synonymous with online scribbling.

39d Acronyms, FWIW

Like 'em or not, acronyms are an essential part of the wired culture. While they *do* connote the scientific and the technical, their use is not limited to scientists and techies. Often, acronyms pick up steam simply with use and become words in themselves.

Embrace acronyms, following these rules of thumb:

- Use vernacular acronyms that your audience knows, that roll off the tongue. In the techno realm, an acronym such as RSI is as recognizable as FBI.

- Find the elegant solution. It isn't necessary to write out *hypertext markup language* each time you invoke HTML, but you might, in an appositive phrase, tag HTML as *the Web's lingua franca*.

- Listen for the colloquial, for those acronyms that enter the vernacular. Expressions like MOO possess all the character of the best words. IBM has earned not just denotation, but connotation. Besides, people *say* them.

Some common acronyms

ASCII	American Standard Code for Information Interchange
BBS	bulletin board system
DOS	disk operating system
FAQ	frequently asked questions
FTP	file transfer protocol
FWIW	for what it's worth
HTML	hypertext markup language
HTTP	hypertext transfer protocol
ISP	Internet service provider
RAM	random access memory
RSI	repetitive strain injury
URL	uniform resource locator

39e When in doubt, close it up.

From computer commands like *whois* and onscreen nouns like *logon*, we have evolved the commandment: "When in doubt, close it up." Words spelled solid — like *videogame* or *gameplay* or *homepage* — may seem odd at first, but the now common modem offers a perfect example of how quickly words move from the strange to the familiar: who even knows that the piece of hardware allowing computers to talk to each other was once called a modulator/demodulator?

We know from experience that new terms often start as two words, then become hyphenated, and eventually end up as one word. Go there now. Here are some words we've decided to spell solid: *desktop, download, email, homepage, menubar, offline, printout, toolbar, trackball, videogame, voicemail, workstation.*

40
Document Design

Many occasions call for you to prepare documents with the greatest of care: a résumé for a big job interview, an application for your first home mortgage, a living will, a report for your boss. To make these documents represent you well, you should design them most carefully.

40a Create a visual structure.

Effective writers use visual elements such as spacing, margins, type styles and sizes, paper, print quality, and page numbers to present documents that are easy on the eye—and easy to understand.

Spacing and margins

For most documents, frame your text with margins of white space of between one inch and one and a half inches. Since the eye takes in only so many chunks of print in one movement, very long lines can be hard to read. When you use wide margins, you can keep the lines of text to a reasonable width. You should also use white space around graphics or lists to make them stand out.

Each page should be a unit. Thus you should not put a heading at the bottom of a page, forcing readers to turn the page to get to the accompanying text. And try not to end a page with a hyphenated word, leaving readers to guess at the second part as they turn the page.

Double-space most academic documents you prepare, and indent new paragraphs five spaces. Certain kinds of writing, however, call for different spacing: letters and memorandums, for example, are usually single-spaced, as are lab reports in some fields.

Word-processing programs allow you to justify, or square off, the right margin—as it is on this page. However, most writers prefer to leave the right margin "ragged," or unjustified.

Appropriate type, paper, and output

Most word-processing systems allow writers to choose among a great variety of fonts (type sizes and typefaces). For most writing, the easy-to-read ten- to twelve-point type size is best for the body of your document, as is a serif face (this is serif type; this is sans serif type). Although a smaller or more unusual font (this is Marigold) might seem attractive at first glance, readers often find such type hard to read, especially when a whole document is in an atypical style.

The quality of the paper you use affects the overall look and feel of your document. For most writing, use 8½- by 11-inch good-quality white bond paper (not erasable bond). If the paper you use has tractor-feed guides, be sure to remove the strips of holes from the sides, and separate the pages. On some occasions, you may wish to use cream-colored bond—for a résumé, perhaps.

Because some computer print is sharper than others, seek out the best-quality printer available; laser printers are generally available in campus computing centers or libraries.

The first page

The first page introduces your document, making an initial impression on readers. For much of your writing, the style of the first page will be conventional: follow the Modern Language Association (MLA) style in the humanities; American Psychological Association (APA) style in many of the social sciences. An example of MLA style is in Chapter 48; of APA in Chapter 50.

For college writing, if you don't need to do a separate title page, consider the following format for your first page, double-spacing throughout:

- Begin about an inch from the top of the paper. Put your name, the course title and number, your instructor's name, and the date, each on separate lines, at the left margin.
- Center the title horizontally. Capitalize the first word and last word of the title and all other words except articles, prepositions, and conjunctions. Do not underline your title or put it in quotation marks. If the title is long, type it on two lines, making the first line longer than the second.
- On the next double-spaced line, begin your text.

For professional and other nonacademic writing, follow the conventions of the field or company.

Pagination

Except for a separate title page, number every page of your document. For college writing, you may need to follow a particular format for pagination (see Chapter 48 for a sample of pagination in an MLA paper; Chapter 50 for an APA paper). If not, beginning with the first page of text, place your last name and an arabic numeral in the upper-right-hand corner of the page, about one-half inch from the top and aligned with the right margin. Do not put the numeral in parentheses or follow it with a period. For work-related writing, you may need to follow a company's set of conventions for pagination and layout. Take the initiative to find out what these conventions are. Most word-processing systems will automatically paginate a document (and include headers) according to your instructions.

40b   Use headings effectively.

In long documents, headings (set-off words and phrases) call readers to attention, announcing a new topic or segment of a topic. As such, headings work with, but do not substitute for, the transitions that guide readers from point to point. Reports in some fields have standard headings—standard in wording and in appearance—which readers expect (and writers therefore must provide). For reports in other fields, you need to decide whether to use headings and what their style should be in terms of type size and face, wording, and placement.

Type size and style of headings

This book uses various levels of headings, distinguished by different type sizes and color—one heading for part titles, another for chapter titles, several kinds of headings within chapters, and other heads for boxes and lists. One way to distinguish levels of headings is by varying type—using all capitals for major, or first-level, headings; capital and lowercase underlined for the second level; plain capitals and lowercase for the third level; and so on. With a computer, you have even more options.

ON A TYPEWRITER	ON A COMPUTER
FIRST-LEVEL HEADING	**FIRST-LEVEL HEADING**
<u>Second-Level Heading</u>	**Second-Level Heading**
Third-Level Heading	*Third-Level Heading*
	<u>Fourth-Level Heading</u>

Consistent wording and placement of headings

Look for the most succinct way to word your headings. Most often, state the topic in a single word, usually a noun (for example, *Toxicity*); in a phrase (*Levels of Toxicity* or *Measuring Toxicity*); in a question that will be answered in the text (*How can toxicity be measured?*); or in an imperative that tells readers what steps to take (*Measure the toxicity*). Whichever structure you choose, make sure you use it consistently for all headings of the same level: all questions, for example, or all gerund phrases, and *not* a mixture of the two.

Typically, within a report, place first-level headings at the left margin; indent a second-level head five spaces from the left; and center a third-level head. Surround headings that you want to display prominently with plenty of white space; headings that are less significant require less space around them. Position each level of head consistently throughout your paper.

40c Use visuals effectively.

Visuals in a written document can help make a point vividly and emphatically. In fact, they can pack extra punch by presenting information more succinctly and more clearly than words alone could do.

In deciding when and where to use visuals, the rule of thumb is simply to choose visuals that will best reinforce your points and most help your readers to understand your document. Here are some tips about when a particular kind of visual is most appropriate.

- Use *tables* to draw attention to particular numerical information. (See Table 1 on the next page or the table in the essay on p. 356.)
- Use *graphs* or *charts* to draw readers' attention to relationships among data. Use *pie charts* to compare a part to the whole. Use *bar charts* and *line graphs* to compare one element with another, to compare elements over time, to demonstrate correlations, and to illustrate frequency. (See Figures 1 and 2 on the following pages.)
- Use *drawings* or *diagrams* to draw attention to dimensions and to details. (See Figure 3 on p. 254.)
- Use *maps* to draw your readers' attention to location and to spatial relationships.
- Use *cartoons* to illustrate or emphasize a point dramatically or to amuse your readers.
- Use *photographs* to draw attention to a graphic scene (such as devastation following an earthquake) or to depict an object.
- Use *overheads* to clarify or summarize your main points, especially if you are presenting part or all of your text orally or in a multimedia format. (See Figure 4 on p. 254.)
- Use a *homepage* from the World Wide Web to reach more and more readers. (See Figure 5 on p. 255.)
- Use *graphics* from the Web to illustrate or clarify your text. (See the essay on p. 315.)

Number your visuals (*Table 1*), and give them titles (*Word Choice by Race*) and perhaps captions or subtitles that provide a link to the text (Seesaw *and* Teeter-totter, *Chicago 1986*). Be sure to identify sources for all visuals, whether you pick up or adapt visuals created by someone else or you create your own visuals based on someone else's data. Place each visual either as close to the appropriate text discussion as possible or in an appendix at the end of your document, with a reference to it within your text.

Some Guidelines for Using Visuals

- Use visuals as part of your written presentation, not as decoration. Preparing visuals should be part of your process of generating ideas and planning for the complete document.

- Refer to the visual in your text before the visual itself appears, explaining its main point. For example: *As Table 1 demonstrates, the cost of a college education has risen dramatically in the last decade.*

- Number and title your visuals.

- If you did not create a particular visual yourself, or if you created a visual using someone else's research, credit your source fully.

- Use decorative touches sparingly if at all. Computer clip art is so easy to generate that you may be tempted to fancy up your visuals, but do so only if the decoration enhances and clarifies your text.

TABLE

Table 1
Word Choice by Race:
Seesaw and *Teeter-totter*, Chicago 1986

	Black	*White*	*Total*
Seesaw	47 (78%)	4 (15%)	51
Teeter-totter	13 (22%)	23 (85%)	36
Total	60	27	87

Source: Michael I. Miller, "How to Study Black Speech in Chicago." *Language Variation in North American English.* Ed. A. Wayne Glowka and Donald M. Lance. NY: MLA, 1993. 166.

PIE CHART

Figure 1
Racial and Ethnic Origin in the United States, 1990

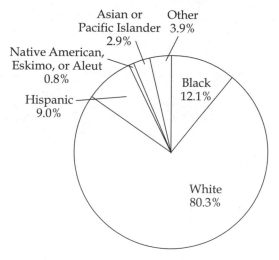

Source: U.S. Bureau of the Census, 1991.

BAR GRAPH

Figure 2
Absence of Third-Person Singular *-s/-es*

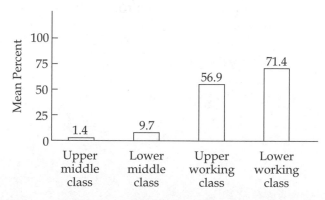

Source: Walt Wolfram, *Dialects and American English.* Englewood Cliffs, NJ: Prentice-Hall, 1991. 95.

DIAGRAM

Figure 3
Spanish-English Bilingualism and the Language Shift Process

RETENTION First and Second Generations		ANGLICIZATION Third and Fourth Generations	
Monolingual Spanish $\longrightarrow$	Simple bilingualism $\longrightarrow$	English bilingualism $\longrightarrow$	Monolingual English

Source: D. Letticia Galindo, "Bilingualism and Language Variation." *Language Variation in North American English.* Ed. A. Wayne Glowka and Donald M. Lance. NY: MLA, 1993. 202.

OVERHEAD

Figure 4
First Slide for Presentation on the World Wide Web

How to Navigate the Web

- Using Netscape

- A Jumping-Off Place for Web Exploration

- Posting Pages on the Web

- The Web, the Future, and You

WORLD WIDE WEB HOMEPAGE

Figure 5
Paula Moore's Homepage for English 367

DOING RESEARCH

Research is formalized curiosity.
It is poking and prying with a
purpose.

— ZORA NEALE HURSTON

DOING RESEARCH

41

Preparing for a Research Project

Your employer asks you to recommend the best new intercom system. You need to plan a week's stay in Tokyo. Your twins want a clown or a magician for their fifth birthday party. An instructor assigns a term paper about an artist. Each of these situations calls for research, for examining various kinds of sources. And each of these situations calls for you to assess the data you collect, to synthesize your findings, and to come up with your own, original recommendation or conclusion. Many tasks that call for research, such as a term paper or a business report, require that your work culminate in a written document.

41a Formulate a research question and a hypothesis.

You first need to formulate a research question about your topic, whether clowns, intercoms, or artists. This research question may be tentatively answered by a hypothesis, a statement of what you anticipate your research will show. As you do your research, you will move from a hypothesis to a working thesis (41c). Both the hypothesis and the working thesis must be manageable, interesting, specific, and arguable—a debatable proposition that can be proved or disproved by research evidence. Here's an example of the move from a general topic to a hypothesis:

TOPIC	the art of Frida Kahlo (1907–1954)
RESEARCH QUESTION	What were the influences on Kahlo's work?
HYPOTHESIS	The events of her own life were the central influence on Kahlo's work.

41b Investigate what you know about your topic.

Once you have formulated a hypothesis, marshal everything you already know about the topic. Here are some strategies for getting all your initial thoughts about the topic down on paper.

- *Brainstorming.* For five minutes, alone or in a group, list everything you know, think of, or wonder about your hypothesis (5a).
- *Freewriting.* For five minutes, write about every reason for believing your hypothesis to be true; then for five minutes, write down every argument that someone opposed to your hypothesis might make (5b).

- *Tapping your memory for sources.* List everything you can remember about *where* you learned about your topic: computer bulletin boards, email, books, magazines, courses, conversations, television. What you know comes from somewhere, and "somewhere" can serve as a starting point.

41c Move from hypothesis to working thesis.

As you gather information and begin examining and evaluating sources, you will probably refine your research question and change your hypothesis significantly. Only after you have explored your hypothesis, tested it, and sharpened it by reading, writing, and talking with others does the hypothesis become a working thesis. For example, through some early research, you may decide that the hypothesis about the artist Kahlo will not in itself lead to an interesting, original research essay (41a). Consequently, you might shift your attention to other influences on Kahlo and come up with the following:

WORKING THESIS	Kahlo's unique style resulted not only from her life events but also from her familiarity with European and Mexican art.

41d Consider the context of the research project.

Audience

Who will be the audience for your research project?

- Who will be interested in the information you gather, and why?
- What do you know about their backgrounds?
- What will they want to know? What will they already know?
- What response do you want to elicit from them?
- What assumptions and beliefs might they already hold about the topic?
- What kinds of evidence will you need to convince them of your view?
- If a supervisor or instructor has assigned the project to you, what other expectations will you need to meet?

Rhetorical stance

Think about your own attitude toward your topic. Are you just curious about it? Do you feel positively about it? dislike it? find it troubling? What influences have shaped your stance?

Purpose

If you have been assigned a specific research project, keep in mind the cue words in that assignment. Does the assignment ask that you *recommend, evaluate, describe, survey, analyze, explain, classify, compare,* or *contrast?* What do such words mean in this field (4a)?

Scope

How many and what kind of sources should you use? Has someone else established such guidelines? Will you be doing any field research—interviewing, surveying, or observing?

Length

What is the anticipated length of your final draft? The amount of research and writing time you need for a five-page essay differs markedly from that for a fifteen-page report. You should also allow extra time in case a problem arises—if materials are not available or if you discover after a first draft that you must do more research.

Deadline

When does the project need to be completed? Do any preliminary materials, such as an outline or a first draft, need to be completed before this date? When you are preparing a research project for an employer, your supervisor may want to see part of your work at an early stage.

Scheduling a Research Project

Date assigned: _____   Try to complete by:

Analyze project; decide on primary purpose and
  audience; choose topic if necessary.   _____

Set aside library time; develop search strategy.   _____

Send for materials needed by mail.   _____

Do background research; narrow topic if necessary.   _____

Decide on research question, tentative hypothesis.   _____

Start working bibliography; track down sources.   _____

Develop working thesis and rough outline.   _____

(Continues)

If necessary, conduct interviews, make observations, or
distribute and collect questionnaires.   _____

Read and evaluate sources; take notes.   _____

Draft explicit thesis and outline.   _____

Prepare first draft.   _____

Obtain and evaluate critical responses.   _____

Do more research if necessary.   _____

Revise draft.   _____

Prepare list of works cited.   _____

Edit revised draft; use spell checker if available.   _____

Prepare final draft.   _____

Do final proofreading.   _____

Final draft due: _____

42

Conducting Research

A few minutes' thought may bring to mind some piece of everyday
research you have done. One couple we know with a passion for ice
cream decided to carry out some research on their city's ice cream, and
after some preliminary reading at the local library about the history
of making ice cream, they literally ate their way through the research
project, ending up with an article they sold to a local magazine. This
chapter describes the kinds of research you will most often be called on
to conduct—library or database research and field research.

42a   Use primary and secondary sources.

A simple way to categorize sources divides them into primary sources,
or firsthand knowledge, and secondary sources, information available
from the research of others. Most research projects depend on both primary and secondary sources.

PRIMARY SOURCES

basic sources of raw information

notes you take in the field

experiments, surveys, interviews you conduct

objects or artwork you examine

literary works you read

performances you attend

diaries, letters, eyewitness accounts, news reports, historical documents

SECONDARY SOURCES

accounts produced by other investigators

other researchers' reports or analyses

critical writing, including reviews and biographies

Often what constitutes a primary or secondary source depends on your purpose. A critic's evaluation of a painting, for instance, is a secondary source if you are writing an essay on that painting, but it serves as a primary source if you are conducting a study of that critic's writing.

42b Select reference works.

Libraries provide two necessary kinds of reference information: general background materials, which will provide an overview of your topic; and specialized materials, which may help answer your research question and develop your working thesis.

GENERAL ENCYCLOPEDIAS

Collier's Encyclopedia, New Encyclopaedia Britannica

SPECIALIZED ENCYCLOPEDIAS

Encyclopedia of Asian History, Cambridge History of Africa, Harvard Guide to American History, Oxford Companion to English Literature

BIOGRAPHICAL RESOURCES

Dictionary of American Biography, Dictionary of National Biography, African American Biographies, Notable American Women, Chicano Scholars and Writers

ALMANACS, YEARBOOKS, NEWS DIGESTS, ATLASES

Facts on File, Statistical Abstracts of the United States, Atlas of World Cultures, National Geographic Atlas of the World

BOOK INDEXES, CD-ROM INDEXES

Books in Print, Cumulative Book Index, Paperbound Books in Print, CD-ROMs in Print

GENERAL PERIODICAL INDEXES/DATABASES

Book Review Digest, InfoTrac, New York Times Index, Readers' Guide to Periodical Literature, LEXIS-NEXIS, Dialog, Dow Jones News/Retrieval

SPECIALIZED PERIODICAL INDEXES AND ABSTRACTS

Arts and Humanities Citation Index, Biological Abstracts, PsycLIT

42c Search computer databases.

You may also search an electronic index or database to find specific articles that may prove to be good references for your research. You conduct a search in an electronic database by entering key words (often referred to as descriptors), and you get back a list of every source that contains those key words. (Some software looks for your key words only in the titles of its sources; some software searches abstracts of sources; and some software searches the full text of sources. Some sophisticated databases allow you to enter a direct question.)

Obviously, then, doing efficient database searches requires that you choose key words carefully. Performing an efficient search also requires that you observe the search logic for a particular database. Let's assume that you are preparing an academic report on urban life as represented in James Joyce's fiction and that you have located the electronic database called *MLA Bibliography of Books and Articles*, a major database for works of and about literature. Using *and* between key words usually indicates that you want to find sources that deal with both key words (for example, Joyce and Ireland, which yields 118 entries). *Or*, on the other hand, instructs the software to call up every source in which either one key word or the other shows up (for example, Joyce and Dublin or Belfast). You can instruct the software to exclude articles that contain a specific term if you type in *not* before the term (for example, Joyce and Ireland not Dublin, which yields 71 entries). In an electronic database search, the *or*, *and*, and *not* are known as Boolean terms.

Some databases require that you use parentheses or quotation marks to search for certain words. Others let you call up every instance in which a key word (*Clinton*, for example) appears near—say, five or ten words from—another key term (*veto*, for example).

Suppose you were working with the MLA database mentioned previously, and you enter the key terms *Kahlo, Frida* and *American literature* as well as the Boolean term *and*; you would find that three articles contain both key terms. Here is the information on those three articles as it would appear on your screen or in a printout at the time this book went to press. (Notice that the MLA format provides information using descriptor words in parentheses—*sau*, for example, is the MLA descriptor for subject-author.)

```
1 MLA
        AUTHOR: Salber, Linde; Stuhlmann, Gunther
        TITLE:  Artists-the Third Sex: A Few Thoughts on the
                Psychology of the Creative Age
        SOURCE: Anais: An International Journal 1993 vii
                p59-68
        SUBJECTS COVERED:
        --(slt) American literature (tim) 1900-1999 (sau)
        Nin, Anais (sau) Kahlo, Frida (sau) Andreas-Salome,
        Lou (sao) psychological approach
        --(slt) German literature (tim) 1800-1899
2 MLA
        AUTHOR: Gambrell, Alice Kathleen Hagood
        TITLE:  The Disquieting Muse: New World Women
                Artists and Modernist Fictions of Alterity
                (Dissertation abstract number: DA9112068;
                Degree granting institution: U of Virginia)
        SOURCE: Dissertation Abstracts International (ISSN
                Pt. A, 0419-4209; Pt. B, 0419-4217; Pt. C,
                1042-7279) 1991 May v51 (11) p3738A
        SUBJECTS COVERED:
        --(slt) American literature (sic) fiction (tim)
        1900-1999 (sau) Doolittle, Hilda (sau) Rhys, Jean
        (sau) Kahlo, Frida (sau) Hurston, Zora Neale (grp)
        men artists (lfe) collaboration
```

3 MLA

```
AUTHOR: Brennan, Karen Morley
TITLE:  Hysteria and the Scene of Feminine
        Representation
SOURCE: Dissertation Abstracts International (ISSN
        Pt. A, 0419-4209; Pt. B, 0419-4217; Pt. C,
        1042-7279) 1990 Oct. v51(4) p1225A
SUBJECTS COVERED:
--(slt) American literature (sic) fiction (tim)
1900-1999 (sau) Nin, Anais (sau) Kahlo, Frida (sau)
Acker, Kathy (lth) hysteria (lth) women (sap)
psychoanalytical approach
```

42d Use the Internet to communicate and to gather data.

The Internet is a great global patchwork quilt of linked computer networks that can help you as a researcher by (1) letting you communicate with individuals and groups all over the world and (2) opening doors to other vast information resources. All you need is an account on a host computer and an Internet address. (An Internet address always consists of a user's name [often referred to as a userid] and the name of the host computer where you have your account, usually separated with an @ symbol: username@hostname.)

Online discussion

MAILING LISTS

The Internet allows you to find and communicate with groups of people who share your research interest—be it intercom systems, Tokyo, or Frida Kahlo. Such interest groups can be found through mailing lists, also called discussion groups or listservs.

USENET

The Internet also gives you access to Usenet, a global collection of interest groups that share news—hence their other name, newsgroups. Instead of mail from these groups automatically coming to your electronic mailbox, as it does from mailing lists, you must electronically visit Usenet groups to get their news.

Similarly, you can connect to an Internet bulletin board system, or BBS, where you can look over messages and files listed on menus. Or you can visit real-time "virtual" conversation spaces in MOOs and MUDs. Above all, you can use email to keep up conversations with all kinds of groups and individuals.

Data gathering

There are many systems on the Internet through which you can access sources, including the World Wide Web, gopher, and others. Here is an overview of what's out there.

WORLD WIDE WEB

The World Wide Web is a network of linked sites, written in hypertext markup language (HTML) and presented in "pages" that can feature sound, graphics, and video. Each site has its own uniform resource locator (URL), or address. Because hypertext is the characterizing feature of the Web, you can leap from one Web site to another and to other kinds of Internet resources—for example, to a gopher menu, a listserv or discussion group, or a Wais search—all with the click of a mouse. To read a hypertext document on the Web, you must have a Web browser software tool, such as Mosaic, Netscape, or Explorer. To do research, you may use a Web search engine such as Yahoo! or Galaxy to help you do key-word searches on the Web. (For more on the Web, see Chapter 39.) If you were using such tools to research the artist Frida Kahlo, for example, you would quickly find this homepage (see the following page), from which you could jump to further resources about Kahlo.

GOPHER

Gopher is a browsing software system that can retrieve data for you from universities, companies, and other organizations. If your host computer has a gopher, you can select the information you want from the gopher's menu of information sources.

Using gopher often involves following a path from one menu to another before you get to a specific document. At times, you may lose track of how you actually located the material of interest to you. To simplify matters, you can use something called a bookmark to identify an important gopher location that you want to revisit. Over time, you may create a bookmark list, a sort of custom menu, that makes it easy for you to get to particular gopher sites.

FRIDA KAHLO WEB SITE

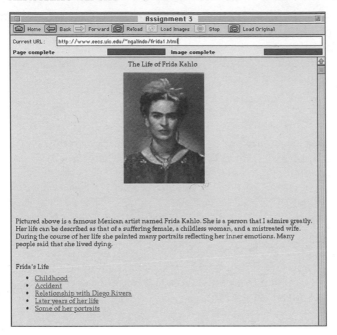

VERONICA AND JUGHEAD

Veronica, one of the menu items provided by gopher, allows you to search a database of all the gopher menus in the world for words that you specify. Veronica then gives you a menu of what it has found for you, and you can go through the menu to evaluate which items might help in your research.

Jughead is the same kind of search engine as Veronica, but instead of searching all the gopher menus in the world, it searches only those in a limited geographical area — say, in a particular university or in one of the fifty states.

ANONYMOUS FTP

Anonymous FTP (file transfer protocol) is a method for calling up and copying (at no cost) a huge and ever-expanding number of public files from host computers all over the Internet. The files, which may not be available via gopher or the World Wide Web, can be short documents or complete magazines (with pictures), audio clips, video clips, and even software that you can download to your computer.

ARCHIE

When you use anonymous FTP, you may know what kind of data you are looking for, but you probably do not know the exact name of the file that contains the data nor the Internet address at which that file resides. The solution is to tell another searching system called Archie what you are looking for. Archie allows you to search FTP sites for access to artwork, books, journals, photographs, sound tracks, and much more. Finally, Archie tells you how to locate the file so that you can copy, or download, it.

WAIS

WAIS (wide area information servers, pronounced *ways*) provides a kind of index to specific files you may have accessed through gopher, allowing you to search for key words within those files. Thus, once you figure out which files or sources might have data important to your research question, you can conduct a search of the documents in those sources by using key words and search logic. The power of WAIS is that it checks not just the titles of documents but each and every word within the documents. In other words, WAIS does what is called a full-text search. WAIS will list all the documents that have the key words you have specified, and it will give you the option of having the complete document appear on your computer screen. The secret to using WAIS is figuring out which sources to search by key words.

TELNET

Telnet is an important system that allows you to make a telephone connection with another computer. Through telnet, you can access on your computer the resources that are available to the other one.

42e Use the library catalog.

A library catalog lists all the library's books. The traditional format for the library catalog is the card catalog. Today some libraries have a microfiche catalog, and many have transferred or are in the process of transferring their records to a computerized catalog. You can use public computer terminals to search for material or log on and access a library catalog from personal computers at remote locations. Most computerized catalogs provide clear instructions on how and when to type in information. As with a card catalog, you can search for holdings by author, title, or subject. With a computerized catalog, you can easily experiment with different subject headings. The computer screen displays entries similar to those in a card catalog but may also indicate whether a book is available or has been checked out and, if so, when it is due to be returned. For example, see the circulation-computer screen entry below, which gives information on an available book.

```
AUTHOR:          Herrera, Hayden
TITLE:           Frida, a biography of Frida Kahlo / by Hayden Herrera.
EDITION:         1st ed.
PUBLISHER:       New York : Harper & Row, c1983.
PHYSICAL DESC:   iii, 507 p., [48] p. of plates : ill.(some col.) ; 25 cm.
NOTES:           Includes bibliographical references and index.
SUBJECTS:        Kahlo, Frida.
                 Painters - Mexico - Biography.

LOCATION         Call#/VOL/NO/COPY          STATUS
UNH/STACK        ND259.K33 H47 1983  c.1    Available
```

Besides identifying a book's author, title, subject, and publication information, each card catalog card or computerized catalog record also lists a call number, the book's identification number. Most academic libraries now use the Library of Congress system, in which call numbers begin with letters of the alphabet. Some libraries still use the older Dewey decimal system; yet others combine systems. Once you have written down the complete call number, look for a library map or a shelving plan to tell you where your book is located. If the stacks are open to library users, take time to browse through the books near the one you have targeted. Very often you will find the other books in the area surrounding your book a more important treasure trove than any bibliography or index.

42f Conduct original research in the field.

Interviews

Some information is best obtained by asking direct questions of other people. If you can talk with an expert—in person, on the telephone, or via the Internet—you might get information you could not have obtained through any other kind of research.

> **Planning an Interview**
>
> - Determine your exact purpose, and be sure it relates to your research question and your hypothesis.
> - Set up the interview well in advance. Specify how long it will take, and if you wish to tape-record the session, ask permission to do so.
> - Prepare a written list of factual and open-ended questions. Brainstorming or freewriting can help you come up with questions. (5a, b) Leave plenty of space for notes after each question. If the interview proceeds in a direction that seems fruitful, do not feel that you have to ask all of your prepared questions.
> - Record the subject, date, time, and place of the interview.
> - Thank those you interview, either in person or in a follow-up letter.

Observation

Trained observers report that making a faithful record of an observation requires intense concentration and mental agility. Here are some tips.

> **Conducting Observation**
>
> - Determine the purpose of the observation, and be sure it relates to your research question and hypothesis.
> - Brainstorm about what you are looking for, but don't be rigidly bound to your expectations.
> - Develop an appropriate system for recording data. Consider using a "split" notebook or page: on one side, record your observations directly; on the other, record your thoughts or interpretations.
> - Be aware that the way you record data will affect the final report, if only in respect to what you include in the notes and what you leave out.
> - Record the date, time, and place of observation.

Opinion surveys

Surveys usually depend on questionnaires. On any questionnaire, the questions should be clear and easy to understand and designed so that you can analyze the answers easily. Questions that ask respondents to say "yes" or "no" or to rank items on a scale are particularly easy to tabulate.

Designing a Questionnaire

- Write out your purpose, and review your research question and hypothesis to determine the kinds of questions to ask.
- Figure out how to reach the respondents you need.
- Draft potential questions, and check to see that each question calls for a short, specific answer.
- Test the questions on several people, and revise questions that are ambiguous, too hard to answer, or take too much time.
- For a questionnaire that is to be mailed, draft a cover letter explaining your purpose. Provide an addressed, stamped return envelope, and be sure to state a deadline.
- On the final version of the questionnaire, leave adequate space for answers.
- Proofread the questionnaire.

43
Evaluating and Using Sources

Every time you pick up *Consumer Reports* to check out its evaluation of an appliance or log on to the Internet to talk to owners of a software program you are interested in, you are calling on sources for help. All research builds on the careful and sometimes inspired use of sources—that research done by others. You will want to make the most of your sources, using the insights you gain from them to help you create powerful prose of your own. This chapter will guide you in this effort.

43a Keep clear records of sources.

As you locate and consider research sources—books, articles, Internet or Web sites, and so on—you should create a working bibliography, a list of the sources that seem most likely to address your research question.

Guidelines for Creating a Working Bibliography

- Use index cards (one for each source), a notebook, or a computer file. Record information on one side only so that you can arrange the entries alphabetically when you prepare the bibliography, or works cited.

- For each *book*, record the following: call number or other location information; author(s) and/or editor(s); title and subtitle, if any; publisher's name and location; year of publication; other information you may find—translator, volume number, edition, and so on. If the book is made up of selections by a variety of authors, record the author(s) and title of the piece you are using and its inclusive page numbers.

- For each *periodical article*, list author(s); editor(s); article title and subtitle; periodical name, volume number, and date; and inclusive page numbers.

- For sources you find listed in *reference books*, note the name of the reference work and its location in case you need to check it again.

- For an *online source*, list the author (if available); title, document, file, or Web page; date of the material; name of the database or other online source; date you accessed the source; and the full electronic address or URL so that you can return to the source.

- For *other electronic sources*, try to obtain a printout of the source information instead of copying it by hand.

For a research essay about the artist Frida Kahlo, you might generate the following working-bibliography cards:

BOOK

> ND 259.K33
> H 47
> 1983
>
>
> Herrera, Hayden. Frida: A Biography
> of Frida Kahlo. New York: Harper,
> 1983.

ARTICLE

Jenkins, Nicholas. "Calla Lilies and Kahlos: The Frida Kahlo Museum in Mexico City." ARTnews Mar. 1991: 104–05.

General Periodicals Index (InfoTrac)

43b   Assess the usefulness of a source.

Since you want the information you glean from sources to be reliable and persuasive, you must evaluate each potential source carefully. Use these guidelines to assess the usefulness of a source.

- *Relevance.* Is the source closely related to your research question?
- *Author's and publisher's credentials and stance.* Is the author an expert on the topic? What is the author's stance on the issue(s) involved, and how does this influence the information in the source? Does the author support or challenge your own views? If you are evaluating a book published by a corporation, government agency, or interest group, what is the publisher's position on the topic? If you are evaluating an article, what kind of periodical published it? popular? academic? alternative?
- *Date of publication.* Recent sources are often more useful than older ones, particularly in the sciences. However, in some fields, the most authoritative works may be the older ones.
- *Level of specialization.* General sources can be helpful as you begin your research, but you may then need the authority or currentness of more specialized sources. On the other hand, extremely specialized works may be too hard to understand.
- *Audience.* Was the source written for the general public? specialists? advocates or opponents?
- *Cross-referencing.* Is the source cited in other works?
- *Length.* Is the source long enough to provide adequate detail?
- *Availability.* Do you have access to the source?

43c Evaluate electronic sources with special scrutiny.

Surfing the Internet or browsing the Web can be fun — and it can also waste a lot of time. You may want to distinguish, then, between free-time browsing and purposeful research, which demands focus, control, and carefully chosen key words to direct your research.

You will probably find working on the Internet both exciting and frustrating, for although these research tools have tremendous potential, they are still in a fairly primitive state. Unlike most library-based research tools, much material on the Internet in general and the World Wide Web in particular is still the work of enthusiastic amateurs. Many people post documents or create homepages, but they often make no attempt to completely cover their issues. As a result, commercial advertisements, one-sided statements, and careless or even false information are all jumbled together with good, reliable data. In this frontier electronic environment, you must be the judge of just how accurate and trustworthy the materials are. In making such judgments, you can rely on the same kind of critical thinking you use to assess the usefulness of any source. In addition, you can improve your evaluation of electronic sources by keeping some key questions in mind.

- Who has posted this document or page — an individual? an interest group? a company? a government agency? What can you determine about the credibility of the individual or group posting the document?
- Who can be held accountable for the information in the document? How well and thoroughly does the document credit its own sources?
- How effectively is the document or page designed? How user-friendly is it? If it is a Web page, are the links helpful? What effects do design, visuals, and sound have on the message?
- What is missing or omitted from the document or page? How do such exclusions affect how you can or cannot use the information?
- What perspective(s) are represented? If only one perspective is represented, how can you balance or expand this viewpoint?

43d Read critically, and synthesize data.

After you have identified a potential source and decided to read it, you still need to determine if it merits a place in your research essay. Keeping these questions in mind can save you time as you dig into sources.

- How does the source material address your research question?
- How does it provide support for your working thesis?
- Does the source offer counterarguments to your working thesis? If so, what responses can you make?
- What is the author's stance or perspective? Is he or she an advocate of something? a strong opponent? an amused onlooker? a specialist? Are there any clues to what forces may have shaped the author's perspective?
- How does this stance affect the author's presentation?
- In what ways do you share — or not share — the author's stance?
- What is the author's tone — cautious? angry? flippant? serious? What words express this tone?
- What is the author's main point?
- How much and what kind of evidence does the author use to support that point?
- How persuasive do you find the evidence?
- Do any of your other sources disagree with this source? If so, how are you going to handle this disagreement?
- What patterns or trends do the author's argument and evidence fall into? Can you synthesize, or group, this author's argument and evidence with arguments and evidence from other sources?
- What inferences, or conclusions, can you draw from those patterns or trends?

43e Take notes: quote, paraphrase, summarize.

When you decide that a source is useful, take careful notes on it. While note-taking methods vary from one researcher to another, you should (1) get down enough information to help you recall the major points of the source; (2) put the information in the form in which you are most likely to incorporate it into your research essay; and (3) note all the information you will need to cite the source accurately.

When you have become more familiar with the general guidelines on taking accurate notes that appear on the following page, then you must decide in each case what kind of notes to take from each source.

Guidelines for Taking Accurate Notes

- Using index cards, a notebook, or a computer file, list the author's name and a shortened title of the source. Your working-bibliography entry for the source will contain full bibliographic information, so you need not repeat it in each note from the source. (43a)

- Record the exact page number from which your note comes. If your note refers to more than one page, indicate which part of the note comes from which page.

- Label each note card with a subject heading.

- After you have written your note, identify it as a quotation, a paraphrase, a summary, a combination of these forms, or some other form—such as your own critical comment—to avoid confusion later. Mark quotations accurately with quotation marks, or paraphrase and summarize completely in your own words to be sure you do not inadvertently plagiarize the source. (43f)

- Read each completed note carefully, and recheck it against the source for the accuracy of quotations, statistics, and specific facts.

Quotation

Quoting involves bringing a source's exact words into your text. Use an author's exact words when the wording is so memorable or expresses a point so well that you cannot improve or shorten it without weakening it; when the author is a respected authority whose opinion supports your own ideas; or when an author challenges or disagrees profoundly with others in the field. Here is an example of an original passage followed by a quotation from it. Note quotation marks, ellipses to mark omitted words, and brackets to signal changed capitalization.

ORIGINAL SOURCE

But Frida was also the product of a bold and brilliant generation that looked back with devotion to its Mexican roots and valued the reality it found there, uncontaminated by foreign influences. She admitted to having a great admiration for her husband's work, as well as that of José Guadalupe Posada, José María Velasco, and Gerardo Murillo (Dr. Atl), and she found great beauty in the highly developed pre-Conquest indigenous arts.   – Martha Zamora, *Frida Kahlo: The Brush of Anguish* (110)

Mexican cultural influences

Zamora, Frida, p. 110

"...Frida was...the product of a bold and brilliant generation that looked back with devotion to its Mexican roots and valued the reality found there, uncontaminated by foreign influences....[S]he found great beauty in the highly developed pre-Conquest indigenous arts."

Guidelines for Quoting Accurately

- Copy quotations carefully, with punctuation, capitalization, and spelling exactly as in the original. (33a)
- It is especially important to enclose the quotation in quotation marks; don't rely on your memory to distinguish your own words from those of the source. (33a)
- Use brackets if you introduce words of your own into the quotation or make changes in it. (34b)
- Use ellipses if you omit material. (34f)
- If you later incorporate the quotation into your research essay, copy it from the note precisely, including brackets and ellipses.
- Record the author's name, shortened title, and page number(s) on which the quotation appears.
- Make sure you have a corresponding working-bibliography entry with complete source information. (43a)
- Label the note with a subject heading.

Paraphrase

When you paraphrase, you put an author's material (including major and minor points, usually in the order they are presented) into *your own words and sentence structures*. If you wish to cite some of the author's words within the paraphrase, enclose them in quotation marks. Here is an example of a paraphrase that resembles an original paragraph too closely.

ORIGINAL SOURCE

Although largely self-taught, and considered by many to be a naive painter, Frida was actually very sophisticated. Intelligent, well-read, and well-informed, she was acquainted with the traditional schools of painting. More important, she recognized the vanguard of Mexican and foreign art not only through her travels but through direct contact with the artists. Direct influences show up in some cases, as in *Magnolias* (1945), reminiscent of the work of Georgia O'Keeffe, or in *Four Inhabitants of Mexico City* (1938), recalling de Chirico. Her earliest works showed an acquaintance with art books; in her first self-portrait for Gómez Arias, she described herself as "your Botticelli," and in letters to him she expressed interest in Modigliani and Piero della Francesca. Her use of suffocating background vegetation is similar to that of Henri Rousseau, the small figures in *What the Water Gave Me* (1938) like something out of Hieronymus Bosch, and the written legends in others like those of the Mexican painter Hermenegildo Bustos.

– MARTHA ZAMORA, *Frida Kahlo: The Brush of Anguish* (110)

UNACCEPTABLE PARAPHRASE: USING THE AUTHOR'S WORDS
AND SENTENCE STRUCTURES

Frida mostly taught herself to paint, but many thought her to be a more *naive painter* than she really was. She was aware of important artists from Mexico and other countries, and some *direct influences* of Georgia O'Keeffe even show up in her work. Early works, for example, refer to Botticelli, Modigliani, della Francesca, and Bosch. Some of her *background vegetation* even recalls that of Rousseau. (110)

Because the italicized phrases are either borrowed from the original without quotation marks or changed only superficially, this paraphrase is unacceptably close to the original. In addition to relying on the exact words of the original, the paraphrase's last sentence follows too closely the structure of the last sentence of the original.

On the following page is an example of an acceptable paraphrase using the writer's own words, including one quotation from the original. This paraphrase appears reworded and worked into the beginning of the ninth paragraph of the sample research essay in Chapter 48.

```
                                           Artistic influences
Zamora, Frida, p. 110

Frida mostly taught herself to paint, but she was not as
unsophisticated as many thought her to be. She was
bright and knowledgeable, familiar with the history
of painting, acquainted with contemporary Mexican and
foreign artists and their work. Some of her paintings
show the influence of O'Keeffe and de Chirico. She
referred to her first self-portrait as "your Botticelli"
and mentioned Modigliani and della Francesca in letters
to Arias. She depicts flora like Rousseau, and uses
small figures like Bosch and captions like Bustos.
                                              (Paraphrase)
```

Guidelines for Paraphrasing Accurately

- Include all main points and any important details from the original source, in the same order in which the author presents them.
- State the meaning in your own words and sentence structures. If you want to include especially memorable language from the original, enclose it in quotation marks.
- Save for another note your own comments, elaborations, or reactions.
- Record the author, shortened title, and the page number(s) on which the original material appeared.
- Make sure you have a corresponding working-bibliography entry.
- Label the note with a subject heading, and identify it as a paraphrase to avoid confusion with a summary.
- Recheck the paraphrase against the original to be sure that the words and sentence structures are your own and that they express the author's meaning accurately.

Summary

A summary is a significantly shortened version of a passage or even a whole chapter or work that captures main ideas *in your own words*. Unlike a paraphrase, a summary uses just enough information to record the points you wish to emphasize. Here is a note card with a summary of the preceding passage by Zamora. It states the author's main points selectively and without using her words.

Artistic influences

Zamora, <u>Frida</u>, p. 110

Frida was well acquainted with historical
and contemporary artists from Europe
and America, whose influence is evident
in her works (particularly in her images
of flora and her rendering of many scenes
in a painting).

(Summary)

Guidelines for Summarizing Accurately

- Include just enough information to recount the main points you want to cite. A summary is usually far shorter than the original.
- Use your own words. If you include any language from the original, enclose it in quotation marks.
- Record the author, shortened title, and page number(s) on which the original material appeared.
- Make sure you have a corresponding working-bibliography entry for the material.
- Label the note with a subject heading, and identify it as a summary to avoid confusion with a paraphrase.
- Recheck against the original any material you plan to use to be sure you have captured the author's meaning and that your words are entirely your own.

43f Recognize plagiarism, and acknowledge sources.

Plagiarism, the use of someone else's words without crediting the other person, breaks trust with the research conversation you are a part of and with readers as well. As a mark of dishonesty, it can destroy the credibility of both research and researcher and can result in serious consequences.

You are probably already aware of cases of deliberate plagiarism—writers who have copied passages directly from source materials. In addition, however, you should be aware of unintended plagiarism—a quotation accidentally used without quotation marks, a paraphrase that too closely resembles the original, background details used without acknowledgment in the mistaken belief that none was necessary. You can avoid unintended plagiarism by understanding what material you must document; by taking systematic, accurate notes; and by giving full credit to sources in both in-text citations and in your list of sources cited.

Materials not requiring acknowledgment

COMMON KNOWLEDGE

If most readers would be likely to know something, you need not mention the source. For example, you do not need to credit a source for the statement that Bill Clinton was elected president in 1992. If, on the other hand, you give the exact number of popular votes he received, you should cite the source for the figure.

FACTS AVAILABLE IN A VARIETY OF SOURCES

If a number of reference books include a certain piece of information, you need not cite a specific source for it. For instance, you do not need to cite a source for the fact that the Japanese bombing of Pearl Harbor failed to destroy the oil tanks and submarines. You would, however, need to credit a source that argued that the failure to destroy the submarines meant that Japan was destined to lose the war.

YOUR OWN FINDINGS FROM FIELD RESEARCH

If you conduct interviews, observation, or surveys, simply announce your findings as your own.

Materials requiring acknowledgment

DIRECT QUOTATIONS

Whenever you use another person's words directly, credit the source. If you quote some of the author's words within a paraphrase or summary, you need to cite the quotation separately, after the closing quotation mark.

FACTS NOT WIDELY KNOWN; ARGUABLE ASSERTIONS

If your readers would be unlikely to know a fact or if an author presents as fact an assertion that may or may not be true, cite the source. To claim, for instance, that Switzerland is amassing an offensive nuclear arsenal would call for the citation of a source, since Switzerland has long been an officially neutral state.

JUDGMENTS, OPINIONS, AND CLAIMS OF OTHERS

Whenever you summarize or paraphrase anyone else's opinion, give the source. Even though the wording should be completely your own, you must acknowledge the source.

STATISTICS, CHARTS, TABLES, AND GRAPHS FROM ANY SOURCE

Credit all statistical and graphic material not derived from your own fieldwork, even if you yourself create the graph from data in another source (40c).

HELP FROM FRIENDS, INSTRUCTORS OR SUPERVISORS, OTHERS

A conference with an instructor may give you the idea you need to clinch an argument. Give credit. Friends may help you conduct surveys. Credit them, too.

Recognizing Plagiarism and Acknowledging Sources

- Maintain an accurate and thorough working bibliography. (43a)
- Establish a consistent note-taking system, listing sources and page numbers and clearly identifying all quotations, paraphrases, summaries, statistics, and graphics. (43e)
- Identify all quotations with quotation marks—both in your notes and in your essay. (43e)
- Be sure your summaries and paraphrases use your own words and sentence structures. (43e)
- Give a parenthetical citation or note for each quotation, paraphrase, summary, arguable assertion or opinion, statistic, and graph that is from a source. (See Chapter 45, 49a, and 51a.)
- Prepare an accurate and complete list of sources cited according to the required documentation style. (See Chapter 47, 49c, and 51b.)

44

Writing a Research Essay

Everyday decisions often call for research and writing. In trying to choose between two jobs in different towns, for example, one person we know made a long list of questions to answer: which job location had the lower cost of living? how did the two locations compare in terms of schools, cultural opportunities, major league sports, and so on? After conducting careful and thorough research he was prepared to draw up a letter of acceptance to one place and a letter of regret to the other. This chapter aims to help you move effectively from research to writing.

44a Refine your writing plans.

For most research writing, drafting should begin well before the deadline. Growing understanding of the subject and response from others may call not only for more drafting but for gathering more information, even refining your research question. Start by reconsidering your purpose, audience, stance, and working thesis:

- What is your central purpose? other purposes, if any?
- What is your stance? Are you an advocate, a critic, a reporter, an observer?
- What audience are you addressing?
- How much background information do you need to present to your audience?
- What support will your readers find convincing—examples? quotations from authorities? statistics? data from your own observation or from interviews?
- Should your tone be that of a colleague, an expert, or a friend?
- How can you establish common ground with your audience?
- What is your thesis trying to establish? Will your audience accept it?

44b Organize, outline, and draft.

To group the many pieces of information that you have collected, examine your notes for connections, finding what might be combined with what, which notes will be more useful and which less useful, which ideas lend support to your thesis and which should be put aside.

Outlines can take various forms and be done at various stages. You may group your notes, as just mentioned, write a draft, and only then outline the draft to study its tentative structure. Or you may develop a working outline from your notes, listing the major points in a tentative order with support for each point. Such a working outline may see you through the rest of the writing process, or you may decide to revise your outline as you go along. Yet another way to proceed is to plot out your organization early on in a formal outline (6c).

Begin drafting wherever you feel most confident. If you have an idea for an introduction, begin there. If you are not sure how you want to introduce the essay but do know how you want to approach one point, begin with that, and return to the introduction later.

Working title and introduction

The title and introduction play special roles, for they set the stage for what is to come. Ideally, the title announces the subject of the essay in an intriguing or memorable way. The introduction should draw readers into the essay and provide any background they will need to understand your discussion. Here are some tips for drafting an introduction to a research essay.

- It is often effective *to open with a question*, especially your research question. Next, you might explain what you will do to answer the question. Then *end with your thesis statement*—in essence, the answer—which grows out of your working thesis.

- Help readers get their bearings by *forecasting your main points*.

- *Establish your own credibility* by telling how you have become knowledgeable about the topic.

- In general, you may *not* want to open with a quotation. In the course of a research essay, you may want to quote several sources, and opening with a quotation from one source may give it too much emphasis.

Conclusion

A good conclusion to a research essay helps readers know what they have learned. Here are some strategies that may help.

- A specific-to-general pattern is frequently appropriate. Open with a reference to your thesis statement, and then expand to a more general conclusion that reminds readers of the significance of your discussion.

- If you have covered several main points, you may want to remind readers of them. Be careful, however, to provide more than a mere summary.
- Try to end with something that will have an impact—a provocative quotation or question, a vivid image, a call for action, or a warning. But guard against sounding "preachy."

44c Incorporate source materials.

Many fields have specific rules for incorporating source materials. Here are some general guidelines.

Direct quotations

Because your essay is primarily your own work, limit your use of quotations to those necessary to your thesis or memorable for your readers. Use direct quotations for the following purposes:

- To incorporate a statement expressed so effectively by the author that it cannot be paraphrased without altering the meaning
- To allow the words of an authority on your topic to contribute to your researching credibility
- To allow an author to state a position in his or her own words
- To create a particular effect

BRIEF QUOTATIONS

Short quotations should run in with your text, enclosed by quotation marks (33b).

> In Miss Eckhart, Welty recognizes a character who shares with her "the love of her art and the love of giving it, the desire to give it until there is no more left" (10).

LONG QUOTATIONS

Quotations longer than four lines (MLA) or forty words (APA) should be set off from the regular text. Begin such a quotation on a new line, and indent every line ten spaces (MLA) or five to seven spaces (APA) from the left margin. This indentation sets off the quotation clearly, so quotation marks are unnecessary. Type the quotation to the right margin, and double-space it as you do the regular text. Introduce long quotations by a signal phrase or a sentence followed by a colon.

> A good sentence arrangement can prevent problems; however, *withitness*, as defined by Woolfolk, works even better:

Withitness is the ability to communicate to students that you are aware of what is happening in the classroom, that you "don't miss anything." With-it teachers seem to have "eyes in the back of their heads." They avoid becoming too absorbed with a few students, since this allows the rest of the class to wander. (359)

This technique works, however, only if students actually believe that their teacher will know everything that goes on.

INTEGRATING QUOTATIONS INTO YOUR TEXT

Carefully integrate quotations into your text so that they flow smoothly and clearly into the surrounding sentences. Use a signal phrase or verb, such as those underlined in the following examples:

In *Death of a Salesman*, Willy Loman dreams the wrong dreams and idealizes the wrong ideals. His misguided perceptions are well captured by Brown: "He has lived on his smile and on his hopes, survived from sale to sale, been sustained by the illusion that he has countless friends in his territory, that everything will be all right . . ." (97).

As Eudora Welty notes, "learning stamps you with its moments. Childhood's learning," she continues, "is made up of moments. It isn't steady. It's a pulse" (9).

SIGNAL VERBS

acknowledges	concludes	emphasizes	replies
advises	concurs	expresses	reports
agrees	confirms	interprets	responds
allows	criticizes	lists	reveals
answers	declares	objects	says
asserts	describes	observes	states
believes	disagrees	offers	suggests
charges	discusses	opposes	thinks
claims	disputes	remarks	writes

When you write about literary and artistic works created in the past, generally follow Modern Language Association (MLA) style and use present-tense verbs, as above. (See Chapter 45.) However, if you are using the style recommendations of the American Psychological Association (APA), use signal phrases in the past tense or the present-perfect form. (See Chapter 49.)

In *Abnormal Psychology*, Comer (1995) emphasized that Shakespeare's Othello blamed behavior on the moon: "She comes more near the earth than she was wont / And makes men mad."

BRACKETS AND ELLIPSES

In direct quotations, enclose in brackets any words you change or add, and indicate any deletions with ellipsis points.

> A farmer, Jane Lee, spoke to the Nuclear Regulatory Commission about the occurrences. "There is something wrong in the [Three Mile Island] area. It is happening within nature itself," she said, referring to human miscarriages, stillbirths, and birth defects in farm animals ("Legacy" 33).

> Economist John Kenneth Galbraith has pointed out that "large corporations cannot afford to compete with one another. . . . In a truly competitive market someone loses. . . . American big business has finally learned that everybody has to protect everybody else's investment" (Key 17).

Paraphrases and summaries

Introduce paraphrases and summaries clearly, usually with a signal phrase that includes the author of the source, as the underlined words in this example indicate.

> Professor of linguistics Deborah Tannen says that she offers her book *That's Not What I Meant!* to "women and men everywhere who are trying their best to talk to each other" (19). Tannen goes on to illustrate how communication between women and men breaks down and then to suggest that a full awareness of "genderlects" can improve relationships (297).

44d Revise and edit your draft.

Try to get feedback from at least two or three readers. Then reread your draft very carefully, making notes for necessary changes and additions. Pay particular attention to how you have used sources, and make sure you have full documentation for all of them. (For more detailed information on revising and editing, see Chapter 8.)

44e Prepare a list of sources cited.

Once you have a final draft with your source materials in place, you are ready to prepare your list of works cited (MLA) or your references (APA or CBE). Create an entry for each source used in your essay. Then double-check your essay against your list of sources cited to see that you have listed every source mentioned in the in-text citations or notes and that you have not listed any sources not cited in your essay. (For guidelines on MLA, APA, and CBE styles, see Chapter 47, 49c, and 51b.)

DOCUMENTING SOURCES, MLA STYLE

Learning the rules the *MLA Handbook* outlines will help you become a writer whose work deserves serious consideration. Similarly, your study of these rules can make you a more discerning reader: knowing how an author is supposed to use sources is essential to judging a text's reliability.

– PHYLLIS FRANKLIN, *MLA Handbook for Writers of Research Papers*

DOCUMENTING SOURCES, MLA STYLE

DIRECTORY TO MLA STYLE

MLA style for in-text citations (Chapter 45)

MLA style for a list of works cited (Chapter 47)

BOOKS

This part of *The Everyday Writer* discusses the basic format for the Modern Language Association (MLA) style and provides examples of various kinds of sources. MLA style is widely used in literature and languages as well as other fields. For further reference, consult the *MLA Handbook for Writers of Research Papers*, fourth edition, 1995.

45

MLA Style for In-text Citations

MLA style requires parenthetical citations in the text of an essay to document quotations, paraphrases, summaries, and other material requiring documentation (43f). Keep your parenthetical citations short, but include the information your readers need to locate the full citation in the list of works cited at the end of the text.

Place a parenthetical citation as near the relevant material as possible without disrupting the flow of the sentence. Pay attention in the following examples to *where* punctuation is placed in relation to the parentheses.

1. AUTHOR NAMED IN A SIGNAL PHRASE

Ordinarily, you can use the author's name in a signal phrase—to introduce the material—and cite the page number(s) in parentheses.

```
Herrera indicates that Kahlo believed in a "vitalistic
form of pantheism" (328).
```

2. AUTHOR NAMED IN PARENTHESES

When you do not mention the author in a signal phrase, include the author's last name before the page number(s) in the parentheses. Use no punctuation between the author's name and the page number(s).

```
In places, Beauvoir "sees Marxists as believing in
subjectivity as much as existentialists do" (Whitmarsh
63).
```

3. TWO OR THREE AUTHORS

Use all the authors' last names in a phrase or in parentheses.

```
Gortner, Hebrun, and Nicolson maintain that "opinion
leaders" influence other people in an organization because
they are respected, not because they hold high positions
(175).
```

4. FOUR OR MORE AUTHORS

Use the first author's name and *et al.* ("and others"), or name all the authors in a phrase or in parentheses.

```
Similarly, as Belenky, Clinchy, Goldberger, and Tarule
assert, examining the lives of women expands our
understanding of human development (7).
```

5. ORGANIZATION AS AUTHOR

Give the full name of a corporate author if it is brief, or, if it is long, give a shortened form in a phrase or in parentheses.

```
In fact, one of the leading foundations in the field of
higher education supports the recent proposals for
community-run public schools (Carnegie Corporation 45).
```

6. UNKNOWN AUTHOR

Use the full title of the work if it is brief, or, if it is long, give a shortened version in a phrase or in parentheses.

```
"Hype," by one analysis, is "an artificially engendered
atmosphere of hysteria" ("Today's Marketplace" 51).
```

7. AUTHOR OF TWO OR MORE WORKS

If your list of works cited has more than one work by the same author, include a shortened version of the title in question in a phrase or in parentheses.

```
Gardner presents readers with their own silliness through

his description of a "pointless, ridiculous monster,

crouched in the shadows, stinking of dead men, murdered

children, and martyred cows" (Grendel 2).
```

8. TWO OR MORE AUTHORS WITH THE SAME LAST NAME

Always include the authors' first *and* last names in the signal phrases or in the parenthetical citations for those works.

```
Children will learn to write if they are allowed to

choose their own subjects, James Britton asserts, citing

the Schools Council study of the 1960s (37-42).
```

9. MULTIVOLUME WORK

Note the volume number first and then the page number(s), with a colon and one space between them.

```
Modernist writers prized experimentation and gradually

even sought to blur the line between poetry and prose,

according to Forster (3: 150).
```

If you name only one volume of the work in your list of works cited, you need include only the page number in the parentheses.

10. LITERARY WORK

Because literary works are often available in many different editions, cite the page number(s) from the edition you used followed by a semicolon and, in addition, give other identifying information that will lead readers to the passage in any edition. Indicate the act and/or scene in a play (37; sc. 1). For a novel, indicate the part or chapter (175; ch. 4).

```
Resisting gossip, Wharton's character Lily says, "What is

truth? Where a woman is concerned, it's the story that's

easiest to believe" (215; bk. 2, ch. 4).
```

For poems, cite the part (if there is one) and line(s), separated by periods. If you are citing only line numbers, use the word *line(s)* in the first reference (lines 33–34).

```
On dying, Whitman speculates "All goes onward and
outward, nothing collapses, / And to die is different
from what anyone supposed, and luckier" (6.129-30).
```

For verse plays, give only the act, scene, and line numbers, separated by periods.

```
As Macbeth begins, the witches greet Banquo as "Lesser
than Macbeth, and greater" (1.3.65).
```

11. WORK IN AN ANTHOLOGY

For an essay, short story, or other piece of prose reprinted in an anthology, use the name of the author of the work, not the editor of the anthology, but use the page number(s) from the anthology.

```
Narratives of captivity play a major role in early
writing by women in the United States, as demonstrated by
Silko (219).
```

12. BIBLE

Identify quotations by chapter and verse (John 3:16). Spell out the names of books mentioned in your text. In a parenthetical citation, use an abbreviation for books with names of five or more letters (*Gen.* for *Genesis*). If you use the King James Version, you do not need to include a works-cited entry.

13. INDIRECT SOURCE

Use the abbreviation *qtd. in* to indicate that you are quoting from someone else's report of a conversation, interview, letter, or the like.

```
As Arthur Miller says, "When somebody is destroyed
everybody finally contributes to it, but in Willy's case,
the end product would be virtually the same" (qtd. in
Martin and Meyer 375).
```

14. TWO OR MORE SOURCES IN THE SAME CITATION

Separate the information with semicolons.

```
Some economists recommend that employment be redefined to
include unpaid domestic labor (Clark 148; Nevins 39).
```

15. ENTIRE WORK OR ONE-PAGE ARTICLE

Include the reference in the text without any page numbers or parentheses.

```
Thomas Hardy's tragic vision is given full vent in his
Jude the Obscure.
```

16. WORK WITHOUT PAGE NUMBERS

If a work has no page numbers or is only one page long, you may omit the page number. If a work uses paragraph numbers instead, use the abbreviation *par(s)*.

```
Whitman considered African American speech "a source of a
native grand opera" in the words of Ellison (par. 13).
```

17. NONPRINT OR ELECTRONIC SOURCE

Give enough information in a signal phrase or parenthetical citation for readers to locate the source in the list of works cited. Usually give the author or title under which you list the source.

```
Kahlo is seated with a Judas doll, identified in the film
Portrait of an Artist: Frida Kahlo as a papier-mâché doll
stuffed with firecrackers to be exploded on the day
before Easter.
```

46

MLA Style for Explanatory and Bibliographic Notes

MLA style allows explanatory notes for information or commentary that does not readily fit into your text but is needed for clarification or further explanation. In addition, MLA style permits bibliographic notes for information about a source. Use superscript numbers in the text to refer readers to the notes, which may appear as endnotes (typed under the heading *Notes* on a separate page after the text but before the list of works cited) or as footnotes at the bottom of the page.

1. SUPERSCRIPT NUMBER IN TEXT

Stewart emphasizes the existence of social contacts in Hawthorne's life so that the audience will accept a different Hawthorne, one more attuned to modern times than the figure in Woodberry.[3]

2. NOTE

[3] Woodberry does, however, show that Hawthorne was often an unsociable individual. He emphasizes the seclusion of Hawthorne's mother, who separated herself from her family after the death of her husband, often even taking meals alone (28). Woodberry seems to imply that Mrs. Hawthorne's isolation rubbed off onto her son.

47

MLA Style for a List of Works Cited

A list of works cited is an alphabetical list of the sources you have referred to in your essay. (If your instructor asks you to list everything you have read as background, call the list *Works Consulted.*) Here are some guidelines for preparing such a list.

- Start your list on a separate page after the text of your essay and any notes.
- Continue the consecutive numbering of pages.
- Type the heading *Works Cited*, neither underlined nor in quotation marks, centered one inch from the top of the page.
- Start each entry flush with the left margin; indent subsequent lines one-half inch (or five spaces if you are using a typewriter.) Double-space the entire list.
- List sources alphabetically by author's last name. If the author is unknown, alphabetize the source by the first major word of the title.

Books

The basic entry for a book includes the following elements:

- *Author*. List the author by last name first, followed by a comma and the first name. End with a period.
- *Title*. Underline the title and subtitle; capitalize all major words. End with a period.
- *Publication information*. Give the city of publication; then add a colon, a space, and a shortened version of the publisher's name (*St. Martin's* for *St. Martin's Press, Inc.; Harcourt* for *Harcourt Brace;* or *Oxford UP* for *Oxford University Press*). End with a comma, the year of publication, and a period.

1. ONE AUTHOR

Herrera, Hayden. <u>Frida: A Biography of Frida Kahlo</u>. New
York: Harper, 1983.

2. TWO OR THREE AUTHORS

Give the first author listed on the title page, last name first; then list the name(s) of the other author(s) in regular order, with a comma between authors and an *and* before the last one.

Appleby, Joyce, Lynn Hunt, and Margaret Jacob. <u>Telling</u>
<u>the Truth about History</u>. New York: Norton, 1994.

3. FOUR OR MORE AUTHORS

Give the first author listed on the title page, last name first, followed by a comma and *et al.* ("and others"), or list all the names.

Belenky, Mary Field, Blythe Clinchy, Jill Goldberger, and
Nancy Tarule. <u>Women's Ways of Knowing</u>. New York:
Basic, 1986.

4. ORGANIZATION AS AUTHOR

Give the name of the group listed on the title page as the author, even if the same group published the book.

American Chemical Society. <u>Handbook for Authors of Papers</u>
<u>in the American Chemical Society Publications</u>.
Washington: American Chemical Soc., 1978.

5. UNKNOWN AUTHOR

Begin the entry with the title, and list the work alphabetically by the first major word of the title after any initial *a, an,* or *the.*

```
The New York Times Atlas of the World. New York: New York
     Times Books, 1980.
```

6. TWO OR MORE BOOKS BY THE SAME AUTHOR(S)

Arrange the entries alphabetically by title. Include the name(s) of the author(s) in the first entry, but in subsequent entries use three hyphens followed by a period.

```
Lorde, Audre. A Burst of Light. Ithaca: Firebrand, 1988.
---. Sister Outsider. Trumansburg: Crossing, 1984.
```

If you cite a work by one author who is also listed as the first coauthor of another work you cite, list the single-author work first, and repeat the author's name in the entry for the coauthored work. Also repeat the author's name if you cite a work in which that author is listed as the first of a different set of coauthors. In other words, use three hyphens only when the work is by *exactly* the same author(s) as the previous entry.

7. EDITOR(S)

Treat an editor as an author, but add a comma and *ed.* (or *eds.*).

```
Wall, Cheryl A., ed. Changing Our Own Words: Essays on
     Criticism, Theory, and Writing by Black Women. New
     Brunswick: Rutgers UP, 1989.
```

8. AUTHOR AND EDITOR

If you have cited the body of the text, begin with the author's name. Then list the editor, introduced by *Ed.* ("Edited by"), after the title.

```
James, Henry. Portrait of a Lady. Ed. Leon Edel. Boston:
     Houghton, 1963.
```

If you have cited the editor's contribution, begin the entry with the editor's name followed by a comma and *ed.* Then list the author's name, introduced by *By,* after the title.

Edel, Leon, ed. <u>Portrait of a Lady</u>. By Henry James.
    Boston: Houghton, 1963.

9. SELECTION IN AN ANTHOLOGY OR CHAPTER IN A BOOK WITH AN EDITOR

List the author(s) of the selection or chapter; its title; the title of the
book in which the selection or chapter appears (underlined); *Ed.* and the
name(s) of the editor(s) in regular order; the publication information;
and the inclusive page numbers of the selection.

Gordon, Mary. "The Parable of the Cave." <u>The Writer on
    Her Work</u>. Ed. Janet Sternburg. New York: Norton,
    1980. 27-32.

If the selection was originally published in a periodical and you are
asked to supply information for this original source, use the following
format. *Rpt.* is the abbreviation for *Reprinted*.

Didion, Joan. "Why I Write." <u>New York Times Book Review</u>.
    9 Dec. 1976: 22. Rpt. in <u>The Writer on Her Work</u>. Ed.
    Janet Sternburg. New York: Norton, 1980. 3-16.

For inclusive page numbers up to 99, note all digits in the second number. For numbers above 99, note only the last two digits and any others
that change in the second number (115-18, 1378-79, 296-301).

10. TWO OR MORE ITEMS FROM AN ANTHOLOGY

Include the anthology itself in your list of works cited.

Donalson, Melvin, ed. <u>Cornerstones: An Anthology of
    African American Literature</u>. New York: St. Martin's,
    1996.

Then list each selection by its author and title, followed by a cross-
reference to the anthology.

Baker, Houston A., Jr. "There Is No More Beautiful Way."
    Donalson 856-63.

Ellison, Ralph. "What America Would Be Like without
    Blacks." Donalson 737-41.

11. TRANSLATION

Begin the entry with the author's name, and give the translator's name, preceded by *Trans.* ("Translated by"), after the title.

```
Zamora, Martha. Frida Kahlo: The Brush of Anguish.
     Trans. Marilyn Sode Smith. San Francisco: Chronicle,
     1990.
```

12. EDITION OTHER THAN THE FIRST

Add the information, in abbreviated form, after the title.

```
Kelly, Alfred H., Winfred A. Harbison, and Herman Belz.
     The American Constitution: Its Origins and
     Development. 6th ed. New York: Norton, 1983.
```

13. ONE VOLUME OF A MULTIVOLUME WORK

Give the volume number after the title, and list the number of volumes in the complete work after the date, using the abbreviations *Vol.* and *vols.*

```
Foner, Philip S., and Ronald L. Lewis, eds. The Black
     Worker. Vol. 3. Philadelphia: Lippincott, 1980. 8
     vols.
```

14. TWO OR MORE VOLUMES OF A MULTIVOLUME WORK

If you cite two or more volumes of a multivolume work, give the number of volumes in the complete work after the title, using the abbreviation *vols.*

```
Foner, Philip S., and Ronald L. Lewis, eds. The Black
     Worker. 8 vols. Philadelphia: Lippincott, 1980.
```

15. PREFACE, FOREWORD, INTRODUCTION, OR AFTERWORD

List the author of the item, the item title, the title of the book, and author. List the inclusive page numbers at the end of the entry.

```
Schlesinger, Arthur M., Jr. Introduction. Pioneer Women:
     Voices from the Kansas Frontier. By Joanna L.
     Stratton. New York: Simon, 1981. 11-15.
```

16. ARTICLE IN A REFERENCE WORK

List the author of the article, if known. If no author is identified, begin with the title. For a well-known encyclopedia, just note the edition and date. If the entries in the reference work are in alphabetical order, you need not give volume or page numbers.

```
Johnson, Peder J. "Concept Learning." Encyclopedia of
     Education. 1971.
"Traquair, Sir John Stewart." Encyclopaedia Britannica.
     11th ed. 1911.
```

17. BOOK THAT IS PART OF A SERIES

Cite the series name as it appears on the title page, followed by any series number.

```
Moss, Beverly J., ed. Literacy across Communities.
     Written Language Series 2. Cresskill: Hampton,
     1994.
```

18. REPUBLICATION

To cite a modern edition of an older book, add the original date, followed by a period, after the title.

```
Scott, Walter. Kenilworth. 1821. New York: Dodd, 1956.
```

19. GOVERNMENT DOCUMENT

Begin with the author, if identified. Otherwise, start with the name of the government, followed by the agency and any subdivision. Use abbreviations if they can be readily understood. Then give the title, and underline it. For congressional documents, cite the number, session, and house; the type (report, resolution, document), in abbreviated form; and number of the material. End with publication information; the publisher is often the Government Printing Office (GPO).

```
United States. Cong. House. Report of the Joint
     Subcommittee on Reconstruction. 39th Cong., 1st sess.
     H. Rept. 30. 1865. New York: Arno, 1969.
U.S. Bureau of the Census. Historical Statistics of the
     United States, Colonial Times to 1870. Washington:
     GPO, 1975.
```

20. PAMPHLET

Treat a pamphlet as you would a book.

<u>Why Is Central America a Conflict Area?</u> Opposing
Viewpoints Pamphlets. St. Paul: Greenhaven, 1984.

21. PUBLISHED PROCEEDINGS OF A CONFERENCE

Treat proceedings as a book, adding any necessary information about the conference after the title.

Martin, John Steven, and Christine Mason Sutherland, eds.
<u>Proceedings of the Canadian Society for the History</u>
<u>of Rhetoric</u>. Calgary, Alberta: Canadian Soc. for the
History of Rhetoric, 1986.

22. PUBLISHER'S IMPRINT

If a book was published by a publisher's imprint (indicated on the title page), hyphenate the imprint and the publisher's name.

Rose, Phyllis. <u>Parallel Lives: Five Victorian Marriages</u>.
New York: Vintage-Random, 1984.

23. TITLE WITHIN A TITLE

Do not underline the title of a book within the title of a book you are citing. Underline and enclose in quotation marks the title of a short work within a book title.

Gilbert, Stuart. <u>James Joyce's</u> Ulysses. New York:
Vintage-Random, 1955.

Periodicals

The basic entry for a periodical includes the following elements:

- *Author.* List the author's last name first, followed by a comma and the first name. End with a period.
- *Article title.* Enclose the complete title in quotation marks, and capitalize all major words. End with a period inside the closing quotation marks.
- *Publication information.* Give the periodical title (excluding any initial *a, an,* or *the*), underlined and with all major words capitalized; the volume num-

ber and, if appropriate, issue number; and the date of publication. For journals, list the year in parentheses, followed by a colon, a space, and the inclusive page numbers. For magazines and newspapers, list the month (abbreviated, except for May, June, and July) or the day and month before the year, and do not use parentheses. For inclusive page numbers, note all digits for numbers 1 to 99, and note only the last two digits and any others that change for numbers above 99 (134–45, 198–201). End with a period.

24. ARTICLE IN A JOURNAL PAGINATED BY VOLUME

Follow the title of the publication with the volume number in arabic numerals.

Norris, Margot. "Narration under a Blindfold: Reading

Joyce's 'Clay.'" PMLA 102 (1987): 206-15.

25. ARTICLE IN A JOURNAL PAGINATED BY ISSUE

Follow the volume number with a period and the issue number.

Lofty, John. "The Politics at Modernism's Funeral."

Canadian Journal of Political and Social Theory 6.3

(1987): 89-96.

26. ARTICLE IN A MONTHLY MAGAZINE

Put the month (or months, hyphenated) before the year. Separate the date and page number(s) with a colon.

Weiss, Philip. "The Book Thief: A True Tale of

Bibliomania." Harper's Jan. 1994: 37-56.

27. ARTICLE IN A WEEKLY MAGAZINE

Include the day, month, and year in that order, with no commas between them.

Van Biema, David. "Parodies Regained." Time 21 Mar.

1994: 46.

28. ARTICLE IN A NEWSPAPER

Give the name of the newspaper, underlined, as it appears on the front page but without any initial *a*, *an*, or *the*. Add the city in brackets after the name if it is not part of the title. Then give the date and the edition if one is listed, and add a colon. Follow the colon with a space, the section number or letter (if given), and then the page number(s). If the article appears on discontinuous pages, give the first page, followed by a plus sign.

```
Markoff, John. "Cyberspace's Most Wanted: Hacker Eludes
     F.B.I. Pursuit." New York Times 4 July 1994, late
     ed.: A1+.
Walsh, Molly. "Tightened Security Offers Peace of Mind."
     Burlington Free Press 5 Aug. 1996: A1.
```

29. EDITORIAL OR LETTER TO THE EDITOR

Use the label *Editorial* or *Letter,* neither underlined nor in quotation marks, after the title or, if there is no title, after the author's name.

```
Magee, Doug. "Soldier's Home." Editorial. Nation 26 Mar.
     1988: 400-01.
```

30. UNSIGNED ARTICLE

Begin with the article title, alphabetizing the entry according to the first word after any initial *a, an,* or *the.*

```
"The Odds of March." Time 15 Apr. 1985: 20+.
```

31. REVIEW

List the reviewer's name and the title of the review, if any, followed by *Rev. of,* not underlined, and the title and author or director of the work reviewed. Then add the publication information for the periodical in which the review appears.

```
Rafferty, Terrence. "Lover-in-Chief." Rev. of The American
     President, dir. Rob Reiner. New Yorker 20 Nov. 1995:
     116-18.
Solinger, Rickie. "Unsafe for Women." Rev. of Next Time,
     She'll Be Dead: Battering and How to Stop It, by
     Ann Jones. New York Times Book Review 20 Mar. 1994:
     16.
```

Electronic sources

Even as electronic sources of information such as bibliographies on CD-ROM and electronic journals accessed through the Internet become more and more important for researchers, documenting these sources remains tricky. Some electronic documents are fluid, changing continually without any notification, making it difficult to cite a "completed" work. Others are more fixed and can be cited much like a book. The MLA guidelines call for much detail, from publication medium to information about printed versions, but they say as well that "if you cannot find some of the information required—for example, the vendor's name—cite what is available."

32. CD-ROM, PERIODICALLY REVISED

Include the author's name, if given, and publication information for print source, if any: title; volume and issue, if appropriate; date; and page numbers. (If the material is not available in print, list only the title and, if given, the date.) Also include the title of the electronic database medium (CD-ROM), name of the company producing the CD-ROM, and electronic publication date: month and year, if possible.

> Natchez, Gladys. "Frida Kahlo and Diego Rivera: The
> Transformation of Catastrophe to Creativity."
> Psychotherapy-Patient 4.1 (1987): 153-74. PsycLIT.
> CD-ROM. SilverPlatter. Nov. 1994.

33. CD-ROM, DISKETTE, OR MAGNETIC TAPE, SINGLE ISSUE

Cite this kind of electronic source, which is *not* regularly updated, much like a book, but add the medium.

> "Communion." The Oxford English Dictionary. 2nd ed.
> CD-ROM. Oxford: Oxford UP, 1992.

34. COMMERCIAL ONLINE DATABASE SERVICE

Some documents and data from online database services will also exist in print form; some will not. Include the publication information: title; volume and issue, if appropriate; date; and page numbers. (If the material is not available in print, list only the title of the material and, if given, the date.) Include the title of the database, medium

(Online), name of the service, and date of access: day, month, and year.

> Johnson, Lawrence B. "Television Grows a Brain." <u>New York</u>
>
>   <u>Times</u> 16 May 1996, late ed.: C1+. <u>New York Times</u>
>
>   <u>Online</u>. Online. America Online. 30 Aug. 1996.

Internet sources

Setting guidelines for regulating and using the information available through the Internet is an ongoing process. While the preceding guidelines for online computer services are derived from the *MLA Handbook for Writers of Research Papers*, the following formats—adapted from the MLA guidelines—are from *Online! A Reference Guide for Using Internet Sources*, by Andrew Harnack and Eugene Kleppinger.

The basic entry for most sources you access via the Internet should include the following elements:

- *Author.* Include the author's name (and email address, in angle brackets), if given, with last name first.
- *Title.* Enclose the title of the document or subject line of the message in quotation marks. End with a period inside the closing quotation marks.
- *Publication date.* Include, if available.
- *Address.* Include the URL, in angle brackets, or the path followed to locate the site or file.
- *Date of access.* End with the date of access, in parentheses, followed by a period.

35. WORLD WIDE WEB SITE

Begin with the author's name, if known. Otherwise, start with the title of the document, in quotation marks, then the title of the complete work, underlined. Include the date of publication or last revision, if known; URL, in angle brackets; and date of access, in parentheses.

> Mullins, Brighde. "Introduction to Robert Hass." <u>Readings</u>
>
>   <u>in Contemporary Poetry at Dia Center for the Arts</u>.
>
>   November 10, 1995. <http://www.diacenter.org/prg
>
>   /poetry/95-96/interhass.html> (24 April 1997).

36. LINKAGE DATA

To cite a file or document accessed through a link with a source document, provide information on both the cited document and the source.

After the title of the document, use the abbreviation *Lkd*. and give the title of the source document to which it is linked, underlined. Give additional linkage details, if applicable, indicated by *at*. End with the source document's URL, in angle brackets, and the date of access, in parentheses.

> Williams, Terry Tempest. "The Politics of Place." Lkd.
>
>   Insight & Outlook: A Program of Ideas, at
>
>   "Transcripts." <http://www.west.net/~insight/>
>
>   (1 May 1997).

37. FTP (FILE TRANSFER PROTOCOL) SITE

After the title of the document, include the date of publication, if available. Then give either the URL in angle brackets or the abbreviation *ftp* and the address of the FTP site, with no closing punctuation, followed by a space and the full path to follow to find the document, with no closing punctuation. End with the date of access, in parentheses.

> Altar, Ted W. "Vitamin B12 and Vegans." 14 Jan. 1993. ftp
>
>   wiretap.spies.com Library/Article/Food/b12.txt
>
>   (28 May 1996).

38. TELNET SITE

Provide the author's name, if known; the title of the document, if shown, in quotation marks; the title of the full work, if applicable, underlined; and the date of publication. Include the word *telnet* and the complete telnet address, with no closing punctuation, and directions to access the publication. End with the date of access, in parentheses.

> Aquatic Conservation Network. "About the Aquatic
>
>   Conservation Network." National Capital Freenet.
>
>   telnet freenet.carleton.ca login as guest, go acn,
>
>   press 1 (28 May 1996).

39. GOPHER SITE

Give the author's name, if known; the title of the document, in quotation marks; date of publication, if known; and any print publication data, underlined where appropriate. Then give either the URL in angle brackets or the word *gopher*, the site name, and the gopher path followed to access information, with slashes to indicate menu selections.

Korn, Peter. "How Much Does Breast Cancer Really Cost?"

    Published in <u>Self</u> Oct. 1994. <gopher://

    nysernet.org:70/00/BCIC/Sources/SELF/94/how-much>

    (5 May 1997).

40. LISTSERV MESSAGE

Provide the author's name and email address, in angle brackets. The subject line from the posting, in quotation marks, and the date of publication are followed by the address of the listserv, in angle brackets. End with the date of access, in parentheses.

Lackey, Noel. <eeinly@ath.ericsson.se> "From Clare

    to Here." 30 Jan. 1995. <nanci@world.std.com>

    (1 May 1997).

To cite a file archived at a listserv or Web address, after the publication date, provide the address of the listserv, in angle brackets; the address for the list's archive, indicated by *via*, in angle brackets; and the date of access, in parentheses.

Lackey, Noel. <eeinly@ath.ericsson.se> "From Clare

    to Here." 30 Jan. 1995. <nanci@world.std.com>

    via <http://www.rahul.net/frankf/Nancy/archives

    /95130.html> (1 May 1997).

41. NEWSGROUP MESSAGE

Include the author's name, if known, and email address, in angle brackets. If the author's name is unknown, cite the email address first. Next, give the subject line from the posting, in quotation marks; the date of publication; the name of the newsgroup, in angle brackets; and the date of access, in parentheses.

Sand, Paul. <psand@unh.edu> "Java Disabled by Default in

    Linux Netscape." 20 Apr. 1996. <keokuk.unh.edu> (10

    May 1996).

42. EMAIL

The author's email address follows the name, in angle brackets. Give the subject line from the posting, in quotation marks, and the date of publication, followed by the kind of communication (Personal email, Distribution list). End with the date of access, in parentheses.

> Talbot, Casey J. <ctalbot@pop.interport.net> "Do This." 26
>
>   Jan. 1996. Personal email. (10 May 1996).

43. SYNCHRONOUS COMMUNICATION

To cite postings in MOOs, MUDs, and IRCs, provide the speaker's name and site name; the title of the event, if appropriate, in quotation marks; and its date. List the type of communication (Group discussion, Personal interview), if necessary. End with the URL in angle brackets or command line directions, and the date of access, in parentheses.

> LambdaMOO. "Seminar Discussion on Netiquette."
>
>   28 May 1996. <telnet://lambda.parc.xerox.edu:8888
>
>   (28 May 1996).

Other sources

44. UNPUBLISHED DISSERTATION

Enclose the title in quotation marks. Add the identification *Diss.*, the name of the university or professional school, a comma, and the year the dissertation was accepted.

> LeCourt, Donna. "The Self in Motion: The Status of the
>
>   (Student) Subject in Composition Studies." Diss. Ohio
>
>   State U, 1993.

45. PUBLISHED DISSERTATION

Cite a published dissertation as a book, adding the identification *Diss.* and the name of the university. If the dissertation was published by University Microfilms International, add *Ann Arbor: UMI*, and the year, and list the UMI number at the end of the entry.

> Botts, Roderic C. Influences in the Teaching of English,
>
>   1917-1935: An Illusion of Progress. Diss.
>
>   Northeastern U, 1970. Ann Arbor: UMI, 1971.
>
>   71-1799.

46. ARTICLE FROM A MICROFORM

Treat the article as you would a printed work, but in addition list the name of the microform and information for locating it.

> Sharpe, Lora. "A Quilter's Tribute." <u>Boston Globe</u> 25 Mar.
>
>   1989: 13. <u>Newsbank: Social Relations</u> 12 (1989): fiche
>
>   6, grids B4-6.

47. INTERVIEW

List the person interviewed, and then list the title, if the interview has one, in quotation marks (or underlined if it is a complete work). If the interview has no title, use the label *Interview*, and identify the source. If you were the interviewer, use the label *Telephone interview, Personal interview,* or *Internet interview,* and give the date it took place.

> Schorr, Daniel. Interview. <u>Weekend Edition</u>. Natl. Public
>
>   Radio. WEVO, Concord. 26 Mar. 1988.
>
> Merget, Astrid. Telephone interview. 16 Mar. 1994.

48. LETTER

If the letter was published, cite it as a selection in a book.

> Frost, Robert. "Letter to Editor of the <u>Independent</u>." 28
>
>   Mar. 1894. <u>Selected Letters of Robert Frost</u>. Ed.
>
>   Lawrance Thompson. New York: Holt, 1964. 19.

If the correspondence was sent to you, follow the form below.

> Moller, Willie. Letter to the author. 10 Sept. 1994.

49. FILM OR VIDEOTAPE

Start with the title, underlined; then name the director, the company distributing the film or videotape, and the date. Other contributors, such as writers or actors, may follow the director's name. If you cite a particular person's work, start with that person's name.

> <u>The Night of the Hunter</u>. Dir. Charles Laughton. Perf.
>
>   Robert Mitchum, Shelley Winters, and Lillian Gish.
>
>   United Artists, 1955.

50. TELEVISION OR RADIO PROGRAM

List the title of the program, underlined, with details (such as narrator, director, actors) after the title, as necessary. Identify the network, local station and city, and broadcast date. If you cite a particular episode, include its title, in quotation marks, before the program's title. If you cite a particular person's work, begin the entry with that person's name.

Hill Street Blues. Writ. Michael Kozoll and Stephen
     Bochco. Perf. Daniel J. Travanti, Joe Spano, and
     Charles Haid. NBC. WNBC, New York. 15 Jan. 1981.

51. RECORDING

Your research interest determines whether the name of the composer, artist, or conductor precedes the title of the recording, which is underlined, or the title of the composition, which is not underlined. If you are not using a compact disc, give the medium before the manufacturer's name. End with the name of the manufacturer and the date.

Grieg, Edvard. Concerto in A-minor, op. 16. Cond. Eugene
     Ormandy. Philadelphia Orch. RCA, 1989.
Velvet Underground. The Velvet Underground and Nicò. LP.
     MGM-Verve, 1967.

52. WORK OF ART

List the artist followed by the work's title, underlined. Add the name of the museum or other location, a comma, and the city.

Kahlo, Frida. Self-Portrait with Cropped Hair. Museum of
     Modern Art, New York.

53. LECTURE OR SPEECH

List the speaker, the title in quotation marks, the name of the sponsoring institution or group, the place, and the date. If the speech is untitled, use a descriptive label (*Lecture, Keynote speech,* etc.).

Stern, Virginia. "Sir Stephen Powle as Adventurer in
     the Virginia Company of London." Seminar on the
     Renaissance. Columbia University. New York, 15 Oct.
     1985.

54. PERFORMANCE

List the title, other appropriate details (such as composer, writer, director), place, and date. If you cite a particular person, begin the entry with that person's name.

Frankie and Johnny in the Clair de Lune. By Terrence

McNally. Dir. Paul Benedict. Westside Arts Theater,

New York. 18 Jan. 1988.

55. MAP OR CHART ·

Cite a map or chart as you would a book with an unknown author, adding the label *Map* or *Chart*.

Pennsylvania. Map. Chicago: Rand, 1985.

56. CARTOON

List the cartoonist's name, the title of the cartoon (if it has one), the word *Cartoon*, and the usual publication information.

Trudeau, Garry. "Doonesbury." Cartoon. Philadelphia

Inquirer 9 Mar. 1988: 37.

57. ADVERTISEMENT

Name the item or organization being advertised, add the word *Advertisement*, and then supply the standard information about the source where the ad appears.

NordicTrack. Advertisement. Cooking Light Jan.-Feb. 1995: 9.

48

A Sample Research Essay, MLA Style

In preparing the following essay, Daniel Taffe followed the MLA guidelines described in the preceding chapters. In order to annotate this essay, we have reproduced it in a smaller space than you would have on a standard (8½- by 11-inch) sheet of paper. The lines shown here are thus considerably shorter than the ones in your essay would be.

Current MLA style does not require a title page; see p. 249 for guidelines on putting your name and title and other information at the top of the first page.

Frida Kahlo: More Than a Life

Heading centered one-third down the page

by Daniel Taffe

Writer's name centered two double spaces below the title

English 231

Professor Connors

15 May 1996

Course number centered two double spaces below the writer's name

Professor's name and the date centered directly below the course number

Writer's last
name and page
number in upper
right-hand corner

1″   Taffe 1

Title centered

Introduction
invites readers to
learn about Kahlo,
provides
background

Visual used,
labeled Fig. 1

Facts cited—
author named
in citation

Major source
introduced

Frida Kahlo: More Than a Life

Who is Frida Kahlo?
Ten or fifteen years
ago, few people would
have known. Today,
however, Kahlo is being
recognized as a major
figure in twentieth-
century art. Her
paintings, primarily
self-portraits, continue
to gain popularity in
the United States and in
her native Mexico. My Birth,
for example, was recently purchased by
Madonna, and Self-Portrait with Loose Hair
sold in 1991 for $1.65 million, a record
price for any Latin American artist (Plagens
et al. 54).

Fig. 1. "Self
Portrait," Frida
Kahlo, from The
Original Frida
Kahlo Home Page

Much of the scholarship on Kahlo and her
art has been produced by Hayden Herrera,
author of Frida: A Biography of Frida Kahlo
and numerous periodical articles about the
artist. Indeed, it is nearly impossible to
read anything about Kahlo without encountering
a reference to Herrera's research. Although
her biography was published almost thirty
years after Kahlo's death, her information

Taffe 2

comes, as Angela Carter notes in her review, from sources remarkably close to the subject. In addition to Kahlo's journal, numerous letters, and medical records, Herrera was able to consult a number of lovers, friends, and relatives, as well as former wives of Kahlo's husband, the artist Diego Rivera (33).

Herrera's interpretation of Kahlo's painting is primarily biographical, as is that of nearly every other Kahlo critic. For example, Herrera describes Kahlo's work as "autobiography in paint" and goes on to label this autobiographical work original, specific, and personal (xii). While this view is certainly not incorrect, it seems limited in important ways. For Frida Kahlo's unique style results not only from autobiographical influences but also from her knowledge of earlier European art, traditional Christian imagery, and Mexican culture.

The autobiographical aspect of Kahlo's work is undoubtedly important and thus worth examining. Her life was eventful, exciting, and often painful. Born in 1907 in a suburb of Mexico City, she was stricken with polio at age six. After a nearly complete recovery, she entered the National Preparatory School to pursue medical training. Tragedy struck again

Annotations (right margin):

Review of source cited

Paraphrase—author named in signal phrase and page numbers identified in parentheses at end of the paraphrase

Notes the biographical focus of most Kahlo criticism

Brief quotation incorporated into text—author named in signal phrase and page numbers identified in parentheses at end of the paraphrase

Explicit thesis stated

First major point: establishes autobiographical elements in Kahlo's work

Subpoint introduces events of Kahlo's life

Taffe 3

Details and
examples
support subpoint

in 1925, however, when a bus she was riding on
was crushed by a trolley car. As Carter
describes:

Long quotation
set off—ellipses
indicate
omissions

> She almost died, and hurt herself so
> badly she never got over it. Her
> spine, collarbone, pelvis and a
> number of ribs were broken; her
> right leg was shattered, her left
> foot crushed; and . . . the steel
> handrail of the bus . . . pierced
> her left side. (33)

While convalescing, Kahlo began to paint,
and soon painting became her career. A few
years later, in 1929, she married Diego
Rivera, who was twice her age and already a
well-known muralist. Their relationship was
volatile; they fought when together and were
miserable when apart. Both carried on many
well-publicized affairs, and they divorced in
1939 only to remarry in 1940. Throughout the
years, Kahlo continued to suffer medical
problems stemming from the accident. After
many operations, in 1953 her right leg was
amputated below the knee. She was devastated,
and her health declined rapidly. She died less
than a year later, in 1954.

As Herrera details in her biography, much
of Kahlo's art grows out of these dramatic

Taffe 4

personal experiences. Self-portraits such as
The Broken Column (Herrera, pl. XXVIII),[1] which
portrays Kahlo encased in a steel orthopedic
corset, nails embedded painfully in her body,
her spine replaced with a broken marble
column, and Remembrance of an Open Wound
(fig. 40), in which a seated Kahlo displays a
bandaged left foot and a large gash on her
left thigh, refer to the physical aftermath of
her accident.

Likewise, The Two Fridas (pl. XIV) and
A Few Small Nips (pl. VIII) directly depict
the pain of her relationship with Rivera. The
first shows two self-portraits, one in Victorian
dress and the other in the Tehuana (Mexican
peasant) costume that Kahlo often wore. Each
Frida has her heart exposed, and an artery
connects the two. The artery originates at a
picture of Rivera held by the Tehuana Frida,
thus linking the lives of the three. But the
Victorian Frida's heart is broken because she
does not have Rivera. She holds the other,
open end of the artery in her hand and tries
to pinch it shut with medical tweezers, but
the red blood drips onto her dress. This
portrait provides a graphic example of the
connection Kahlo felt to Rivera and of her

Explanatory note
indicates source
of paintings

Second subpoint
builds on first
major point by
relating details of
Kahlo's physical
pain to particular
paintings

Examines two
works in detail
for their autobio-
graphical
elements

Third subpoint
builds on first
major point by
relating details of
Kahlo's personal
relationship with
her husband to
particular
paintings

Detailed
description of
one painting

devastating sense of loss because of his
infidelity.

Shortly after a separation precipitated
by Rivera's affair with her sister, Kahlo
completed <u>A Few Small Nips</u> (pl. VIII). The
work is her most violent, the clearest
expression of the pain she suffered in her
marriage. The painting, as Martha Zamora
notes, is based on a true story: a man stabbed
his girlfriend to death and when confronted
with the murder said, "But I only gave her a
few small nips" (50). Kahlo's painting
portrays a young woman lying in bed, naked but
for one sock and shoe. Her body is covered
with bleeding gashes, and her face has a pale,
almost bluish tint; she is clearly dead.
Splashes of blood spatter the bed, the floor,
even the frame of the painting. And they
spatter the man standing over her. A ribbon
bearing the words "<u>unos cuantos piquetitos</u>"
("a few small nips") is held at the top of the
painting by two birds, one black and one
white. Although not exact likenesses, the
man's features suggest that he represents
Rivera, and the woman's suggest that she is
Kahlo.

Paraphrase and
brief quotation—
author identified
in signal phrase

Detailed descrip-
tion of a second
painting

Taffe 6

If Kahlo's work is often personal, however, it is not untutored or untaught. In fact, Kahlo was clearly familiar with, and also clearly influenced by, earlier art, including traditional Christian and Mexican imagery (Zamora 110). Indeed, it would be surprising, given her background, if she had not been acquainted with a wide range of art, both European and Mexican. Kahlo was well educated--the National Preparatory School she attended spawned some of Mexico's greatest minds. Herrera identifies Kahlo's father as a scholarly European who emigrated to Mexico, where he became a photographer (5-7), and says that Kahlo studied her father's collection of German literature and philosophy books (19) as well as many art books, particularly those reproducing Italian Renaissance paintings (64). And Zamora notes that Kahlo referred to her first self-portrait, given to a close friend, as "your Botticelli" (110). Her relationship with Rivera and her travels in Europe no doubt served further to broaden her awareness of contemporary art and its roots in earlier styles and themes.

A careful study of Kahlo's art reveals both stylistic and larger thematic influences on her

Reiteration of thesis and second major point: the influence of earlier art

Source identified in parentheses following a paraphrase. For the original passage and the paraphrased notes on the passage, see p. 280.

Supporting details

Summary of long passage—author named in signal phrase and page numbers identified in parentheses

Second source cited to corroborate main point

Subpoint: the influence of other artists

work. One of her striking conventions is the
use of a stylized facial "mask," like that in
her first self-portrait, <u>Self-Portrait Wearing
a Velvet Dress</u> (pl. I). In this painting, the
mask is simply a blank stare devoid of any
evidence of emotion. As Kahlo sits facing the
viewer, she does not smile, but neither does
she appear overly sad. In many of her later
self-images, however, the mask is streaked by
tears, which, combined with the expressionless
face, tell far more about the subject than
would any realistic expression.

Certainly, there is an autobiographical
basis for the mask; it hides the subject's
pain much as Kahlo hid her pain from her
friends during her life. But as Professor
Richard Honeywell points out, the mask also
suggests the influence of a painting by
Hieronymus Bosch (1450-1516), <u>Bearing of the
Cross</u> (reproduced in Delavoy 59).[2] The masks of
the figures in Bosch's painting, which depicts
Christ being led to the site of his
crucifixion, are horrid grimaces. As Delavoy
explains, Bosch realized that a mask could
"never convey the human quality of a real face
treated expressively" (58). The effect of the

Information from
interview cited

Bibliographic note
acknowledges
help

"Reproduced in"
shows that the
citation is for the
painting, not for
Delavoy's text

Taffe 8

masks is perhaps greater than that of actual
faces, however, because of the horror they
evoke. In much the same way, Kahlo's mask
creates an effect, albeit a different one.
Her mask hides emotion, yet in doing so shows
her pain powerfully.

    Another stylistic influence appears in
Kahlo's use of landscape. In both The Broken
Column and Tree of Hope (pl. XXX), Kahlo's
physical suffering, depicted as cuts in her
chest and back and in the nails embedded in
her flesh, is mirrored in the gouges scarred
into the barren terrain in the backdrop, which
projects an aura of pain and hopelessness.
This use of landscape, according to Honeywell,
is a familiar element in paintings such as
The Triumph of Death by Francesco Traini
(reproduced in Gardner 59), paintings Kahlo
would have undoubtedly seen. Traini's violent,
ragged landscape, featuring tall cliffs
dropping out of sight, augments the power of
his elaborate depiction of several young
aristocrats confronting three corpses.

    Another major influence on Kahlo's work,
religion, provided her with a number of themes
and subjects. Her own religious upbringing was
mixed. Herrera indicates that her mother was

The influence of
Bosch supports
the subpoint

Second stylistic
influence—
Traini's land-
scape supports
the subpoint

Subpoint: the-
matic influence—
religion

devoutly Catholic and her father, "by birth
Jewish," was "by persuasion an atheist" (6);
she says that Kahlo herself, while professing
no organized religion (283), nevertheless
believed in a "vitalistic form of pantheism"
(328). Although most of her religious imagery
is specifically Christian, her most directly

Supporting examples and details

religious subject is <u>Moses</u> (fig. 69), which
Zamora identifies as having been commissioned
by José Domingo Lavin in 1945 (102). A complex
work detailing the birth of its subject, it
resembles in composition Bosch's <u>Garden of
Earthly Delights</u> (reproduced in Delavoy 88-89)
and Traini's <u>The Triumph of Death</u>, both of
which contain many little scenes to help tell
the whole story.

First religious theme—the Last Supper—further supports the subpoint

The story of the Last Supper has been
depicted by many artists, the most famous
version being that of Leonardo da Vinci
(reproduced in Hartt 452-53). In 1940, Kahlo
contributed to this tradition <u>The Wounded
Table</u> (fig. 55), painted after her divorce. As

Film cited by title

Explanation of unfamiliar term provided in parentheses

explained in the film <u>Portrait of an Artist:
Frida Kahlo</u>, it depicts, from left to right, a
young boy and girl (her sister's children), a
Judas doll (a papier-mâché figure stuffed with

Taffe 10

firecrackers to be exploded on the day before
Easter), Kahlo, a skeleton, and a young deer.
Kahlo thus occupies the central position of
Jesus, with a symbol of betrayal on her right,
of death on her left, and of innocence at
either end of the table. Blood on the floor
underneath her skirt reveals that she has
already been wounded.

It is not surprising that another
Christian theme explored by Kahlo is martyrdom,
particularly the martyrdom of Saint Sebastian.
A popular Renaissance subject, Sebastian's
death was depicted by, among others, Antonio
del Pollaiuolo and Antonello da Messina, both
in 1475. In both portrayals, Sebastian has
been tied to a post and shot full of arrows.
Kahlo uses the Saint Sebastian theme in two
paintings, again substituting herself for the
central character. In The Broken Column,
described previously, Kahlo is passive,
almost fatalistically calm, as she stands
bound to her column by her metal corset, her
flesh pierced by nails. In The Little Deer
(pl. XXXI), a deer with Kahlo's head and a
body pierced with arrows runs through a wood.
Together the two images suggest that Kahlo

Second religious
theme—
martyrdom of
Saint Sebastian—
further supports
the subpoint

Taffe 11

found echoes of her physical and emotional torment in the tradition of Christian martyrdom.

In Mexico, as Herrera notes, this tradition is powerfully influenced by the "bloodiness and self-mortification" of the Aztec tradition (283). Indeed, in much of Kahlo's work, the Christian imagery shows a Mexican influence. Rivera and Kahlo owned a collection of nineteenth-century retablos, described by Nicholas Jenkins as "votive paintings on tin, each about the size of a postcard, melodramatically relating the facts of an intercession by God: here a child rescued from a burning bed, there a man rescued from drowning" (105). In 1932, Kahlo completed Henry Ford Hospital (pl. IV), her first work on a metal surface. Although the painting does not adhere to the strict characteristics of a retablo, Herrera argues that both Rivera and Kahlo viewed it as one (151). Instead of a divine deliverance, the painting tells the story of a calamity: Kahlo's miscarriage.

Yet another example of Christian imagery filtered through Mexican culture is My Birth (pl. VI). In this painting, the Virgin Mary

Final subpoint: Mexican influence — retablos

Examples support the final subpoint

Additional example of Mexican influence supports the final subpoint

Taffe 12

gazes out of a framed portrait above a bed
covered in white. On the bed is a woman
giving birth, her head and shoulders covered,
suggesting that she is dead. The child
being born--Kahlo--also appears to be dead.
According to Herrera, this painting is based
on a well-known Aztec sculpture of a woman
giving birth to a man's head, a sculpture and
a tradition with which Kahlo was well
acquainted (158).

Thus, despite a desire on the part of
many critics and admirers to see her as an
almost entirely original artist, evidence
suggests that Kahlo's art strongly reflects a
number of influences from earlier paintings
and from her own Mexican culture. While her
work is clearly informed by her life
experience, she had a deep understanding of
European and Mexican artistic traditions, an
understanding that powerfully shaped her
creation of what the art world has come to
identify as uniquely Kahlo. Just eight days
before she died, Herrera tells us, Kahlo wrote
in bright red paint on her last painting "VIVA
LA VIDA" (LONG LIVE LIFE) (440). Those who
study her art are increasingly likely to
answer, "Viva la Kahlo."

Conclusion: summary of argument and echo of thesis

Quotation reproduced in all capital letters, as it appeared in the source; translation of Spanish provided in parentheses

Taffe 13

Notes

Heading centered

Double space ⟶

Indent five spaces
to superscript
numeral

Explanatory note

Bibliographic
note

1″

¹ All cited Kahlo paintings are reproduced
in Herrera and identified by the plate or
figure number assigned by her. Color plates
(pl.) follow p. 162 and p. 290; black-and-
white illustrations (fig.) follow p. 130 and
p. 226.

² I wish to thank Professor Honeywell, who
in our interview suggested that I consult
several standard histories of Western art,
such as Gardner, Janson, and Hartt.

Taffe 14

Works Cited · Heading centered

· Double space

Carter, Angela. "A Ribbon around a Bomb." Rev. · First line of each entry flush with left margin
    of <u>Frida: A Biography of Frida Kahlo</u>, by
    Hayden Herrera. <u>New Statesman & Society</u> · Weekly periodical
    12 May 1989: 32-33.

Delavoy, Robert L. <u>Bosch</u>. Trans. Stuart · Translation
    Gilbert. Cleveland: World, 1984.

Gardner, Helen. <u>Art through the Ages</u>. 7th ed. · One volume of multivolume work
    Vol. 2. New York: Harcourt, 1980. 3 vols.

Hartt, Frederick. <u>History of Italian</u>
    <u>Renaissance Art</u>. Englewood Cliffs:
    Prentice, 1981. · Subsequent lines of each entry indented five spaces

Herrera, Hayden. <u>Frida: A Biography of Frida</u>
    <u>Kahlo</u>. New York: Harper, 1983.

Honeywell, Richard. Telephone interview. 15 · Interview
    Apr. 1991.

Janson, H. W. <u>Key Monuments in the History of</u>
    <u>Art</u>. New York: Abrams, 1959.

Jenkins, Nicholas. "Calla Lilies and Kahlos: · Monthly periodical
    The Frida Kahlo Museum, Mexico City."
    <u>ARTnews</u> Mar. 1989: 104-05.

Natchez, Gladys. "Frida Kahlo and Diego · Online computer service
    Rivera: The Transformation of Catastrophe
    to Creativity." <u>Psychotherapy-Patient</u> 4.1
    (1987): 153-74. PsycINFO. Online. Dialog.
    12 July 1994.

Plagens, Peter, et al. "Frida on Our
Minds." <u>Newsweek</u> 27 May 1991:
54-55.

<u>Portrait of an Artist: Frida Kahlo</u>. Dir.
Eila Hershon. RM Arts/Hershon/WDR,
1983.

Zamora, Martha. <u>Frida Kahlo: The Brush of
Anguish</u>. Trans. Marilyn Sode Smith.
San Francisco: Chronicle, 1990.

Article by more
than four authors

Film

DOCUMENTING SOURCES, APA AND CBE STYLES

Many disciplines have their own carefully crafted documentation styles, and these styles differ according to what information is valued most highly. Thus in the sciences and social sciences, where timeliness of publication is crucial to keeping up with the most current research, the date of publication comes up front, right after the author's name.

DOCUMENTING SOURCES, APA AND CBE STYLES

Chapters 49 and 50 discuss the basic formats prescribed by the American Psychological Association (APA), guidelines that are widely used in the social sciences. For further reference, consult the *Publication Manual of the American Psychological Association*, fourth edition, 1994. Chapter 51 deals with formats prescribed by the Council of Biology Editors.

DIRECTORY TO APA STYLE

49

APA Style

49a APA style for in-text citations

APA style requires parenthetical citations in the text to document quotations, paraphrases, summaries, and other material from a source (43f). These in-text citations correspond to full bibliographic entries in a list of references at the end of the text.

1. AUTHOR NAMED IN A SIGNAL PHRASE

Generally, use the author's name in a signal phrase to introduce the cited material, and place the date, in parentheses, immediately after the author's name. For a quotation, the page number, preceded by *p.*, appears in parentheses after the quotation. For electronic texts or other works without page numbers, paragraph numbers may be used instead.

Key (1983) has argued that the placement of women in print advertisements is subliminally important.

As Briggs (1970) observed, parents play an important role in building their children's self-esteem because "children value themselves to the degree that they have been valued" (p. 14).

Position the page reference in parentheses two spaces after the final punctuation of a long, set-off quotation.

2. AUTHOR NAMED IN PARENTHESES

When you do not mention the author in a signal phrase in your text, give the name and the date, separated by a comma, in parentheses at the end of the cited material.

One study has found that only 68% of letters received by editors were actually published (Renfro, 1979).

3. TWO AUTHORS

Use both names in all citations. Use *and* in a signal phrase, but use an ampersand (&) in parentheses.

```
Murphy and Orkow (1985) reached somewhat different
conclusions by designing a study that was less dependent
on subjective judgment than were previous studies.
```

```
A recent study that was less dependent on subjective
judgment resulted in conclusions somewhat different from
those of previous studies (Murphy & Orkow, 1985).
```

4. THREE TO FIVE AUTHORS

List all the authors' names for the first reference.

```
Belenky, Clinchy, Goldberger, and Tarule (1986) have
suggested that many women rely on observing and listening
to others as ways of learning about themselves.
```

In subsequent references, use just the first author's name plus *et al.*

```
From this experience, observed Belenky et al. (1986),
women learn to listen to themselves think, a step toward
self-expression.
```

5. SIX OR MORE AUTHORS

Use only the first author's name and *et al.* in *every* citation.

```
As Mueller et al. (1980) demonstrated, television holds
the potential for distorting and manipulating consumers as
free-willed decision makers.
```

6. ORGANIZATION AS AUTHOR

If the name of an organization or a corporation is long, spell it out the first time, followed by an abbreviation in brackets. In later citations, use the abbreviation only.

FIRST CITATION (Centers for Disease Control [CDC], 1990)

LATER CITATION (CDC, 1990)

7. UNKNOWN AUTHOR

Use the title or its first few words in a signal phrase or in parentheses.

The school profiles for the county substantiated this trend (Guide to Secondary Schools, 1983).

8. TWO OR MORE AUTHORS WITH THE SAME LAST NAME

If your list of references includes works by different authors with the same last name, include the authors' initials in each citation.

G. Jones (1984) conducted the groundbreaking study of retroviruses.

9. TWO OR MORE SOURCES WITHIN THE SAME PARENTHESES

List sources by different authors in alphabetical order by author's last name, separated by semicolons: (Chodorow, 1978; Gilligan, 1982). List works by the same author in chronological order, separated by commas: (Gilligan, 1977, 1982).

10. SPECIFIC PARTS OF A SOURCE

Use abbreviations (chap., p., and so on) in a parenthetical citation to name the part of a work you are citing.

Montgomery (1988, chap. 9) argued that his research yielded the opposite results.

11. PERSONAL COMMUNICATION

Cite any personal letters, email, electronic bulletin-board correspondence, telephone conversations, or interviews with the person's initial(s) and last name, the identification *personal communication*, and the date.

J. L. Morin (personal communication, October 14, 1990) supported with new evidence the claims made in her article.

49b   APA style for content notes

APA style allows you to use content notes to expand or supplement your text. Indicate such notes in your text by superscript numerals. Type the notes themselves on a separate page after the last page of the text, under the heading *Footnotes,* centered at the top of the page. Double-space all entries. Indent the first line of each note five to seven spaces, but begin subsequent lines at the left margin.

SUPERSCRIPT NUMERAL IN TEXT

The age of the children involved was an important factor in the selection of items for the questionnaire.[1]

FOOTNOTE

[1] Marjorie Youngston Forman and William Cole of the Child Study Team provided great assistance.

49c   APA style for a list of references

The alphabetical list of the sources cited in your document is called *References.* (If your instructor asks that you list everything you have read as background — not just the sources you cite — call the list *Bibliography.*) Here are some guidelines for preparing such a list.

- Start your list on a separate page after the text of your document but before any appendices or notes.
- Type the heading *References,* neither underlined nor in quotation marks, centered one inch from the top of the page.
- Begin your first entry. Do not indent the first line of each entry, but indent subsequent lines one-half inch or five spaces. Double-space the entire list.
- List sources alphabetically by authors' last names. If the author of a source is unknown, alphabetize the source by the first major word of the title.

The APA style specifies the treatment and placement of four basic elements — author, publication date, title, and publication information.

- *Author.* List all authors last name first, and use only initials for first and middle names. Separate the names of multiple authors with commas, and use an ampersand before the last author's name.

- *Publication date*. Enclose the date in parentheses. Use only the year for books and journals; use the year, a comma, and the month or month and day for magazines. Do not abbreviate.
- *Title*. Underline titles and subtitles of books and periodicals. Do not enclose titles of articles in quotation marks. For books and articles, capitalize only the first word of the title and subtitle and any proper nouns or proper adjectives. Capitalize all major words in a periodical title.
- *Publication information*. For a book, list the city of publication (and the country or postal abbreviation for the state if the city is unfamiliar), a colon, and the publisher's name, dropping *Inc., Co.,* or *Publishers*. For a periodical, follow the periodical title with a comma, the volume number (underlined), the issue number (if appropriate) in parentheses and followed by a comma, and the inclusive page numbers of the article. For newspapers and for articles or chapters in books, include the abbreviation *p.* ("page") or *pp.* ("pages").

The following APA-style examples appear in the "hanging indent" format, in which the first line aligns on the left and the subsequent lines indent one-half inch or five spaces. Unless your instructor suggests otherwise, it is the format we recommend. Note, however, that for manuscripts submitted to journals, APA requires the reverse (first lines indented, subsequent lines flushed left), assuming that the citations will be converted by a typesetting system to a hanging indent.

Books

1. ONE AUTHOR

Lightman, A. (1993). <u>Einstein's dreams.</u> New York: Warner
    Books.

2. TWO OR MORE AUTHORS

Newcombe, F., & Ratcliffe, G. (1978). <u>Defining females:</u>
    <u>The nature of women in society.</u> New York: Wiley.

3. ORGANIZATION AS AUTHOR

Institute of Financial Education. (1983). <u>Income property</u>
    <u>lending.</u> Homewood, IL: Dow Jones-Irwin.

Use the word *Author* as the publisher when the organization is both the author and the publisher.

American Chemical Society. (1978). <u>Handbook for authors of</u>
<u>papers in American Chemical Society publications.</u>
Washington, DC: Author.

4. UNKNOWN AUTHOR

<u>National Geographic atlas of the world.</u> (1988).
Washington, DC: National Geographic Society.

5. EDITOR

Solomon, A. P. (Ed.). (1980). <u>The prospective city.</u>
Cambridge, MA: MIT Press.

6. SELECTION IN A BOOK WITH AN EDITOR

West, C. (1992). The postmodern crisis of the black
intellectuals. In L. Grossberg, C. Nelson, & P.
Treichler (Eds.), <u>Cultural studies</u> (pp. 689-705).
New York: Routledge.

7. TRANSLATION

Durkheim, E. (1957). <u>Suicide</u> (J. A. Spaulding & G.
Simpson, Trans.). Glencoe, IL: Free Press of
Glencoe.

8. EDITION OTHER THAN THE FIRST

Kohn, M. L. (1977). <u>Class and conformity: A study in</u>
<u>values</u> (2nd ed.). Chicago: University of Chicago
Press.

9. ONE VOLUME OF A MULTIVOLUME WORK

Baltes, P., & Brim, O. G. (Eds.). (1980). <u>Life-span</u>
<u>development and behavior</u> (Vol. 3). New York: Basic
Books.

10. ARTICLE IN A REFERENCE WORK

Ochs, E. (1989). Language acquisition. In International
     encyclopedia of communications (Vol. 2, pp. 390-393).
     New York: Oxford University Press.

If no author is listed, begin with the title.

11. REPUBLICATION

Piaget, J. (1952). The language and thought of the child.
     London: Routledge & Kegan Paul. (Original work
     published 1932)

12. GOVERNMENT DOCUMENT

U.S. Bureau of the Census. (1975). Historical statistics
     of the United States, colonial times to 1870.
     Washington, DC: U.S. Government Printing Office.

13. TWO OR MORE WORKS BY THE SAME AUTHOR(S)

List two or more works by the same author in chronological order.
Repeat the author's name in each entry.

Macrorie, K. (1968). Writing to be read. New York:
     Hayden.

Macrorie, K. (1970). Uptaught. New York: Hayden.

Periodicals

14. ARTICLE IN A JOURNAL PAGINATED BY VOLUME

Shuy, R. (1981). A holistic view of language. Research in
     the Teaching of English, 15, 101-111.

15. ARTICLE IN A JOURNAL PAGINATED BY ISSUE

Maienza, J. G. (1986). The superintendency:
     Characteristics of access for men and women.
     Educational Administration Quarterly, 22(4),
     59-79.

16. ARTICLE IN A MAGAZINE

Gralla, P. (1994, April). How to enter cyberspace. PC
      Computing, 60–62.

17. ARTICLE IN A NEWSPAPER

Browne, M. W. (1988, April 26). Lasers for the
      battlefield raise concern for eyesight. The New York
      Times, pp. C1, C8.

18. EDITORIAL OR LETTER TO THE EDITOR

Russell, J. S. (1994, March 27). The language instinct
      [Letter to the editor]. The New York Times Book
      Review, 27.

19. UNSIGNED ARTICLE

What sort of person reads Creative Computing? (1985,
      August). Creative Computing, 8, 10.

20. REVIEW

Larmore, C. E. (1989). [Review of the book Patterns of
      moral complexity]. Ethics, 99, 423–426.

21. PUBLISHED INTERVIEW

McCarthy, E. (1968, December 24). [Interview with Boston
      Globe Washington staff]. Boston Globe, p. B27.

22. TWO OR MORE WORKS BY THE SAME AUTHOR IN THE SAME YEAR

List works alphabetically by title, and place lowercase letters (*a, b,*
etc.) after the dates.

Murray, F. B. (1983a). Equilibration as cognitive
      conflict. Developmental Review, 3, 54–61.

Murray, F. B. (1983b). Learning and development through
social interaction. In L. Liben (Ed.), Piaget and
the foundations of knowledge (pp. 176-201).
Hillsdale, NJ: Erlbaum.

Electronic sources

In the 1994 edition of its *Publication Manual,* the APA acknowledges that set standards for referencing online information have yet to emerge. However, the APA offers general guidelines for referencing electronic sources (for example, CD-ROMs) and recommends that writers follow standard APA format for listing the author, date, and title of electronic sources. The date should consist of the year of publication or the year of the most recent update if it is available. If the year of publication is not available, use the exact date of the search that turned up the item. Following the title, in brackets, indicate the kind of electronic source (CD-ROM).

23. CD-ROM ABSTRACT

Natchez, G. (1987). Frida Kahlo and Diego Rivera:
The transformation of catastrophe to creativity
[CD-ROM]. Psychotherapy-Patient, 8, 153-174. Abstract
from: SilverPlatter File: PsycLIT Item: 76-11344

24. MATERIAL FROM AN INFORMATION SERVICE OR DATABASE

Belenky, M. F. (1984). The role of deafness in the moral
development of hearing impaired children. In A.
Areson & J. De Caro (Eds.), Teaching, learning and
development. Rochester, NY: National Institute for
the Deaf. (ERIC Document Reproduction Service No.
ED 248 646)

25. SOFTWARE OR COMPUTER PROGRAM

SuperCalc3 Release 2.1 [Computer program]. (1985). San
Jose, CA: Computer Associates, Micro Products
Division.

Internet sources

With the exception of guidelines for citing some kinds of electronic sources, such as an online journal article available via email or FTP, *the Publication Manual of the American Psychological Association* does not have guidelines for citing World Wide Web sites and other Internet sources. The following formats—adapted from APA style to include Internet sources—are from *Online! A Reference Guide for Using Internet Sources*, by Andrew Harnack and Eugene Kleppinger.

The basic entry for most sources you access via the Internet should include the following elements:

- *Author.* Give the author's name, if available.
- *Date of publication.* Include the year of Internet publication or the year of the most recent update, if available.
- *Title.* Enclose the title of the document or subject line of the message in quotation marks. End with a period inside the quotation marks.
- *Address.* Include the URL, in angle brackets, or other retrieval information. (For more on citing details of online sources, see 39a.)
- *Date of access.* End with the date of access, in parentheses, followed by a period.

26. WORLD WIDE WEB SITE

Begin with the author's name, if known. Otherwise, start with the date of publication or last revision, in parentheses. Give the full title of the document, followed by a period, then the title of the complete work, if applicable, underlined. Finally, list the URL (full http address), enclosed in angle brackets, and the date of access, in parentheses.

```
Burka, L. P. (1993). A hypertext history of multi-user
    dimensions. MUD History. <http://www.ccs.neu.edu
    /home/lpb/mud-history.html> (1994, December 5).

Shade, L. R. (1993). Gender issues in computer
    networking. <http://www.mit.edu:8001/people
    /sorokin/women/lrs.html> (1996, May 28).
```

27. LINKAGE DATA

To cite a file or document accessed through a link with a source document, provide information on both the cited document and the source. After the title of the document, use the abbreviation *Lkd.* and give the title of the source document to which it is linked, underlined. Give additional linkage details, if applicable, indicated by *at.* End with the source's URL, in angle brackets, and the date of access, in parentheses.

```
Ross, J. (1996). Plays in which Jason Ross has appeared.

    Lkd. UNH Campus Wide Information System, at "Public

    Pages." <http//:www.unh.edu:70/1/unh> (1996, May 10).
```

28. FTP (FILE TRANSFER PROTOCOL) SITE

Give the author's name; the date of publication, if available, in parentheses; and the title of the document. The abbreviation *ftp* is followed by the address of the FTP site, with no closing punctuation, and the full path to follow to find the document, with no closing punctuation. End with the date of access, in parentheses.

```
Jagota, A. (n.d.). Introduction to the theory of neural

    computation. ftp cs.buffalo.edu users/jagota/hkp

    .ps.z (1996, May 8).
```

29. TELNET SITE

Provide the author's name; date of publication, in parentheses; the title of the document; and the title of the full work, if applicable, underlined. Include the word *telnet,* followed by the complete telnet address, with no closing punctuation, and directions to access the document. End with the date of access, in parentheses.

```
Aquatic Conservation Network. (n.d.). About the Aquatic

    Conservation Network. National Capital Freenet.

    telnet freenet.carleton.ca login as guest, go acn,

    press 1 (1996, May 28).
```

30. GOPHER SITE

Give the author's name, if known; the date of publication, in parentheses; the title of the document; and any print publication information, underlined where appropriate. Then give the URL, enclosed in angle brackets, or list the word *gopher*, the site name, and the path followed to access information, with slashes to indicate menu selections.

> Quittner, J. (1993, November 7). Far out: Welcome to
>
> their world built of MUD. Newsday. gopher University
>
> of Koeln/About MUDs, MOOs, and MUSEs
>
> in Education/Selected Papers/newsday (1994,
>
> December 5).

31. LISTSERV MESSAGE

Provide the author's name, if known, and the author's email address, in angle brackets. The date of publication, in parentheses, is followed by the subject line from the posting. Give the address of the listserv, enclosed in angle brackets. End with the date of access, in parentheses.

> Seabrook, R. H. C. <rseabrook@uva.edu> (1994,
>
> January 4). Community and progress.
>
> <cybermind@jefferson.village.virginia.edu> (1994,
>
> January 4).

To cite a file which can be retrieved from a list's server or Web address, after the publication date, include the address of the listserv, enclosed in angle brackets; the address or URL for the list's archive, indicated by *via*, in angle brackets; and the date of access, in parentheses.

> Seabrook, R. H. C. <rseabrook@uva.edu> (1994,
>
> January 22). <cybermind@jefferson.village
>
> .virginia.edu> via <listserv@jefferson.village.edu>
>
> (1994, January 29).

32. NEWSGROUP MESSAGE

To document information posted in a newsgroup discussion, include the author's name, if known, and the author's email address, enclosed in angle brackets. The date of publication, in parentheses, is followed by the subject line from the posting. Give the name of the newsgroup, in angle brackets, and end with the date of access, in parentheses.

```
Sand, P. <psand@unh.edu> (1996, April 20). Java disabled
    by default in Linux Netscape. <keokuk.unh.edu> (1996,
    May 10).
```

33. EMAIL MESSAGE

The APA's *Publication Manual* discourages including email in a list of references, and suggests citing email only in text. It is good practice, however, to document email messages in the list of references, especially when their content is scholarly. To cite email correspondence, provide the author's name, followed by the author's email address, in angle brackets. Give the date of publication, in parentheses, the subject line from the posting, followed by the kind of communication (Personal email, Office communication) in square brackets. End by listing the date of access, in parentheses.

```
Talbot, C. J. <ctalbot@pop.interport.net> (1996, January
    26). Do this [Personal email]. (1996, May 10).
```

34. SYNCHRONOUS COMMUNICATION

To cite synchronous communications such as those posted in MOOs, MUDs, and IRCs, provide the speaker's name, if known, or the name of the site; the date of the event, in parentheses; the title of the event, if appropriate; and the kind of communication (Group Discussion, Personal Interview) in square brackets. Include the address using a URL (enclosed within angle brackets) or command-line directions, and the date of access, in parentheses.

```
LambdaMOO. (1996, May 28). Seminar discussion on
    netiquette. <telnet://lambda.parc.xerox.edu:8888>
    (1996, May 28).
```

Other sources

35. TECHNICAL OR RESEARCH REPORTS AND WORKING PAPERS

Wilson, K. S. (1986). <u>Palenque: An interactive</u>
<u>multimedia optical disc prototype for children</u>
(Working Paper No. 2). New York: Center for
Children and Technology, Bank Street College of
Education.

36. PAPER PRESENTED AT A MEETING OR SYMPOSIUM, UNPUBLISHED

Cite the month of the meeting, if it is available.

Engelbart, D. C. (1970, April). <u>Intellectual implications</u>
<u>of multi-access computing.</u> Paper presented at the
meeting of the Interdisciplinary Conference on
Multi-Access Computer Networks, Washington, DC.

37. DISSERTATION, UNPUBLISHED

Leverenz, C. A. (1994). <u>Collaboration and difference in</u>
<u>the composition classroom.</u> Unpublished doctoral
dissertation, Ohio State University, Columbus.

38. POSTER SESSION

Ulman, H. L., & Walborn, E. (1993, March). <u>Hypertext in</u>
<u>the composition classroom.</u> Poster session presented
at the Annual Conference on College Composition and
Communication, San Diego.

39. FILM OR VIDEOTAPE

Hitchcock, A. (Producer & Director). (1954). <u>Rear window</u>
[Film]. Los Angeles: MGM.

40. TELEVISION PROGRAM, SINGLE EPISODE

Begin with the names of the script writers, and give the name of the director, in parentheses, after the episode title.

Kuttner, P. K., Moran, C., & Scholl, E. (1994, July 19).

Passin' it on (W. Chamberlain, Executive Director).

In D. Zaccardi (Executive Producer), P.O.V. New York:

Public Broadcasting Service.

41. RECORDING

For recordings by an artist other than the writer, begin with the writer's name, followed by the date of copyright. Give the recording date if it is different from the copyright date.

Colvin, S. (1991). I don't know why. [Recorded by A.

Krauss and Union Station]. On Every time you say

goodbye [Cassette]. Cambridge, MA: Rounder Records.

(1992)

50

A Sample Research Essay, APA Style

An introductory psychology class was given the assignment to write a brief literature review related to one aspect of child development. Students were asked to summarize three journal articles addressing the topic and to draw some conclusions based on their findings. Here is Laura Brannon's essay, a literature survey reviewing the three articles and drawing conclusions about what they show and mean. In preparing the following paper, Brannon based citations and references on APA guidelines.

In order to annotate this essay, we have reproduced it in a smaller space than you will have on a standard (8½- by 11-inch) sheet of paper. The lines shown here are thus considerably shorter than the lines in your essay will be.

Shortened title
and page number
appear on every
page

Early Detection 1

Heading centered
and double-
spaced

Early Detection of Child Abuse

Laura Brannon

Professor Phelan

Psychology 101

May 20, 1995

Early Detection 2

Early Detection of Child Abuse

There is no simple one-word answer to the question of what causes child abuse. The abuse of children results from a complex interaction among parent, child, and environmental factors. This complexity does not necessarily mean, however, that potential victims and abusers cannot be identified before serious damage is done. Researchers have examined methods of detecting potential or actual child abuse.

Prediction of Child Abuse: Interviews

In a study by Altemeier, O'Connor, Vietze, Sandler, and Sherrod (1984), 1,400 women between 9 and 40 weeks pregnant were interviewed to test their abusive tendencies. Four researchers were present (with an inter-rater agreement of 90% or better). The Maternal History Interview included questions about the mother's own childhood, self-image, support from others, parenting philosophy, attitudes towards pregnancy, and health-related problems (including substance abuse). Maternal and paternal stresses during the preceding year were measured with a modified Life Stress Inventory. Any information not

Title centered

Paragraphs indented five spaces

Double spacing used throughout

Minimum of one-inch margin on all sides

First-level heading centered

Subjects of study identified

Materials described

Right margin not justified

included in the standard interview but felt by
the researchers to make the mother at high
risk for abuse of her child--for example,
being overtly untruthful--was also recorded.
When the infants were 21 to 48 months old, the
Juvenile Court and the Department of Human
Services were checked for reports of their

Results analyzed

abuse or neglect.

Although the interview predicted abuse
($\underline{p}$ < .001), its ability to predict decreased
with time; for example, although "six of seven
families reported for abuse within the first
nine months following the interview were high
risk, . . . after 24 months only one of seven
had been assigned to this group" (Altemeier et

Page noted for
specific source

al., 1984, p. 395). The researchers point out
some shortcomings of their study, particularly
the high rate of false positives. (Only 6% of
the high-risk population was reported for
abuse, 22% if failure to thrive and neglect
were included.) Although many incidents of

Biases and possi-
ble improve-
ments in the
study listed

abuse may go unreported (possibly accounting
for some of the false positives), this false-
positive percentage should be reduced. Also,
it would be preferable if the role of
subjective judgments in the method for
prediction could be reduced as well.

Early Detection 4

Toward Improving Child Abuse Prediction

A later study by Murphy, Orkow, and
Nicola (1985) was less dependent on subjective
judgments. In this study, 587 women between
three and six months pregnant were interviewed
using the Family Stress Checklist. This
checklist has 10 factors: parent beaten or
deprived as a child; parent with record of
criminal activity or mental illness; parent
suspected of abuse in the past; parent with
low self-esteem, social isolation, or
depression; parent with multiple crises or
stresses; parent with violent temper outbursts;
parent with rigid, unrealistic expectations of
child's behavior; parent's harsh punishment of
a previous child; child difficult and/or
provocative or perceived to be by parents; and
child unwanted or at risk of poor bonding.
Each item is scored as either no risk (0),
risk (5), or high risk (10); consequently, an
individual's score can range from 0 to 100.

Scores of 40 or above represent high
risk: 7% of the tested mothers were in this
range. Although all of the items were somewhat
more common among the high-risk group, the
following factors were almost totally absent
from the low-scoring population and increased

Second-level
heading
underlined and
flush left

Signal phrase
identifies authors
with date of
source in
parentheses

Additional
subjects
identified

Materials
described

Methods for
analyzing results
explained

as total scores increased: criminal activity,
serious mental illness, suspicions of past
abuse, violent temper outbursts, rigid
expectations of the child's behavior, and
harsh punishment of a previous child.

After the children reached an age of one
to two years, their medical charts were
reviewed. A negative rating meant no signs of
abuse. "Mild neglect" was signified by the
mother's failure to provide sufficient medical
care or her complaint that the baby was
spoiled, difficult, or a poor feeder; "child
neglect" was signified by the mother's failure
to provide food, clothing, shelter, or
supervision for the child or by the child's
being "accident-prone" or failing to thrive;
and "child abuse" was signified by the child's
having broken bones, bruises, burns, or welts
either verified or strongly suspected to have
been inflicted by the parent. The Family

**Results from
second study
analyzed
statistically**

Stress Checklist was 80% effective at
predicting neglect and abuse. There were fewer
false positives than in the previous study:
the checklist was correct 89.4% of the time in
predicting which parents would not be likely
to be abusive. Variables such as age, marital
status, and parenting experience did not

Early Detection 6

significantly differentiate the high-risk
mothers from those with low risk.
Early Detection of Child Abuse: Injuries
       Johnson and Showers (1985) analyzed 616
child abuse reportings. Boys were reported
abused more often than girls (56% to 44%),
and black children were reported abused at a
rate disproportionate to their population
distribution and general hospitalization rate
(p < .001). Also, although more men than women
were reported for abuse (51%), mothers abused
their children more often. The type, cause,
and locations of the injuries varied with the
child's age and race, but not sex. Johnson and
Showers present a table with data on how
injuries vary with age and race, reproduced as
Table 1.

Table used to
show results

Table 1

How Injuries Vary With Age and Race

Child's age or race	Highest risk type	Highest risk cause	Highest risk location
0–4 years	Broken bones Hemorrhage Burns	Hot liquid Grid/heater Iron	Skull Brain Feet Genitalia Buttocks Hips
4–8	Erythema and marks	Cord Belt/strap	Not significant
8–12	---	Foot Fist	---
12–17	Lacerations Pain- tenderness Swelling	Foot Fist	Scalp Nose Neck
Blacks	Lacerations Erythema	Cord Belt/strap Switch/stick Knife Iron	Arms Thighs
Whites	Bruises	Board/paddle Open hand	Buttocks Face

Note. From "Injury Variables in Child Abuse," by
C. F. Johnson and J. Showers, 1985, Child Abuse and
Neglect: The International Journal, 9, p. 211.

Early Detection 8

Conclusions

Overall, the findings of these studies
seem to indicate that tests can be devised to
predict potential child abusers. The study by
Murphy et al. (1985), which relies less on
subjective judgments, has a significantly
lower false-positive rate than the earlier
study by Altemeier et al. (1984). Therefore,
although such tests have not yet been
perfected, they appear to be improving.

The two studies tried to integrate the
complex relationships among child, parent, and
environmental factors that are involved in
child abuse. Ideally, if potential abusers
could be identified early enough, they could
undergo treatment even before the child is
born. Of course, a parent could not be
separated from a child on the basis of one
test, and, therefore, the results should
remain confidential to avoid any potential for
abuse of the test itself.

Whereas the tests look carefully at the
parent's situation, the injury variables
analyzed in the Johnson and Showers study
(1985) focus attention on the child. If
teachers, neighbors, relatives, or other
people notice that children have frequent

Results
interpreted

Implications of
these studies for
those who seek to
prevent child
abuse noted in
conclusion

injuries (especially with the locations,
types, and causes associated with different
ages and races), abuse can be detected early
and perhaps stopped.

References

Altemeier, W. A., O'Connor, S., Vietze, P., Sandler, H., & Sherrod, K. (1984). Prediction of child abuse: A prospective study of feasibility. Child Abuse and Neglect: The International Journal, 8, 393-400.

Johnson, C. F., & Showers, J. (1985). Injury variables in child abuse. Child Abuse and Neglect: The International Journal, 9, 207-215.

Murphy, S., Orkow, B., & Nicola, R. (1985). Prenatal prediction of child abuse and neglect: A prospective study. Child Abuse and Neglect: The International Journal, 9, 225-235.

51

CBE Style

Writers in the natural sciences, the physical sciences, and mathematics can find recommendations for documentation style in the manual of the Council of Biology Editors (CBE): *Scientific Style and Format: The CBE Manual for Authors, Editors, and Publishers*, sixth edition, 1994.

DIRECTORY TO CBE STYLE

51a   CBE style for in-text citations

In CBE style, citations within an essay follow one of two formats.

- The citation-sequence format calls for a superscript number ([1]) or a number in parentheses after any mention of a source.

- The name-year format calls for the last name of the author and the year of publication in parentheses after any mention of a source. If the last name appears in a signal phrase, the name-year format allows for giving only the year of publication in parentheses.

Dr. Edward Huth, chairperson of the CBE Style Manual Committee, recommends either the name-and-year or the superscript system rather than the number-in-parentheses system—and suggests that student writers check a current journal in the field or ask an instructor about the preferred style in a particular course or discipline.

1. IN-TEXT CITATION USING CITATION-SEQUENCE SUPERSCRIPT FORMAT

In his lengthy text, Gilman[1] provides the most complete discussion of this phenomenon.

For the citation-sequence system, you would also use a superscript *1* ([1]) for each subsequent citation of this work by Gilman.

2. IN-TEXT CITATION USING NAME-YEAR FORMAT

In his lengthy text, Gilman provides the most complete discussion of this phenomenon (Gilman 1994).

Maxwell's two earlier studies of juvenile obesity (1988, 1991) examined only children with diabetes.

The classic examples of such investigations (Morrow 1968; Bridger and others 1971; Franklin and Wayson 1972) still shape the assumptions of current studies.

51b CBE style for a list of references

The citations in the text of an essay correspond to items on a list called *References*.

- If you use the citation-sequence superscript format, number and list the references in the sequence in which the references are *first* cited in the text.
- If you use the name-year format, list the references, unnumbered, in alphabetical order.

In the following examples, you will see that the citation-sequence format calls for listing the date after the publisher's name in references for books and after the periodical name in references for articles. The name-year format calls for listing the date immediately after the author's name in any kind of reference.

Books

1. ONE AUTHOR

CITATION-SEQUENCE SUPERSCRIPT

[1] Freidson E. Profession of medicine. New York: Dodd-Mead; 1972. 802 p.

NAME-YEAR

Freidson E. 1972. Profession of medicine. New York: Dodd-Mead. 802 p.

2. TWO OR MORE AUTHORS

CITATION-SEQUENCE SUPERSCRIPT

[2] Stalberg E, Trontelj JV. Single fiber electromyography: studies in healthy and diseased muscle. New York: Raven; 1994. 291 p.

NAME-YEAR

Stalberg E, Trontelj JV. 1994. Single fiber electromyography: studies in healthy and diseased muscle. New York: Raven. 291 p.

3. ORGANIZATON AS AUTHOR

Any organization abbreviation is placed at the beginning of the name-year entry and is used in the corresponding in-text citation.

CITATION-SEQUENCE SUPERSCRIPT

[3] World Health Organization. World health statistics annual: 1993. Geneva: World Health Organization; 1994.

NAME-YEAR

[WHO] World Health Organization. 1994. World health
    statistics annual: 1993. Geneva: WHO.

4. BOOK PREPARED BY EDITOR(S)

CITATION-SEQUENCE SUPERSCRIPT

[4] Berge ZL, Collins MP, editors. Computer mediated
    communication and the online classroom. Cresskill,
    NJ: Hampton Pr; 1995. 230 p.

NAME-YEAR

Berge ZL, Collins MP, editors. 1995. Computer mediated
    communication and the online classroom. Cresskill,
    NJ: Hampton Pr. 230 p.

5. SECTION OF A BOOK WITH AN EDITOR

CITATION-SEQUENCE SUPERSCRIPT

[5] Adler M. Stroke. In: Dulbecco R, editor. Encyclopedia of
    human biology. San Diego: Academic; 1991. p 299-308.

NAME-YEAR

Adler M. 1991. Stroke. In: Dulbecco R, editor.
    Encyclopedia of human biology. San Diego: Academic.
    p 299-308.

6. CHAPTER OF A BOOK

CITATION-SEQUENCE SUPERSCRIPT

[6] Castro J. The American way of health: how medicine is
    changing and what it means to you. Boston: Little,
    Brown; 1994. Chapter 9, Why doctors, hospitals, and
    drugs cost so much; p 131-53.

NAME-YEAR

Castro J. 1994. The American way of health: how medicine
    is changing and what it means to you. Boston:
    Little, Brown. Chapter 9, Why doctors, hospitals, and
    drugs cost so much; p 131-53.

7. PUBLISHED PROCEEDINGS OF A CONFERENCE

CITATION-SEQUENCE SUPERSCRIPT

[7] [Anonymous]. International Conference on the Bus '86;
    1986 Sep 9-10; London. [London]: Institution of
    Mechanical Engineers; 1986. 115 p.

The place of publication was not stated but inferred and placed in brackets.

NAME-YEAR

[Anonymous]. 1986. International Conference on the Bus
    '86; 1986 Sep 9-10; London. [London]: Institution of
    Mechanical Engineers. 115 p.

Periodicals

For rules on abbreviating journal titles, consult the *CBE Manual*, or ask an instructor or librarian to refer you to other examples.

8. ARTICLE IN A JOURNAL PAGINATED BY VOLUME

CITATION-SEQUENCE SUPERSCRIPT

[8] Finkel MJ. Drugs of limited commercial value. New Engl J
    Med 1980;302:643-4.

NAME-YEAR

Finkel MJ. 1980. Drugs of limited commercial value. New
    Engl J Med 302:643-4.

9. ARTICLE IN A JOURNAL PAGINATED BY ISSUE

CITATION-SEQUENCE SUPERSCRIPT

[9] Fagan R. Characteristics of college student
    volunteering. J Vol Admin 1992;11(1):5-18.

NAME-YEAR

Fagan R. 1992. Characteristics of college student
    volunteering. J Vol Admin 11(1):5-18.

10. ARTICLE IN A WEEKLY JOURNAL

CITATION-SEQUENCE SUPERSCRIPT

[10] Kerr RA. How many more after Northridge? Science 1994
    Jan 28;263(5146):460-1.

NAME-YEAR

Kerr RA. 1994 Jan 28. How many more after Northridge?
    Science 263(5146):460-1.

11. ARTICLE IN A MAGAZINE

CITATION-SEQUENCE SUPERSCRIPT

[11] Jackson R. Arachnomania. Natural History 1995 Mar:28-31.

NAME-YEAR

Jackson R. 1995 Mar. Arachnomania. Natural History:28-31.

12. ARTICLE IN A NEWSPAPER

CITATION-SEQUENCE SUPERSCRIPT

[12] Christopher T. Grafting: playing Dr. Frankenstein in
    the garden. New York Times 1995 Feb 19;Sect Y:21
    (col 1).

NAME-YEAR

Christopher T. 1995 Feb 19. Grafting: playing
    Dr. Frankenstein in the garden. New York Times;
    Sect Y:21(col 1).

Electronic sources

13. ELECTRONIC JOURNAL ARTICLES

CITATION-SEQUENCE SUPERSCRIPT

[13] Cisler S. MediaTracks. Public Access Comput Syst Rev
    [serial online] 1990;1(3):109-15. Available from:
    Public Access Computer Systems Forum PACS-L via the
    INTERNET. (Accessed 1990 Nov 29).

[14] Harrison CL, Schmidt PQ, Jones JD. Aspirin compared
with acetaminophen for relief of headache. Online J
Therap [serial online] 1992 Jan 2;Doc nr 1:[4320
words; 10 paragraphs]. 5 figures; 10 tables.
(Accessed 1992 Dec 26).

The abbreviation *nr* stands for "number."

NAME-YEAR

Cisler S. 1990. MediaTracks. Public Access Comput Syst
Rev [serial online];1(3):109-15. Available from:
Public Access Computer Systems Forum PACS-L via the
INTERNET. (Accessed 1990 Nov 29).

Harrison CL, Schmidt PQ, Jones JD. 1992 Jan 2. Aspirin
compared with acetaminophen for relief of headache.
Online J Therap [serial online];Doc nr 1:[4320 words;
10 paragraphs]. 5 figures; 10 tables. (Accessed 1992
Dec 26).

14. ELECTRONIC BOOKS (MONOGRAPHS)

CITATION-SEQUENCE SUPERSCRIPT

[15] Martindale online [monograph online]. London:
Pharmaceutical Society of Great Britain; 1989
[updated 1989 Dec]. Available from: Dialog. Accessed
1990 Jan 10.

NAME-YEAR

[PSGB] Pharmaceutical Society of Great Britain. 1989.
Martindale online [monograph online]. London: PSGB;
[updated 1989 Dec]. Available from: Dialog. Accessed
1990 Jan 10.

SPECIAL KINDS OF WRITING

Once one can write, one can write
on many topics. . . . Indeed,
dealing with notational systems
altogether may be a chief survival
skill.

— HOWARD GARDNER

SPECIAL KINDS OF WRITING

52

Oral Presentations

When the Gallup Poll reports on what U.S. citizens say they fear most, the findings are always the same: public speaking is apparently more frightening to us than anything else, scarier even than an attack from outer space or nuclear holocaust. This chapter aims to allay any such fears *you* may have by offering guidelines that can help you prepare for and deliver successful oral presentations.

Editing Text for Oral Presentations

- How does your presentation fulfill your purpose? (52a)
- How do you appeal to your audience's interests? (52a)
- How does the introduction get the audience's attention? Does it provide necessary background information? (52b)
- How do you guide listeners? Are your transitions explicit? Do you repeat key words or ideas? (52c)
- Have you used straightforward sentences and concrete terms? (52c)
- Have you marked your text for pauses and emphasis? (52d)
- How, if at all, do you use visuals? Are they large enough to be seen? Would other visuals be helpful? (52e)

52a Consider your task, purpose, and audience.

Consider how much time you have to prepare, how long the presentation is to be, and whether visual aids, handouts, or other accompanying materials are called for. If you are making a group presentation, you will need time to divide duties and to practice with your colleagues.

Consider the purpose of your presentation. Are you to lead a discussion? present a proposal? teach a lesson? give a report? engage a group in an activity? And who will be the audience? Ask yourself what they know about your topic, what opinions they already hold about it, and what they need to know and understand to follow your presentation and accept your point of view.

52b   Work on your introduction and conclusion.

Listeners tend to remember beginnings and endings most readily, so try to make these elements memorable. Consider, for example, using a startling statement, opinion, or question; a vivid anecdote; or a powerful quotation. (See 7f for examples.) Linking your subject to the experiences and interests of your listeners will help them remember you and your presentation.

52c   Use explicit structure and signpost language.

Organize your presentation clearly and carefully, and, toward the beginning of your presentation, give an overview of your main points. (You may wish to recall these points again toward the end of the talk.) Throughout your presentation, pause between major points, and use signpost language to mark your movement from one idea to the next. Signpost language acts as an explicit transition in your talk: *The second crisis point in the breakup of the Soviet Union occurred hard on the heels of the first* instead of *Another thing about the breakup of the Soviet Union. . . .* (For a list of transitions, see p. 48.) Avoid long, complicated sentences, and remember that listeners can hold on to concrete verbs and nouns more easily than they can grasp abstractions. You may need to deal with abstract ideas, but try to provide concrete examples for each.

52d   Prepare your text for ease of presentation.

Depending on the audience and your personal preferences, you may decide to prepare a full text of your presentation. If so, double- or triple-space it, and use fairly large print so that it will be easy to read. Try to end each page with the end of a sentence so that you won't have to pause while you turn a page. Or you may prefer to work from a detailed topic outline or from note cards. In any case—full text, outline, or notes—be sure to mark the places where you want to pause and to highlight the words you want to emphasize.

Of the following paragraphs, the first is from an essay that is intended to be read. The second paragraph presents the same information but is intended for oral presentation. Note how the second text uses signpost language, repetition, vivid concrete examples, and uncomplicated sentence structure to make it easy to follow by ear. Note also how the writer has marked her text for emphasis and pauses.

A PARAGRAPH FROM A WRITTEN ESSAY

The decision about a major or other course of study is crucial because it determines both what we study and how we come to think about the world. The philosopher Kenneth Burke explains that we are inevitably affected not only by our experiences but also by the terminologies through which our perceptions of those experiences are filtered. Burke calls these filters "terministic screens" and says that they affect our perception, highlighting some aspects of an experience while obscuring others. Thus the terminologies (or languages) we use influence how we see the world and how we think about what we see.

THE PARAGRAPH REVISED FOR ORAL PRESENTATION

Why is our decision about a major so crucial? I can give two important reasons. First, our major determines what we study. *Pause* Second, it determines how we come to think about the world. The philosopher Kenneth Burke explains these influences this way: our experience, he says, influences what we think about ideas and the world. But those experiences are always filtered through language, through words and terminologies. Burke calls these terminologies "terministic screens," a complicated-sounding term for a pretty simple idea. Take, for example, the latest hike in student fees on our campus. The Board of Trustees and the administration use one set of terms to describe the hike: "modest and reasonable," they call it. Students I know use entirely different terms: "exorbitant and unjust," they call it. Why the difference? Because their terministic screens are entirely different. *Pause* Burke says we all have such screens made up of language, and these screens act to screen out some things for us and to screen in, or

```
highlight, others. Burke's major point is this: the terms
and screens we use have a big influence on how we see the
world and how we think about what we see.
```

52e Use visuals.

Think of visuals—charts, graphs, photographs, summary statements, or lists—not as mere add-ons but as one of your major means of conveying information. Because of their importance, they must be large enough to be easily seen and/or read by your audience. Many speakers use overhead projections throughout a presentation to help keep themselves on track and to guide their audience. Posters, flip charts, and chalkboards can make strong visual statements as well.

Most important, make sure that all visuals engage and help your listeners, rather than distract them from your message. Check the effectiveness of your visuals by trying them out on other people before you give your presentation. (See 40c for an example of an overhead slide.)

52f Practice your presentation.

Prepare a draft of your presentation, including all visuals, far enough in advance to allow for several run-throughs. Some speakers audiotape or videotape their rehearsals and then base their revisions on the tape-recorded performance. Others practice in front of a mirror or in front of colleagues or friends, getting comments on content and style.

Once you are comfortable giving the presentation, make sure you will stay within the allotted time. One good rule of thumb is to allow roughly two and a half minutes per double-spaced eight-and-a-half by eleven-inch page of text (or one and a half minutes per five by seven-inch card).

When the time comes to stand up before your real audience, pause before you begin to speak, concentrating on your opening lines. During your presentation, face the audience at all times, and make eye contact as often as possible. You may want to choose two or three people to look at and "talk to," particularly if you are addressing a large group. Allow time for the audience to respond and ask questions. Try to keep your answers short so that others may participate in the conversation. At the conclusion of your presentation, remember to thank your audience.

53

Writing about Literature

Literature might be called an art of story, and story might in turn be called a universal form of language, for every culture we know of has a tradition of storytelling. No doubt stories have touched your life too, whether the stories you first heard were bedtime stories told by a parent, the stories you and your friends created during play, or the stories you and your colleagues tell on the job. Indeed, we might even say that a major goal of living is to create the story of our own lives, a story we can take pleasure and pride in telling. Thinking and writing about literature can give you insight into human motives, character, and potential—others' as well as your own.

53a Become a strong reader of literature.

As a reader of literature, you are not an empty cup into which the "meaning" of a literary work is poured. If such were the case, literary works would have exactly the same meanings for all of us, and reading would be a fairly boring affair. If you have ever gone to a movie with a friend and each come away with a completely different understanding or response, you already have ample evidence that literature never has just one meaning. The following guidelines will help you exercise your powers of interpretation and of making meaning.

Reading Literature

- *Read the work first for an overall impression.* How did the work make you feel? What about it is most remarkable? Are you confused about anything in it?

- *Reread the work, annotating* in the margins to "talk back," asking questions, pointing out anything that seems out of place, puzzling, or ineffective.

- *What is the genre*—gothic fiction? tragic drama? lyric poetry? creative nonfiction? What is noteworthy about the form of the work?

- *What is the point of view, and who is the narrator?* How reliable and convincing does the narrator seem? What in the work builds up or suspends your faith in the narrator's credibility?

(Continues)

- *What do you see as the major themes* of the work? How do plot, setting, character, point of view, imagery, and sound support the themes?
- *What may have led the author to address these themes?* Consider the time and place represented in the work as well as when and where the writer wrote the work. Also consider the social, political, or even personal forces that may have affected the writer.
- *Who are the readers the writer seems to address?* Do they include you? Do you sympathize with a particular character? Why?
- *Review your thoughts and any notes you have made.* What interests you most? Freewrite for fifteen minutes or so about your overall response to this work and about the key point you would like to make about it.

53b A glossary of literary terms

To analyze the sounds in a literary work, you might use the following terms:

alliteration   the repetition of initial sounds to create special emphasis or rhythm as in this sentence from Eudora Welty: "Monsieur Boule inserted a *d*elicate *d*agger in Mademoiselle's left side and *d*eparted with a posed immediacy."

meter   the rhythm of a line of verse, as determined by kind of foot— iambic, dactylic, and so on—and number of feet—pentameter, tetrameter—in a line. Iambic pentameter indicates five feet of iambs (two syllables, with the stress falling on the second of the two), as in the following line: *An aged man is but a paltry thing.* Blank verse refers to unrhymed iambic pentameter; free verse is the label for poetry without a fixed meter or rhyme scheme.

onomatopoeia   the use of words whose sounds call up, or "echo," their meaning: *hiss* or *sizzle*, for example.

rhyme scheme   the pattern of end rhymes in a poem, usually designated by the letters *a, b, c.* A Shakespearean sonnet typically follows a rhyme scheme of *abab cdcd efef gg.*

rhythm   in metrical poetry, the beat or pattern of stresses; in prose, the effect created by repetition, parallelism, and variation of sentence length and structure.

stanza   a division of a poem: a four-line stanza is called a quatrain; a two-line stanza, a couplet.

Use the following terms to discuss imagery, the general label applied to vivid descriptions that evoke a picture or appeal to other senses:

allusion   an indirect (that is, unacknowledged) reference in one work to another work or to a historical event, biblical passage, and so on.

analogy   a comparison of two things that are alike in some respect, often to explain one of the things or to represent it more vividly by relating it to the second. A simile is an explicit analogy; a metaphor, an implied one.

figurative language   hyperbole, metaphor, simile, personification, and other figures of speech that enrich description and create meaning (24d).

symbolism   the use of one thing to represent another thing or idea, as the flag symbolizes patriotism.

Helpful terms for analyzing the elements and structures of narrative include the following:

characters   the people in a story, who may act, react, and change during the course of a story. In Amy Dierst's essay on *The Third Life of Grange Copeland* (53d), she examines the characters in the novel in order to interpret its meaning.

dialogue   the conversation among characters, which can show how they interact and suggest why they act as they do. Monologue is a speech by one character, spoken to him- or herself or aloud to another character.

heteroglossia   a term referring to the many voices in a work. In Dickens's *Hard Times*, the "voice" of mass education speaks alongside the voices of fictional characters.

implied author   the "author" that is inferred from or implied by the text, as distinct from the real person/author. In *The Adventures of Huckleberry Finn*, for example, the real author is the flesh and blood Samuel Clemens (or Mark Twain); the implied author is the "author" we imagine as Clemens in the text.

intertextuality   the system of references in one text to other texts through quotations, allusions, parodies, or thematic references. Larson's *Far Side* Frankenstein cartoons refer intertextually to the original novel, *Frankenstein*, as well as to movie versions and to other works focusing on the delights — and limits — of science.

irony   the suggestion of the opposite, or nearly the opposite, as in saying that being caught in a freezing downpour is "delightful."

narrator   the person telling a story. In *The Adventures of Huckleberry Finn*, the narrator is Huck himself. In poetry, the narrator is known as the speaker. Both narrator and speaker can be referred to as the persona. See also *point of view*.

paradox   a seemingly contradictory statement that may nonetheless be true. The ultimate Christian paradox is that in death one ultimately finds life.

parody an imitation intended for humorous effect, as in the current take-off on the magazine *Martha Stewart Living: Is Martha Stewart Living?*

plot the events selected by the writer to reveal the conflicts, or struggles, among or within characters, often arranged chronologically but sometimes including flashbacks to past events. Traditionally, the plot begins with exposition, which presents background information; rises to a climax, the point of greatest tension; and ends with a resolution and denouement, which contain the outcome.

point of view the perspective from which the work is presented by a character in the work or by a narrator or speaker; terms relating to point of view include omniscient narrator, limited third-person narrator, first-person narrator, and unreliable narrator.

protagonist the hero or main character, often opposed by an antagonist.

setting the scene of the work, including time, physical location, and social situation.

style the writer's choice of words and sentence structures.

theme a major and often recurring idea; the larger meaning of a work, including any thoughts or insights about life or people in general.

tone the writer's attitude, conveyed through specific word choices and structures.

Editing Your Writing about Literature

- What is your thesis? How could it be stated more clearly?

- What support do you offer for your thesis? Check to be sure you include concrete instances drawn from the text you are writing about.

- How do you organize your essay? Do you move chronologically through the work of literature? Do you consider major elements such as images or characters one by one? If you cannot discern a clear relationship among your points, you may have to rearrange them, revise your materials, or substitute better evidence in support of your thesis.

- Check all quotations to make sure each supports your thesis and that you have properly used signal phrases, indentations (necessary for longer quotations), and citations in parentheses.

- If you quote, paraphrase, or summarize secondary sources, do you cite and document thoroughly and accurately following MLA guidelines? (See Chapters 45–48.)

- Be sure to use present-tense verbs when discussing works of literature: *Alice Walker's Grange Copeland displays his frustration through neglect.* Use past tense only to describe historical events: *Thus sharecropping, like slavery before it, contributed to the black man's feeling of powerlessness.* (44c)

53c Consider your assignment, purpose, and audience.

When you write about literature, you will often be responding to an assignment given by an instructor.

- Study the assignment carefully, noting any requirements about use of sources or overall length.

- Check the assignment for key words that specify a certain purpose. *Analyze*, for example, implies that you should look at one or more parts of the literary work and relate it to, say, a point or theme of the work.

- Consider the audience for your essay—your instructor, most likely, and perhaps others as well.

53d Select a critical stance.

Writers often adopt one of three stances in writing about literature:

- *a text-based stance*, which supports a thesis, or main point, by focusing on specific features in the literary text in question

- *a context-based stance*, which supports a thesis by focusing on the context, or outside environment, in which the literary text exists

- *a reader-based stance*, which creates a thesis based on the response of a particular reader to the literary text and an interpretation that grows out of his or her personal response

The following essay, which is slightly abridged, demonstrates a text-based response to an assignment that asked students to "analyze some aspect of one of the works read" in an introductory literature class. Because the assignment called for an analysis of a work read by the entire class, the writer, Amy Dierst, could assume she need not review the plot; she could also assume that an analysis of characters and themes was an appropriate form of interpretation. Dierst makes a claim—her thesis—about the role of men in *The Third Life of Grange Copeland*; she then substantiates her thesis by citing passages from the primary source, the novel itself, as well as from secondary sources, other readers' interpretations of the novel. (See p. 315 for a full sample essay, which includes a complete title page following MLA style.)

The Role of Men in

The Third Life of Grange Copeland

Many observers of American society charge that it
has created a distorted definition of manhood and
produced men who, in their need to assert control of
their lives, release their frustration at the expense of
women. In her novel The Third Life of Grange Copeland,
Alice Walker addresses this theme from the point of view
of black men and women, for whom racism heightens the
distortion and its consequences. She suggests that by
stifling black men's sense of freedom and control, a
racist society creates frustrations that are released in
family violence and inherited by their children. Because
his wife and children are the only aspect of the black
man's life that he can control, they become the scapegoat
upon which his frustrations are released. As Walker's
title suggests, she sees redemption, or spiritual rebirth
into a new life, as the best defense against society's
injustice. Though Walker's male characters have been
labeled by some as either heartlessly cruel or
pathetically weak (Steinem 89), many of them, like Grange
Copeland, do change during the course of a work.
Individual transformation stimulates the potential for
change in the social system as a whole.

In this novel, Walker shows how the social and
economic system of the 1920s offered a futile existence
to southern black families. Grange Copeland, like most
southern black men of his era, lived and worked on a farm
owned and operated by a white man. This system, called
sharecropping, did not allow for future planning or
savings, for everything earned was returned to the white
man's pocket for rent. Thus sharecropping, like slavery
before it, contributed to the black man's feelings of

powerlessness. In his desperation and helplessness, Grange turns to exert power in the one place he is dominant, his home. He releases his frustration by abusing his family in a weekly cycle of cruelty:

> By Thursday, Grange's gloominess reached its peak and he grimaced respectfully, with veiled eyes, at the jokes told by the man who drove the truck [the white farm owner, Mr. Shipley]. On Thursday night, he stalked the house from room to room, pulled himself up and swung from the rafters. Late Saturday night Grange would come home lurching drunk, threatening to kill his wife and Brownfield [his son], stumbling and shooting his shotgun. (Walker 12)

At other times, Grange displays his frustration through neglect, a more psychologically disturbing device that later affects Brownfield's emotional stability. Grange's inability to rise above his own discontent with his life and express feeling toward his son becomes his most abusive act. Eventually, he abandons his family completely for a new life in the North. Even when he says good-bye, "even in private and in the dark and with his son, presumably asleep, Grange could not bear to touch his son with his hand" (Walker 121).

Brownfield picks up where Grange left off, giving his father's violent threats physical form by beating his own wife and children regularly. Although he, too, blames the whites for driving him to brutality, Walker suggests that his actions are not excusable on these grounds. By the time he reaches adulthood, sharecropping is not a black man's only option and cannot be used as a scapegoat. Nevertheless, he chooses to relinquish his freedom and work for Mr. Shipley.

By becoming the overseer on Mr. Shipley's plantation, Brownfield positions himself for the same failure that ruined his father. As Trudier Harris notes, over time Brownfield's loss of control of his life turns his feelings of depression and lost pride into anger, and his own destructive nature turns him toward violence and evil (240). Unable or unwilling to take responsibility for himself, Brownfield blames his own inadequacies on his wife, Mem, who bears the brunt of his anger:

> Brownfield beat his once lovely wife now, regularly, because it made him feel briefly good. Every Saturday night he beat her, trying to pin the blame for his failure on her by imprinting it on her face, and she . . . repaid him by becoming a haggard . . . witch. (Walker 55)

Brownfield demonstrates his power by stripping Mem, a former schoolteacher, of anything that would threaten his manhood. Reasoning that her knowledge is a power that he cannot have and therefore she does not deserve, he wants her to speak in her old dialect so that she will not appear to be more intelligent than he does. He also wants her to be ugly because her ugliness makes it easier for him to justify beating her. He wants her to reach a state of ultimate degradation where any strength of her character will be quickly extinguished by a blow to the face or a kick in the side. In fact, "he rather enjoyed her desolation because in it she had no hopes. She was totally weak, totally without view, without a sky" (Walker 59). In a final attempt to release his frustration, as Paul Theroux suggests, Brownfield kills Mem, literally and symbolically obliterating the remainder of her identity--her face (2).

But in the face of this brutality and degradation,

Walker raises the possibility of a different fate for
black men and women. While in the North, Grange undergoes
a spiritual rebirth and, as Karen Gaston notes, comes to
understand that white injustice is not alone responsible
for the cruelty of black men toward their families (278).
He also realizes that to weaken and destroy a wife and
family is not a sign of manhood:

> You gits just as weak as water, no feeling of
> doing nothing yourself, you begins to destroy
> everybody around you, and you blame it on
> crackers [whites]. Nobody's as powerful as we
> make out to be, we got our own souls, don't we?
> (Walker 207)

Grange redeems his spirit in his "third life" with
his granddaughter, Ruth. His objective now is not to
destroy what he loves but to cherish it. . . .

Here is Amy Dierst's list of works cited in her essay.

Works Cited

Gaston, Karen C. "Women in the Lives of Grange
     Copeland." College Language Association Journal 24
     (1981): 276-86.

Harris, Trudier. "Violence in The Third Life of Grange
     Copeland." College Language Association Journal 19
     (1975): 238-47.

Steinem, Gloria. "Do You Know This Woman? She Knows You--A
     Profile on Alice Walker." Ms. June 1982: 89-94.

Theroux, Paul. Rev. of The Third Life of Grange
     Copeland, by Alice Walker. Bookworld 4 Sept.
     1970: 2.

Walker, Alice. The Third Life of Grange Copeland. New
     York: Harcourt, 1970.

54

Professional and Business Communication

From requesting a credit report to protesting a public official's stand on an issue to thanking a community group for help during a family emergency, much everyday business is conducted in writing. Professional and business communication follows various formats—proposals and reports, letters and memos, email, and faxes. This chapter provides information essential to using these formats effectively.

Editing Business and Professional Communication

- *Be clear.* Use simple words and straightforward sentences with active verbs. Use topic sentences to help readers follow your points.

- *Be concise.* Use the words you need to make your point but no more. Don't give readers information they don't need. Try to keep paragraphs short—in general, six lines or fewer.

- *Be courteous.* Write in a friendly, conversational tone. Imagine how you would respond if you were the reader.

- *Be correct.* Use a spell checker, and then proofread carefully.

- *Be consistent.* If you refer to someone as *Susan* in one sentence, don't switch to *Sue* in the next. If you use kilograms in one part of a letter, don't switch to pounds in another.

- *Be complete.* Include all the information readers need. You don't want them to have to call or write you for important, but missing, details.

54a Use a conventional format for memos.

Memos constitute the most common form of printed correspondence sent *within* an organization. In established business or professional relationships, memos travel between organizations as well. Since they usually deal with only one subject, memos tend to be brief.

Guidelines for Writing Memos

- State your topic in a subject line.
- Begin with the most important information, and move on from there.
- Try to involve readers in your opening paragraph, and attempt to build goodwill in your conclusion.
- Focus each paragraph on one idea pertaining to the subject.
- Emphasize specific action—exactly what you want readers to do, and when.
- Initial your memo next to your name.

Sample memo

```
Date:     November 10, 1995
To:       Members of the Shipping Department
From:     Willie Smith, Supervisor WS
Subject:  Scheduling holiday time
```

With orders running 25 percent higher than average this season, I can give everyone an opportunity to work overtime and still enjoy the company's traditional half day off for holiday shopping. I must submit the department schedule by tomorrow at 5:00 p.m., however, so I will need to know your preferences right away.

Please fill out the attached form with the days and hours you can work overtime and your first and second choices for time off. Return it to me before you leave today.

I will try to accommodate everybody's preferences. If we work together, December should be good for all of us--on and off the job.

54b Use email to save time, money, and paper.

Email has revolutionized correspondence. Containing basically the same elements as a memo, an email note can speedily reach individuals and groups all over the world—often for the cost of a local phone call. The following example illustrates a common use of email: to get a quick response to a pressing question (in this case, advice on a possible job opening).

Sample email

```
Subj: Job description
Date: 96-09-18 18:16:39 EDT
From: kristinsmp@aol.com
To:   alunsfor@aol.com
File: jobad.doc


I am attaching a job advertisement I just found, posted
on one of the listservs I subscribe to. Would you be
willing to talk with me more about it--either by email,
fax, or phone? I'd like to talk about my qualifications
for the job and how I might go about making a successful
application. Eagerly awaiting your reply,


Kristin Bowen
kristinsmp@aol.com
(212) 726-0300
```

54c Use a conventional format for letters.

When you send a business or professional letter, you are writing either as an individual or as a representative of an organization. In either case, and regardless of the purpose of the letter, it should follow certain conventions. Whenever possible, you should write to a specific person.

Many letters use the block format, in which all text aligns at the left margin. Some writers prefer a different style, using paragraph indents and aligning the return address, date, close, and signature on the right.

A sample letter of application, block format

<table>
<tr><td>

837 Siuslaw Highway
Corvallis, OR 97330
February 12, 1996

Ms. Suzanne Camdon
Director of Public Information
Northern California Bureau of Tourism
1421 Fairfax St.
San Francisco, CA 94120

Dear Ms. Camdon:

I would like to be considered for the opening you listed
at Oregon State's placement office for a public relations
writer. I will receive my degree in journalism this June,
and I think my education as well as my professional
experience might be appropriate for the position.

I recently completed an internship with the Willamette
Valley Visitor's Association, details of which are on
the enclosed résumé. In this letter, I want especially
to emphasize that I learned, in general, how to develop
a good travel story, meet deadlines for print and
electronic media, and work with members of the
hospitality industry.

Of special interest to you may be my work on the
Willamette Spring Winery Tour (some samples of which
are attached). Following the campaign I developed,
wineries reported a 27 percent increase in visitors
over the previous year.

In a week or so, I will phone to see if I might speak
with you in order to learn more about this position. In
the meantime, I can be reached at (541) 555-1763 or at
asaunders@cla.orst.edu. I look forward to talking with
you soon.

Sincerely yours,

Andrew Saunders
Andrew Saunders

enc.

</td><td>

return address at
least 1"
from edge

1 or 2 double
spaces

inside address

double space

salutation

double space

double space
between
paragraphs

double space

close

2 double spaces

double space

</td></tr>
</table>

Guidelines for Writing Effective Letters

- Open cordially, and be polite—even if you have a complaint.
- State the reason for your letter clearly and specifically. Include whatever details will help your reader to see your point and respond.
- If appropriate, make clear what you hope your reader will do.
- Express appreciation for your reader's attention.
- Make response simple by including your telephone or fax number or email address, and, if appropriate, a self-addressed, stamped envelope.

54d Use a conventional format for résumés.

Often, a letter of application and a résumé travel together. A letter of application, or cover letter, emphasizes specific parts of the résumé, telling how your background is suited to a particular job. A résumé summarizes your experience and qualifications and provides support for your letter. An effective résumé is brief, usually one or two pages.

Research indicates that employers usually spend less than a minute scanning a résumé. Remember that they are interested not in what they can do for you but what you can do for them. They expect a résumé to be typed or printed neatly on high-quality paper and to read easily, with clear headings, adequate spacing, and a conventional format. Such conventions may be hard to accept because you want your résumé to stand out from the crowd, but a *well-written* résumé may be the best way to distinguish yourself.

Your résumé may be arranged chronologically (in reverse chronological order) or functionally (around skills or expertise). Either way, you will probably include the following:

1. *Name, address, phone and fax numbers, and email address*, usually centered at the top.
2. *Career objective(s)*. List immediate or short-term goals and specific jobs for which you realistically qualify.
3. *Educational background*. Include degrees, diplomas, majors, and special programs or courses that pertain to your field of interest. List honors and scholarships and your grade-point average if it is high.
4. *Work experience*. Identify each job—whether a paying job, an internship, or military experience—with dates and names of organizations. Describe your duties by carefully selecting strong action verbs. Highlight any of your activities that improved business in any way.

5. *Skills, personal interests, activities, and awards.* Identify your technology skills. If space permits, list hobbies, offices held, volunteer work, and awards.

6. *References.* Provide the names of two or three people who know your work well, first asking their permission. Give their titles, addresses, and phone or fax numbers. Or simply say that your references are available on request.

Sample résumé

Andrew Saunders
837 Siuslaw Highway
Corvallis, OR 97330
(541) 555-1763
asaunders@cla.orst.edu

CAREER OBJECTIVE:
A challenging public-relations position in the travel and tourism industry.

EDUCATION:
B.A., Journalism (to be awarded June 1996)
Oregon State University
Major: Public Relations
Minor: Psychology
Major G.P.A.: 3.4/4.0

Core Courses:
- Writing for public relations
- Magazine production and design
- News writing and editing

PUBLIC RELATIONS
EXPERIENCE:

Public Relations Intern
Willamette Valley Visitor's
    Association
Eugene, OR
April-December 1995
- Wrote and placed news releases.
- Served as liaison with West Coast newspapers.
- Helped with design of and proofread monthly newsletter.
- Developed and managed campaign for annual Willamette Valley Winery Tour.

Publicity Chairperson
Oregon State University
    Coalition for the Homeless
September 1994-June 1995
- Planned successful food drive.
- Created and implemented public-awareness campaign.

Andrew Saunders   2

OTHER WORK
EXPERIENCE: Supervisor
                         Sherwin-Williams Company
                         Portland, OR
                         June 1993-June 1994
                         - Supervised warehouse operations
                            and eight-person staff.
                         - Maintained computerized order
                            system.

                         Inside Salesperson
                         Sherwin-Williams Company
                         Eugene, OR
                         Summers 1991-93

PROFESSIONAL
ORGANIZATIONS: Public Relations Student
                         Society of America
                         - Vice President, Oregon State
                            University Chapter, 1995

                         Society of Professional
                             Journalists/Sigma Delta Chi

REFERENCES: Martin Anderson
                         Manager
                         Willamette Valley Visitor's
                             Association
                         4281 Valley River Rd.
                         Eugene, OR 97403
                         (541) 555-6333
                         (541) 555-1234 (FAX)

                         Professor Shirley Sinclair
                         Department of Journalism
                         Oregon State University
                         Corvallis, OR 97330
                         (541) 555-2000 ext. 541
                         ssinclair@coj.orst.edu

FOR MULTILINGUAL WRITERS

The history of the American people, the story of the peoples native to this continent and of those who immigrated here from every corner of the world, is told in the rich accents of Cherokee, Spanish, German, Dutch, Yiddish, French, Menomenie, Japanese, Norwegian, Arabic, Aleut, Polish, Navajo, Thai, Portuguese, Caribbean creoles, and scores of other tongues.

– HARVEY DANIELS

FOR MULTILINGUAL WRITERS

55

Nouns and Noun Phrases

Everyday life is filled with nouns and noun phrases: orange juice, the morning news, a bus to work, meetings, a slice of pizza for lunch, email, Diet Coke, errands, dinner with friends, a chapter in a good book. No matter what your first language is, it includes nouns. This chapter will focus on some of the ways English nouns differ from those in some other languages.

55a Know how to use count and noncount nouns.

The nouns *tree* and *grass* differ both in meaning and in the way they are used in sentences.

> The hill was covered with trees.
> The hill was covered with grass.

Tree is a count noun and *grass* a noncount noun. These terms do not mean that grass cannot be counted but only that English grammar requires that if we count grass, we express it indirectly: *one blade of grass, two blades of grass*, not *one grass, two grasses*.

Count nouns usually have singular and plural forms: *tree, trees*. Noncount nouns usually have only a singular form: *grass*.

Count nouns refer to distinct individuals or entities: *a doctor, a book, a tree; doctors, books, trees*. Noncount nouns refer to indeterminate masses or collections: *milk, ice, clay, blood, grass*.

COUNT	NONCOUNT
people (plural of *person*)	humanity
tables, chairs, beds	furniture
letters	mail
pebbles	gravel
beans	rice
facts	information
words	advice

Some words can be either count or noncount, depending on meaning.

COUNT	Before there were video games, children played with *marbles*.
NONCOUNT	The floor of the palace was made of *marble*.

When you learn a noun in English, you need to learn whether it is count, noncount, or both. Two dictionaries that supply this information are the *Oxford Advanced Learner's Dictionary* and the *Longman Dictionary of American English*.

55b State singular and plural forms explicitly.

Look at this sentence from a traffic report:

All four bridges into the city are crowded with cars right now.

This sentence has three count nouns; one is singular (*city*), and two are plural (*bridges, cars*). If you speak a language with nouns that generally have no distinct plural forms (for example, Chinese, Japanese, or Korean), you might argue that no information would be lost if the sentence were *All four bridge into the city are crowded with car right now.* After all, *four* indicates that *bridge* is plural, and obviously there would have to be more than one car if the bridges are crowded. But English requires that every time you use a count noun, you ask yourself whether you are talking about one item or more than one, and that you choose a singular or a plural form accordingly.

Since noncount nouns have no plural forms, they can be quantified only with a preceding phrase: *one quart of milk, three pounds of rice, several bits of information.* The noun in question remains singular.

55c Use determiners appropriately.

A noun together with all its modifiers constitutes a noun phrase, and the noun around which the modifiers cluster is called the head. For example, in *My adventurous sister is leaving for New Zealand tomorrow*, the noun phrase *my adventurous sister* consists of two modifiers (*my* and *adventurous*) and the head *sister.*

Words like *my, our,* and *this* are determiners. They are common and important words in the English language. Determiners identify or quantify the noun head.

COMMON DETERMINERS

- *a/an, the*
- *this, these, that, those*
- *my, our, your, his, her, its, their*

- possessive nouns and noun phrases (*Sheila's, my friend's*)
- *whose, which, what*
- *all, both, each, every, some, any, either, no, neither, many, much, (a) few, (a) little, several,* and *enough*
- the numerals *one, two,* etc.

Using determiners with singular count nouns

Every noun phrase with a singular count noun head must begin with a determiner.

▶ *my*
  ⌃adventurous sister

▶ *the*
  ⌃big, bad wolf

▶ *that*
  ⌃old neighborhood

If there is no reason to use a more specific determiner, use *a* or *an*: *a big, bad wolf; an old neighborhood.*

    Notice that every noun phrase need not begin with a determiner, only those whose head is a singular count noun. Noncount and plural count nouns sometimes have determiners, sometimes not: *This grass is green* and *Grass is green* are both acceptable, though different in meaning.

Remembering which determiners go with which types of noun

- *This* or *that* goes with singular count or noncount nouns: *this book, that milk.*
- *These, (a) few, many, both,* or *several* goes with plural count nouns: *these books, those plans, a few ideas, many students, both hands, several trees.*
- *(A) little* or *much* goes with noncount nouns: *a little milk, much affection.*
- *Some* or *enough* goes with noncount or plural count nouns: *some milk, some books; enough trouble, enough problems.*
- *A, an, every,* or *each* goes with singular count nouns: *a book, every child, each word.*

55d Choose articles that convey your intended meaning.

The definite article *the* and the indefinite articles *a* and *an* are challenging to multilingual speakers. Many languages have nothing directly comparable to them, and languages that do have articles differ from English in the details of their use.

Using the

Use the definite article *the* with nouns whose identity is known or is about to be made known to readers. The necessary information for identification can come from the noun phrase itself, from elsewhere in the text, from context, from general knowledge, or from a superlative.

▶ Let's meet at ^*the* fountain in front of Dwinelle Hall.

The phrase *in front of Dwinelle Hall* identifies the specific fountain.

▶ Last Saturday, a fire that started in a restaurant spread to a neighboring dry-goods store. ^*The* Store was saved, although it suffered water damage.

The word *store* is preceded by *the*, which directs our attention to the information in the previous sentence, where the store is identified.

▶ Professor to student in her office: "Please shut ^*the* door when you leave."

The professor expects the student to understand that she is referring to the door in her office.

▶ ~~Pope~~ ^*The pope* is expected to visit Africa in October.

There is only one living pope, and so his identity is clear.

▶ Willie is now ^*the* best singer in the choir.

The superlative *best* identifies the noun *singer*.

Using a *or* an

Use *a* before a consonant sound: *a car*. Use *an* before a vowel sound: *an uncle*. Pay attention to sounds rather than to spelling: *a house, an hour*.

A or *an* tells readers they do not have enough information to identify what the noun refers to. The writer may or may not have a particular thing in mind but in either case will use *a* or *an* if the reader lacks the information necessary for identification. Compare these sentences:

I need *a* new *parka* for the winter.

I saw *a parka* that I liked at Dayton's, but it wasn't heavy enough.

The parka in the first sentence is hypothetical rather than actual. Since it is indefinite to the writer, it clearly is indefinite to the reader, and is used with *a*, not *the*. The second sentence refers to a very specific actual parka, but since the writer cannot expect the reader to know which one it is, it is used with *a* rather than *the*.

If you want to speak of an indefinite quantity, rather than just one indefinite thing, use *some* with a noncount noun or a plural count noun.

> This stew needs *some* more *salt*.

> I saw *some plates* that I liked at Gump's.

Zero article

If a noun appears without *the, a* or *an*, or any other determiner (even if it is preceded by other adjectives), it is said to have a zero article. The zero article is used with noncount and plural count nouns: *cheese, hot tea, crackers, ripe apples* (but not *cracker* or *ripe apple*). Use the zero article to make generalizations.

> In this world nothing is certain but *death* and *taxes*. —BENJAMIN FRANKLIN

The zero article indicates that Franklin refers not to a particular death or specific taxes but to death and taxes in general.

Here English differs from many other languages—Greek or Spanish or German, for example—that would use the definite article to make generalizations. In English, a sentence like *The snakes are dangerous* can refer only to particular, identifiable snakes, not to snakes in general.

It is sometimes possible to make general statements with *the* or *a/an* and singular count nouns.

> *First-year college students* are confronted with a wealth of new experiences.

> *A first-year student* is confronted with a wealth of new experiences.

> *The first-year student* is confronted with a wealth of new experiences.

These sentences all make the same general statement, but the last two are more vivid than the first. The second focuses on a hypothetical student taken at random, and the third sentence, which is characteristic of formal written style, projects the image of a typical student as representative of the whole class.

55e Arrange modifiers carefully.

Some modifiers can precede the noun head, and others can follow, and you need to learn both the obligatory and preferred positions for modifiers in order to know what can go where.

- Phrases or clauses follow the noun head: *the tiles on the wall, the tiles that we bought in Brazil.*
- Determiners go at the very beginning of the noun phrase: *these old-fashioned tiles. All* or *both* precedes any other determiners: *all these tiles.* Numbers follow any other determiners: *these six tiles.*
- Noun modifiers go directly before the noun head: *these kitchen tiles.*
- All other adjectives go between determiners and noun modifiers: *these old-fashioned kitchen tiles.* If there are two or more of these adjectives, their order is variable, but there are strong preferences, described below.
- Subjective adjectives (those that show the writer's attitude) go before objective adjectives (those that merely describe): *these beautiful old-fashioned kitchen tiles.*
- Adjectives of size generally come early: *these beautiful large old-fashioned kitchen tiles.*
- Adjectives of color generally come late: *these beautiful large old-fashioned blue kitchen tiles.*
- Adjectives derived from proper nouns or from nouns that refer to materials generally come after color terms and right before noun modifiers: *these beautiful large old-fashioned blue Portuguese ceramic kitchen tiles.*
- All other objective adjectives go in the middle, and adjectives for which a preferred order does not exist are separated by commas: *these beautiful large decorative, heat-resistant, old-fashioned blue Portuguese ceramic kitchen tiles.*

It goes without saying that the interminable noun phrase presented as an illustration in the last bulleted item is a monstrosity that would be out of place in almost any conceivable kind of writing. You should always budget your use of adjectives.

56

Verbs and Verb Phrases

When there are things to do, verbs tell us what they are — from the street signs that say *stop* or *yield*, to email commands, such as *send* or *delete*. Verbs can be called the heartbeat of prose, especially in English. With rare exceptions, you cannot deprive an English sentence of its verb without killing it. If you speak Russian or Arabic, you might wonder what is wrong with the sentence *Where Main Street?* But unlike those and many other languages, English sentences must have a verb: *Where is* Main Street? This chapter will focus on some of the ways English verbs differ from verbs in other languages.

56a A review of verb phrases

Verb phrases can be built up out of a main verb (MV) and one or more auxiliaries (17b).

> My cat *drinks* milk.
> My cat *is drinking* milk.
> My cat *has been drinking* milk.
> My cat *may have been drinking* milk.

Verb phrases have strict rules of order. If you try to rearrange the words in any of these sentences, you will find that most alternatives are impossible. You cannot say *My cat* drinking is *milk* or *My cat* have may been drinking *milk*. The only permissible rearrangement is to move the first auxiliary to the beginning of the sentence in order to form a question: Has *my cat* been drinking *milk?*

Auxiliary and main verbs

In *My cat may have been drinking milk*, the main verb *drinking* is preceded by three auxiliaries: *may*, *have*, and *been*.

- *May* is a modal, which must be followed by the base form (*have*).
- *Have* indicates that the tense is perfect, and it must be followed by a past participle (*been*).
- *Been* (or any other form of *be*), when it is followed by a present participle (such as *drinking*), indicates that the tense is progressive.
- A form of *be* can also represent passive voice, but then the following verb form must be a past participle, as in *My cat may have been bitten by a dog.*

Auxiliaries must be in the following order: modal + perfect *have* + progressive *be* + passive *be*.

>   PERF PASS   MV
> ▶ Sonya *has been invited* to stay with a family in Prague.

>   PERF PROG   MV
> ▶ She *has been taking* an intensive course in Czech.

>   MOD PROG   MV
> ▶ She *must be looking* forward to her trip eagerly.

Only one modal is permitted in a verb phrase.

>   MOD MV
> ▶ Sonya *can speak* a little Czech already.

>   MOD PROG   MV
> ▶ She *will be studying* for three more months.

>   *will be able to speak*
> ▶ She ~~will can speak~~ Czech much better soon.
>   ^

Every time you use an auxiliary, you should be careful to put the next word in the appropriate form.

Modal + base form

Use the base form of the verb after *can, could, will, would, shall, should, may, might*, and *must*.

> Alice *can read* Latin.
> Paul *should have* studied.
> They *must be* going to a fine school.

In many other languages, modals like *can* or *must* are followed by the infinitive (*to* + base form). Do not substitute an infinitive for the base form.

> ▶ Alice can ~~to~~ read Latin.

Perfect have, has, *or* had + *past participle*

To form the perfect tenses, use *have, has,* or *had* with a past participle.

> Everyone *has gone* home.
> They *have been* working all day.

Progressive be + *present participle*

A progressive form of the verb is signaled by two elements, a form of the auxiliary *be* (*am, is, are, was, were, be,* or *been*) and the *-ing* form of the next word: *The children are studying.* Be sure to include both elements.

>   *are*
> ▶ The children studying in school.
>   ^

>   *studying*
> ▶ The children are ~~study~~ in school.
>   ^

Some verbs are rarely used in progressive forms. These are verbs that express unchanging conditions or mental states rather than deliberate actions: *believe, belong, cost, hate, have, know, like, love, mean, need, own, resemble, think, understand, weigh.*

Passive be + past participle

Use *am, is, are, was, were, being, be,* or *been* with a past participle to form the passive voice.

> Tagalog *is spoken* in the Philippines.

Notice that the difference between progressive *be* and passive *be* is that the following word ends in the *-ing* of the present participle with the progressive, but with the passive, the following word never ends in *-ing* and instead becomes the past participle.

> Meredith *is* studying music.

> Natasha *was* taught by a famous violinist.

If the first auxiliary in a verb phrase is *be* or *have,* it must show either present or past tense, and it must agree with the subject: *Meredith has played in an orchestra.*

Notice that although a modal auxiliary may also show present or past tense (for example, *can* or *could*), it never changes form to agree with the subject.

> ▶ Michiko ~~cans~~ play two instruments.
>   ^*can*

56b Use present and past tenses carefully.

Every English sentence must have at least one verb or verb phrase that is not an infinitive, a gerund, or a participle without any auxiliaries. Furthermore, every such verb or verb phrase must have a tense.

In some languages, such as Chinese and Vietnamese, the verb form never changes regardless of when the action of the verb takes place, and the time of the action is simply indicated by other expressions such as *yesterday, last year,* and *next week.* In English, the time of the action must be clearly indicated by the tense form of each and every verb, even if the time is obvious or indicated elsewhere in the sentence.

> ▶ During the Cultural Revolution, millions of young people ~~cannot~~ go to
>   ^*could not*
> school and ~~are~~ sent to the countryside.
>   ^*were*

In some languages (Spanish, for example), words end in either a vowel or a single consonant, not in one consonant followed by another. Remember to add the *-s* of the present-tense third-person singular and the *-ed* of the past tense.

> ▶ Last night I ~~call~~ my aunt who ~~live~~ in Santo Domingo.

with *called* written above *call* and *lives* written above *live*.

56c Understand perfect and progressive verb phrases.

The perfect and progressive auxiliaries combine with the present or past tense, or with modals, to form complex verb phrases with special meanings.

Distinguishing the simple present and the present perfect

My sister *drives* a bus.

The simple present (*drives*) merely tells us about her current occupation. But if you were to add the phrase *for three years*, it would be incorrect to say *My sister drives a bus for three years*. You need to set up a time frame that encompasses the past and the present, and therefore you should use the present perfect or the present perfect progressive.

My sister *has driven* a bus for three years.

My sister *has been driving* a bus for three years.

Distinguishing the simple past and the present perfect

Since she started working, she *has bought* a new car and a VCR.

The clause introduced by *since* sets up a time frame that runs from past to present, and requires the present perfect (*has bought*) in the subsequent clause. Furthermore, the sentence does not say exactly when she bought the car or the VCR, and that indefiniteness also calls for the perfect. It would be less correct to say *Since she started working, she bought a new car and a VCR*. But what if you should go on to say when she bought the car?

She *bought* the car two years ago.

It would be incorrect to say *She has bought the car two years ago* because the perfect is incompatible with definite expressions of time. In this case, use the simple past (*bought*) rather than the present perfect (*has bought*).

Distinguishing the simple present and the present progressive

When an action is in progress at the present moment, use the present progressive. Use the simple present for actions that frequently occur during a period of time that might include the present moment (though such an assertion makes no claim that the action is taking place now).

> My sister *drives* a bus, but she *is taking* a vacation now.
>
> My sister *drives* a bus, but she *takes* a vacation every year.

Many languages, such as French and German, use the simple present (*drives, takes*) for both types of sentence. In English, it would be incorrect to say *But she takes a vacation now.*

Distinguishing the simple past and the past progressive

> Sally *spent* the summer in Italy.

You might be tempted to use the past progressive (*was spending*) here instead of the simple past, since spending the summer involves a continuous stretch of time of some duration, and duration and continuousness are typically associated with the progressive. But English speakers use the past progressive infrequently and would be unlikely to use it in this case except to convey actions that are simultaneous with other past actions. For example:

> Sally *was spending* the summer in Italy when she *met* her future husband.

Use the past progressive to focus on duration, continuousness, and simultaneousness, and especially to call attention to past action that went on at the same time as something else.

56d Use modals appropriately.

Consider the following passage:

> College course work *will* call on you to do much reading, writing, research, talking, listening, and note-taking. And as you probably have already realized, you *will not* — or *need not* — always carry out all these activities in solitude. Far from it. Instead, you *can* be part of a broad conversation that includes all the texts you read.

This passage contains four modal auxiliaries: *will, will not, need not,* and *can.* These modals tell the reader what the writer judges to be the options available — in this case, in college work. The passage begins with *will*, which makes a firm prediction of what the reader is to expect. It continues with a firm negative prediction (*will not*) but immediately revises it to a more tentative forecast (*need not*) and finally opens up a new vista of possibilities for the reader (*can*).

The most commonly used modals

The nine basic modal auxiliaries are *can, could, will, would, shall, should, may, might,* and *must*. There are a few others as well, in particular *ought to*, which is close in meaning to *should*. Occasionally *need* can be a modal rather than a main verb.

Using modals to refer to the past

The nine basic modals are the pairs *can/could, will/would, shall/should, may/might,* and the loner *must*. In earlier English, the second member of each pair was the past tense of the first. To a limited degree, the second form still functions as a past tense, especially in the case of *could*.

> Ingrid *can* ski.
>
> Ingrid *could* ski when she was five.

But for the most part, in present-day English, all nine modals typically refer to present or future time. When you want to use a modal to refer to the past, you follow the modal with a perfect auxiliary.

> If you have a fever, you *should* see a doctor.
>
> If you had a fever, you *should have seen* a doctor.

In the case of *must*, refer to the past by using *had to*.

> You *must* renew your visa by the end of this week.
>
> You *had to* renew your visa by the end of last week.

Using modals to make requests or to give instructions

The way modals contribute to human interaction is most evident in requests and instructions. Imagine making the following request of a flight attendant:

> *Will* you bring me a pillow?

You have expressed your request in a demanding manner, and the flight attendant might resent it. A more polite request:

> *Can* you bring me a pillow?

This question acknowledges that fulfilling the request may not be possible.

Another way of softening the request is to use the past form of *will*, and the most discreet choice is the past form of *can*.

> *Would* you bring me a pillow?
>
> *Could* you bring me a pillow?

Using the past of modals is considered more polite than using their present forms because it makes any statement or question less assertive.

Now consider each of the following instructions:

1. You *can* submit your report on disk.
2. You *may* submit your report on disk.
3. You *should* submit your report on disk.
4. You *must* submit your report on disk.
5. You *will* submit your report on disk.

Instructions 1 and 2 give permission to submit the paper on disk, but do not require it; of these, 2 is more formal. Instruction 3 adds a strong recommendation; 4 allows no alternative; and 5 implies, "Don't even think of doing otherwise."

Using modals to reveal doubt and certainty

Modals indicate how confident the writer is about the likelihood that what is being asserted is true. Look at the following set of examples, which starts with a tentative suggestion and ends with full assurance.

> Please sit down; you *might* be tired.
>
> Please sit down; you *may* be tired.
>
> Please sit down; you *must* be tired.

56e Use participial adjectives appropriately.

Many verbs refer to feelings—for example, *bore, confuse, excite, fascinate, frighten, interest*. The present and past participles of such verbs can be used as ordinary adjectives. Use the past participle to describe a person having the feeling:

> The *frightened* boy started to cry.

Use the present participle to describe the thing (or person) causing the feeling:

> The *frightening* dinosaur display gave him nightmares.

Be careful not to confuse the two types of adjectives.

>   *interested*
> ▶ I am ~~interesting~~ in African literature.
>   ^

>   *interesting.*
> ▶ African literature seems ~~interested.~~
>   ^

57

Prepositions and Prepositional Phrases

If you were traveling by rail and asked for directions, it would not be helpful to be told to "take the Chicago train." You would need to know whether to take the train *to* Chicago or the one *from* Chicago. Words such as *to* and *from* which show the relations between other words are prepositions. Not all languages use prepositions to show such relations, and English differs from other languages in the way prepositions are used. This chapter provides guidelines for using prepositions in English.

57a   Use prepositions idiomatically.

Even if you usually know where to use prepositions, you may have difficulty from time to time knowing which preposition to use. Each of the most common prepositions, whether in English or in other languages, has a wide range of different applications, and this range never coincides exactly from one language to another. See, for example, how English speakers use *in* and *on*.

> The peaches are *in* the refrigerator.

> The peaches are *on* the table.

> Is that a diamond ring *on* your finger?

If you speak Spanish

Spanish uses one preposition (*en*) in all these sentences, a fact that might lead you astray in English.

>   *on*
> ▶ Is that a ruby ring ~~in~~ your finger?
>   ^

There is no easy solution to the challenge of using English prepositions idiomatically, but the following strategies can make it less formidable.

Strategies for Using Prepositions Idiomatically

1. Keep in mind typical examples of each preposition.

   IN   **The peaches are *in* the refrigerator.**

   There are still some pickles *in* the jar.

   Here the object of the preposition *in* is a container that encloses something.

   ON   **The peaches are *on* the table.**

   The book you are looking for is *on* the top shelf.

   Here the object of the preposition *on* is a horizontal surface that supports something with which it is in direct contact.

2. Learn other examples that show some similarities and some differences in meaning.

   IN   **You shouldn't drive *in* a snowstorm.**

   Here there is no container, but like a container, the falling snow surrounds and seems to enclose the driver.

   ON   **Is that a diamond ring *on* your finger?**

   A finger is not a horizontal surface, but like such a surface it can support a ring with which it is in contact.

3. Use your imagination to create mental images that can help you remember figurative uses of prepositions.

   IN   **Michael is *in* love.**

   Imagine a warm bath in which Michael is immersed (or a raging torrent, if you prefer to visualize love that way).

   ON   **I've just read a book *on* computer science.**

   Imagine a shelf labeled COMPUTER SCIENCE on which the book you have read is located.

4. Try to learn prepositions not in isolation but as part of a system. For example, in identifying the location of a place or an event, the three prepositions *in, on*, and *at* can be used.

   (Continues)

> *At* specifies the exact point in space or time.
>
> AT **There will be a meeting tomorrow *at* 9:30 A.M. *at* 160 Main Street.**
>
> Expanses of space or time within which a place is located or an event takes place might be seen as containers and so require *in*.
>
> IN **I arrived *in* the United States *in* January.**
>
> 5. *On* must be used in two cases: with the names of streets (but not the exact address) and with days of the week or month.
>
> ON **The airlines office is *on* Fifth Avenue.**
>
> **I'll be moving to my new apartment *on* September 30.**

57b Use two-word verbs idiomatically.

Some words that look like prepositions do not always function as prepositions. Consider the following two sentences.

The balloon rose *off* the ground.

The plane took *off* without difficulty.

In the first sentence, *off* is a preposition that introduces the prepositional phrase *off the ground*. In the second sentence, *off* neither functions as a preposition nor introduces a prepositional phrase. Instead, it combines with *took* to form a two-word verb with its own meaning. Such a verb is called a phrasal verb, and the word *off*, when used in this way, is called an adverbial particle. Many prepositions can function as particles to form phrasal verbs.

The verb + particle combination that makes up a phrasal verb is a tightly knit entity that usually cannot be torn apart.

The plane *took off* without difficulty. [not *took* without difficulty *off*]

The exceptions are the many phrasal verbs that are transitive, meaning that they take a direct object (16k). Some transitive phrasal verbs have particles that may be separated from the verb by the object.

I *picked up my baggage* at the terminal.

I *picked my baggage up* at the terminal.

If a personal pronoun is used as the direct object, it must separate the verb from its particle.

I *picked it up* at the terminal.

In some idiomatic two-word verbs, the second word is a preposition. With such verbs, the preposition can never be separated from the verb.

We *ran into* our neighbor on the plane. [not *ran* our neighbor *into*]

Every comprehensive dictionary includes information about the various adverbial particles and prepositions that a verb can combine with, but only some dictionaries distinguish verb + particle from verb + preposition. The *Longman Dictionary of American English* is one that does.

58

Clauses and Sentences

Sound bites surround us, from Nike's "Just do it" to Avis's "We try harder." These short simple sentences may be memorable, but they don't tell us very much. Ordinarily, we need more complex sentences to convey meaning. The sentences of everyday discourse are not formed in the same way in every language. This chapter will focus on clauses and sentences in English.

58a Express subjects explicitly.

English sentences consist of a subject and a predicate. This simple statement defines a gulf separating English from many other languages, which leave out the subject when it can easily be inferred. Not English. With few exceptions, English demands that an explicit subject accompany an explicit predicate in every sentence. Though you might write *Went from Yokohoma to Nagoya* on a postcard to a friend, in most varieties of spoken and written English, the extra effort of explicitly stating who went is not simply an option but an obligation.

In fact, every dependent clause must have an explicit subject.

▶ They flew to London on the Concorde because ^*it* was fast.

English even requires a kind of "dummy" subject to fill the subject position in certain kinds of sentences. Consider the following sentences:

It is raining.

There is a strong wind.

If you speak Spanish

Speakers of Spanish might be inclined to leave out dummy subjects. In English, however, *it* and *there* are indispensable.

▶ ~~Is~~ raining.
   It is
   ^

▶ ~~Has~~ a strong wind.
   There is
   ^

58b   Express objects explicitly.

Transitive verbs typically require that objects also be explicitly stated, and in some cases even other items of information as well (16k). For example, it is not enough to tell someone *Give!* even if it is clear what is to be given to whom. You must say *Give it to me* or *Give her the passport* or some other such sentence. Similarly, saying *Put!* or *Put it!* is insufficient when you mean *Put it on the table*.

58c   Be careful of English word order.

You should not move subjects, verbs, or objects out of their normal positions in a sentence. In the following sentence, each element is in its appropriate place:

    SUBJECT VERB OBJECT   ADVERB
▶ **Omar reads books voraciously.**

> Note, however, that this sentence would also be acceptable if written as: *Omar voraciously reads books.*

If you speak Turkish, Korean, or Japanese

In these languages, the verb must come last. You may have to make a special effort never to write such a sentence as *Omar books voraciously reads*, which is not acceptable in English.

If you speak Russian

Because Russian permits a great deal of freedom in word order, you must never interchange the position of subject and object (*Books reads*

Omar voraciously is not acceptable English). Also, avoid separating the verb from its object (*Omar reads voraciously books*). (See 16j and k for more on subjects and objects; see 20b for more on disruptive modifiers.)

 Use noun clauses appropriately.

Examine the following sentence:

> In my last year in high school, my adviser urged that I apply to several colleges.

This is built up out of two sentences, one of them (B) embedded in the other (A):

> A. In my last year in high school, my adviser urged B.
>
> B. I (should) apply to several colleges.

When these are combined as in the first sentence above, sentence B becomes a noun clause introduced by *that* and takes on the role of object of the verb *urged* in sentence A. Now look at the following sentence:

> It made a big difference that she wrote a strong letter of recommendation.

Here the two component sentences are C and D:

> C. D made a big difference.
>
> D. She wrote a strong letter of recommendation.

In this case the noun clause formed from sentence D functions as the subject of sentence C, so that the combination reads as follows:

> That she wrote a strong letter of recommendation made a big difference.

This is an acceptable sentence but somewhat top-heavy. Usually when a lengthy noun clause is the subject of the sentence, it is moved to the end. When that is done, the result is *Made a big difference that she wrote a strong letter of recommendation*. If you speak Italian or Spanish or Portuguese, you might see nothing wrong with such a sentence. In English, however, the subject must be stated. The "dummy" element *it* comes to the rescue and sets things right:

▶ <del>Made</del> a big difference that she wrote a strong letter of recommendation.
  It made

58e Know when to use infinitives and gerunds.

Knowing when to use infinitives or gerunds may be a challenge to multilingual writers. Though there is no simple explanation that will make it an easy task, here are some hints that will help you.

> My adviser urged me *to apply* to several colleges.

> Her *writing* a strong letter of recommendation made a big difference.

Why was an infinitive chosen for the first and a gerund for the second? In general, *infinitives* tend to represent intentions, desires, or expectations, while *gerunds* tend to represent facts. The gerund in the second sentence calls attention to the fact that a letter was actually written; the infinitive in the first sentence conveys the message that the act of applying was something desired, not an accomplished fact.

The distinction between fact and intention is not a rule but only a tendency, and it can be superseded by other rules. Use a gerund—never an infinitive—directly following a preposition.

> ▶ This fruit is all right for ~~to eat.~~ *eating.*

You can also get rid of the preposition and keep the infinitive.

> ▶ This fruit is all right ~~for~~ to eat.

> ▶ This fruit is all right *for us* to eat.

The association of fact with gerunds and of intention with infinitives can help you know in the majority of cases whether to use an infinitive or a gerund when another verb immediately precedes.

Gerunds

> Jerzy *enjoys going* to the theater.
> We *resumed working* after our coffee break.
> Kim *appreciated getting* candy from Sean.

In all of these cases, the second verb is a gerund, and the gerund indicates that the action or event that it expresses actually has happened. Verbs like *enjoy, resume*, and *appreciate* can be followed only by gerunds, not by infinitives. In fact, even when these verbs do not convey clear facts, the verb that comes second must still be a gerund.

> Kim *would appreciate getting* candy from Sean, but he hardly knows her.

Infinitives

Kumar *expected to get* a good job after graduation.

Last year, Fatima *decided to become* a math major.

The strikers have *agreed to go* back to work.

Here it is irrelevant whether the actions or events referred to by the infinitives did or did not materialize; at the moment indicated by the verbs *expect, decide,* and *agree,* those actions or events were merely intentions. These three verbs, as well as many others that specify intentions (or negative intentions, like *refuse*), must always be followed by an infinitive, never by a gerund.

A few verbs can be followed by either an infinitive or a gerund. With some, such as *begin* or *continue,* the choice makes little difference in meaning. With others, however, the difference in meaning is striking.

Using an infinitive to state an intention

Carlos was working as a medical technician, but he *stopped to study* English.

The infinitive indicates that Carlos intended to study English when he left his job. We are not told whether he actually did study English.

Using a gerund to state a fact

Carlos *stopped studying* English when he left the United States.

The gerund indicates that Carlos actually did study English, but later stopped.

Checking when to use a gerund or an infinitive

A full list of verbs that can be followed by an infinitive and verbs that can be followed by a gerund can be found in the *Index to Modern English,* by Thomas Lee Crowell Jr. (McGraw-Hill, 1964).

58f Use adjective clauses carefully.

Adjective clauses can be a challenge. Look at the following sentence, and then see what can go wrong:

▶ The company *Yossi's uncle invested in* went bankrupt.

The subject is a noun phrase in which the noun *company* is modified by the article *the* and the adjective clause *Yossi's uncle invested in*. The sentence as a whole says that a certain company went bankrupt, and the adjective clause identifies the company more specifically by saying that Yossi's uncle had invested in it.

One way of seeing how the adjective clause fits into the sentence is to rewrite it like this: *The company (Yossi's uncle had invested in it) went bankrupt.* This is not a normal English sentence, but it helps to demonstrate a process which leads to the sentence we started with. Note the following steps:

1. Change the personal pronoun *it* to the relative pronoun *which: The company (Yossi's uncle had invested in which) went bankrupt.* That still is not acceptable English.
2. Move either the whole prepositional phrase *in which* to the beginning of the adjective clause, or just move the relative pronoun: *The company in which Yossi's uncle had invested went bankrupt* or *The company which Yossi's uncle had invested in went bankrupt.* Both of these are good English sentences, the former somewhat more formal than the latter.
3. If no preposition precedes, substitute *that* for *which* or leave out the relative pronoun entirely. *The company that Yossi's uncle had invested in went bankrupt* or *The company Yossi's uncle had invested in went bankrupt.* Both of these are good English sentences, not highly formal, but still acceptable in much formal writing.

Speakers of some languages find adjective clauses difficult in different ways. Following are some guidelines that might help:

If you speak Korean, Japanese, or Chinese

If you speak Korean, Japanese, or Chinese, the fact that the adjective clause does not precede the noun that it modifies may be disconcerting, both because that is the position of such clauses in the East Asian languages and because other modifiers, such as determiners and adjectives, do precede the noun in English.

If you speak Farsi, Arabic, or Hebrew

If you speak Farsi, Arabic, or Hebrew, you may expect the adjective clause to follow the noun as it does in English, but you might need to remind yourself to change the personal pronoun (*it*) to a relative pronoun (*which* or *that*) and then to move the relative pronoun to the beginning of the clause. You may mistakenly put a relative pronoun at the beginning but keep the personal pronoun, thus producing incorrect sentences such as *The company that Yossi's uncle invested in it went bankrupt.*

If you speak a European or Latin American language

If you are a speaker of some European or Latin American languages, you are probably acquainted with adjective clauses very much like those of English, but you may have difficulty accepting the possibility that a relative pronoun that is the object of a preposition can be moved to the beginning of the clause while leaving the preposition stranded. You might, therefore, move the preposition as well even when the relative pronoun is *that*, or you might drop the preposition altogether, generating such incorrect sentences as *The company in that Yossi's uncle invested went bankrupt* or *The company that Yossi's uncle invested went bankrupt.*

Finally, the fact that the relative pronoun can sometimes be omitted may lead to the mistaken notion that it can be omitted in all cases. Remember that you cannot omit a relative pronoun that is the subject of a verb.

▶ Everyone ^who^ invested in that company lost a great deal.

58g Understand conditional sentences.

English pays special attention to whether or not something is a fact, or to the degree of confidence we have in the truth or likelihood of an assertion. English distinguishes among many different types of conditional sentences, that is, sentences that focus on questions of truth and that are introduced by *if* or its equivalent. The following examples illustrate a range of different conditional sentences. Each of these sentences makes different assumptions about the likelihood that what is stated in the *if*-clause is true, and then draws the corresponding conclusion in the main clause.

> If you *practice* (or *have practiced*) writing frequently, you *know* (or *have learned*) what your chief problems are.

This sentence assumes that what is stated in the *if*-clause may very well be true; the alternatives in parentheses indicate that any tense that is appropriate in a simple sentence may be used in both the *if*-clause and the main clause.

> If you *practice* writing for the rest of this term, you *will* (or *may*) *get* a firmer grasp of the process.

This sentence makes a prediction about the future and again assumes that what is stated may very well turn out to be true. Only the main clause uses the future tense (*will get*) or some other modal that can indicate future time (*may get*). The *if*-clause must use the present tense, even though it too refers to the future.

> If you *practiced* (or *were to practice*) writing every single day, it *would* eventually *seem* much easier to you.

This sentence casts some doubt on the likelihood that what is stated will be put into effect. In the *if*-clause, the verb is either past—actually, past subjunctive (17h)—or *were to* + the base form, though it refers to future time. The main clause has *would* + the base form of the main verb.

> If you *practiced* writing on Mars, you *would find* no one to show your work to.

This sentence contemplates an impossibility at present or in the foreseeable future. As with the preceding sentence, the past subjunctive is used in the *if*-clause, although past time is not being referred to, and *would* + the base form is used in the main clause.

> If you *had practiced* writing in ancient Egypt, you *would have used* hieroglyphics.

This sentence shifts the impossibility back to the past; obviously you are not going to find yourself in ancient Egypt. But since past forms have already been used in the preceding two sentences, this one demands a form that is "more past": the past perfect in the *if*-clause, and *would* + the present perfect form of the main verb in the main clause.

ONLINE WRITING AND RESEARCHING

Visit us at *The Everyday Writer* Web site. Find answers to the most frequently asked questions about writing. Or bring questions to the site's chat space to get response from other writers, teachers, or even the authors. Find links to other useful writing resources on the Web. Look for us at *www.smpcollege.com/smp_english.everyday_writer*.

FOR MULTILINGUAL WRITERS

REVISION SYMBOLS

abb	abbreviation 36a–g		//	faulty parallelism 7e, 11
ad	adjective/adverb 19		para	paraphrase 43e–f, 44c
agr	agreement 18, 21f		pass	inappropriate passive 12c, 17g
awk	awkward			
cap	capitalization 35		ref	unclear pronoun reference 21g
case	case 21a			
cliché	cliché 8b, 24d		run-on	run-on (fused) sentence 22
co	coordination 10a			
coh	coherence 7e, 13		shift	shift 12
com	incomplete comparison 9e		slang	slang 24a
			sp	spelling 27
concl	weak conclusion 7f, 44b		sub	subordination 10b
cs	comma splice 22		sum	summarize 43e–f, 44c
d	diction 24		sexist	sexist language 21f, 25c
def	define 7c		t	tone 8b, 24a, 24d, 43d
dm	dangling modifier 20d		trans	transition 7e, 15b
doc	documentation 45–48, 49–50, 51		u	unity 7a, 13
			vague	vague statement
emph	emphasis unclear 13		verb	verb form 17a–d
ex	example needed 13		vt	verb tense 17e–h
frag	sentence fragment 23		wv	weak verb 17
fs	fused sentence 22		wrdy	wordy 14
hyph	hyphen 38		ww	wrong word 8b, 24a–b
inc	incomplete construction 9b–e		. ? !	period, question mark, exclamation point 31
intro	weak introduction 7e, 44b		,	comma 29
			;	semicolon 30
it	italics (or underlining) 37		'	apostrophe 32
jarg	jargon 24a		" "	quotation marks 33
lc	lowercase letter 35		() []—	parentheses, brackets, dash 34a–c
lv	language variety 26			
mix	mixed construction 9a		: / ...	colon, slash, ellipsis 34d–f
mm	misplaced modifier 20a		∧	insert
ms	manuscript form 40		∩	transpose
no ,	no comma 29j		◡	close up
num	number 36h–j		X	obvious error
¶	paragraph 7			

CONTENTS